Writing Clearly
Grammar for Editing
THIRD EDITION

JANET LANE AND ELLEN LANGE
University of California, Davis

HEINLE
CENGAGE Learning

Australia • Brazil • Japan • Korea • Mexico • Singapore • Spain • United Kingdom • United States

Writing Clearly
Grammar for Editing
Third Edition
by Janet Lane and Ellen Lange

Publisher: Sherrise Roehr

Acquisitions Editor: Thomas Jefferies

Director of Global Marketing: Ian Martin

Director of U.S. Marketing: Jim McDonough

US Academic Marketing Manager:
  Emily Stewart

Manufacturing Manager: Marcia Locke

Sr. Manufacturing Buyer: Marybeth Hennebury

Director of Content and Media Production:
  Michael Burggren

Sr. Content Project Manager: Maryellen Killeen

Cover Design: Muse Group

Interior Design: Muse Group

Composition: Nesbitt Graphics, Inc.

ISBN-13: 978-1-111-35197-7

ISBN-10: 1-111-35197-X

Heinle
20 Channel Center Street
Boston, MA 02210
USA

Cengage Learning is a leading provider of customized learning solutions with office locations around the globe, including Singapore, the United Kingdom, Australia, Mexico, Brazil, and Japan. Locate your local office at **www.cengage.com/global**

Cengage Learning products are represented in Canada by Nelson Education, Ltd.

Visit Heinle online at **elt.heinle.com**

Visit our corporate website at **www.cengage.com**

Printed in the United States of America
6 7 8 9 10 11 20 19 18 17

Contents

SECTION 3

BEYOND GRAMMAR: OTHER WAYS
TO MAKE YOUR WRITING CLEAR   **319**

APPENDIX A   337

STEPS TO WRITING AND REVISING

APPENDIX B   338

EDITING SYMBOLS
ERROR AWARENESS SHEET

APPENDIX C   345

ADDITIONAL EXERCISES FOR PRACTICE:
EDITING FOR A VARIETY OF ERRORS

ANSWERS TO PRE-TESTS   350

INDEX   I-1

DEDICATION

To our students, who inspired us to write this book and to our colleagues for all their support and friendship over the years.

ACKNOWLEDGMENTS

We are indebted to our students at the University of California, Davis, whose continuing interest in reducing the errors in their writing prompted us to undertake a third edition of *Writing Clearly*.

While writing this revision, we have been fortunate to have had the encouragement and guidance of our publisher, Heinle|Cengage, including Tom Jefferies, Acquisitions Editor, Academic ESL, who helped us visualize the third edition. We especially thank Eric Brendenberg, National Sales Manager, whose initial encouragement set everything in motion. We thank our editor, Jennifer Bixby, whose excellent suggestions strengthened the text and whose enthusiasm for exactness motivated us as writers. Our appreciation also goes to Content*Ed Publishing Solutions, and, in particular, to Sally Giangrande, Director of Operations, and Charlotte Sturdy, Project Manager, for keeping us on task and moving towards publication.

We are also indebted to those students who so generously contributed their sentences, paragraphs, and essays as examples for this textbook, making this third edition a richer text.

PHOTO CREDITS

Unit 1: p. 1 Adrin Shamsudin/Shutterstock.com; p. 3 Chris Schmidt/istockphoto.com; p. 29 tl Benis Arapovic/Shutterstock.com, cl rgerhardt/Shutterstock.com, bl John Kershner/Shutterstock.com; **Unit 2:** p.31 Benis Arapovic/Shutterstock.com; p. 55 tl technotr/iStockphoto.com, cl bikeriderlondon/ Shutterstock.com, bl zoran simin/iStockphoto; **Unit 3:** p. 57 mangostock/Shutterstock.com; p. 78 tl DAVID BOYER/National Geographic Stock, cl Amy Nichole Harris/Shutterstock.com, bl Vuk Vukmirovic/Shutterstock.com; **Unit 4:** p. 79 Craig Hale/iStockphoto.com; p. 102 tl CROM/ Shutterstock.com, cl Deborah Cheramie/iStockphoto.com, bl Elena Elisseeva/Shutterstock.com; **Unit 5:** p. 103 James Morgan/Shutterstock.com, p. 122 tl luoman/iStockphoto.com, cl Losevsky Pavel/ Shutterstock.com, bl Mario Savoia /Shutterstock.com; **Unit 6:** p. 123 Deklofenak/Shutterstock.com; p. 156 tl Jeffrey M. Frank/Shutterstock.com, cl prodakszyn/Shutterstock.com, bl JustASC, 2008/ Shutterstock.com; **Unit 7:** p.157 kaczor58/Shutterstock.com; p.176 tl Ryan Klos/iStockphoto, cl Joggie Botma/Shutterstock.com, bl baranq/Shutterstock.com; **Unit 8:** p. 177 James Brey/iStockphoto.com; p. 197 tl Songquan Deng/Shutterstock.com, cl TataN/Shutterstock.com, bl Supri Suharjoto/Shutterstock. com; **Unit 9:** p. 199 Stewart Cohen/Blend Images/Jupiter Images; p. 216 tl Tom Grill /Corbis Premium RF / Alamy, cl Don Smetzer / Alamy, bl iofoto/Shutterstock.com; p. 217 Somjade Boonyarat/ Shutterstock.com; **Unit 10:** p. 219 Nicole S. Young/iStockphoto.com; p. 236 tl Nosha/Shutterstock.com, cl Leslie Banks/iStockphoto, bl Rich Legg/iStockphoto.com; **Unit 11:** p. 237 Chin Kit Sen/Shutterstock Images; p. 253 tl Carmen Martínez Banús/Maica/iStockphoto.com, cl anastasia tsoupa/iStockphoto.com, bl iofoto/Shutterstock.com; **Unit 12:** p. 255 Dmitry Naumov/Shutterstock.com; p. 268 tl Loskutnikov/ Shutterstock.com, cl Keith Brofsky/ Photodisc /Jupiter Images, bl Steve Froebe/iStockphoto.com; **Unit 13:** p. 269 Charlie Edward/Shutterstock.com; p. 281 tl mediaphotos/iStockphoto.com, cl biffspandex/iStockphoto.com, bl gary718, 2009/Shutterstock.com; **Unit 14:** p. 283 Peter Weber / Shutterstock.com; p. 300 tl Niels Laan / iStockphoto.com, cl Golden Pixels LLC / Shutterstock.com, bl Brzi/iStockphoto.com; **Unit 15:** p. 301 Jiri Miklo/Shutterstock.com; p.317 tl Sergey Rusakov / Shutterstock.com, cl Felix Manuel Burgos-Trujillo/iStockphoto.com, bl Shai Halud / Shutterstock.com

TO THE TEACHER

Introduction

Writing Clearly: Grammar for Editing, Third Edition, is designed to help high-intermediate and advanced English language learners become aware of those language problems commonly found in their writing, focusing on error analysis rather than on a comprehensive study of grammar. Through using this textbook, students will not only learn to analyze their specific sentence-level weaknesses but will also develop strategies for reducing errors and becoming proficient self-editors.

Whom is this text written for?

The primary audience for this textbook is English language learners who need to improve their sentence accuracy as writers in academic or professional settings. In addition, it addresses the needs of Generation 1.5 writers, immigrant students who have resided in the United States for a long time and who have been mostly educated in an English-language environment. *Writing Clearly* guides these writers from proficiency in oral skills to proficiency in academic writing skills. *Writing Clearly* is also highly suited for use with English as a foreign language learners who want to improve their academic and professional writing.

Why did we write this text?

Writing Clearly: Grammar for Editing had its start in 1988 as a handbook for writing instructors at the University of California, Davis. At that time, the instructors working with nonnative English speakers did not have a standardized set of editing symbols or any guide for differentiating more serious errors from less serious ones. Therefore, they had no organized way of identifying, categorizing, or prioritizing their students' errors. We undertook the challenge to meet this need. First, we examined over 2,000 papers written by English language learners to determine the 15 most common errors student writers were making. These 15 errors were then ranked according to how seriously they affected writing clarity. We identified the specific problems common to each error and then provided examples of each problem and the relevant grammar rule. The handbook proved so helpful to instructors that we decided to develop it into a student textbook. We firmly believe this textbook's success and usefulness is directly related to the fact that it was generated from the source material our students provided us with.

By teaching English language learners how to self edit and reduce their grammar errors, *Writing Clearly* addresses today's heightened emphasis on writing in all content areas of an academic curriculum. Students must pass proficiency exams or meet writing requirements before moving forward in their studies or degree programs. In the business world, there is also increased pressure to communicate via e-mail. This text will enable students to meet the challenges of learning to write clearly by helping them become independent learners and better editors of their own work.

How is this text organized and how does it work?

The book is divided into three sections:

Section 1 (Units 1–9), Global Errors; Section 2 (Units 10–15), Local Errors; and Section 3, Beyond Grammar: Other Ways to Make Your Writing Clear

(Global Errors, Local Errors) Each unit guides students through all aspects of an error. First, they learn to recognize and understand the error, and then they learn to correct it in controlled exercises. Finally, they learn to edit for the error in their own writing by writing and revising a response to a writing topic. Most importantly, students learn which problems they have with an error and whether they are dealing with global (more serious) or local (less serious) errors. In this way, they can first address those errors that most affect sentence clarity in their writing.

Section 3, *Beyond Grammar* has five parts: Expand Your Vocabulary, Achieve an Academic Writing Style, Avoid Nonidiomatic and Unclear Sentences, Improve Flow of Ideas, and Revise Your Writing. Each part focuses on an aspect of writing that goes beyond grammatical errors and focuses on clarity and style.

What are the features of each unit?

- **Unit Opener**: Each unit opens with three clearly-defined learning goals for students to work towards and one or more photo-based discussion questions.

- **Learn What the Error Is**: The error is defined and explained, and identified as global (more serious) or local (less serious). Its editing symbol is introduced, and specific suggestions for reducing the error are given.

- **Check Your Understanding**: Two questions test students' grasp of essential information necessary to understand the error.

- **Grammar Journal**: Students apply what they have just learned about the error by writing responses in their journals.

- **Pre-test**: Through a pre-test, students discover what they already know about the error. This self-assessment helps them decide what aspects of the error they need to work on and helps teachers decide which parts of the unit to emphasize.

- **Understand Common Problems**: Each of the common problems illustrates a different aspect of the error with examples of incorrect and correct sentences provided. Students are offered self-help strategies for reducing the error.

- **Review Grammar Solutions**: Grammar rules and academic usage are carefully explained and clearly illustrated with examples and user-friendly charts.

- **Improve Your Writing Style**: These suggestions move students beyond grammatical correctness and empower them to make stylistic choices about the grammatical point.

- **Practice What You Have Learned**: Students are given progressively more difficult exercises to practice what they have learned in the unit with an emphasis on grammar in context and on editing.

- **Post-test**: Students take a comprehensive post-test on the material presented in the unit so that they can evaluate what they have learned.

- **Apply What You Have Learned to Writing**: Students select from three photo-based writing topics and apply what they have learned to a writing assignment.

What is new in this edition?

- **New organization and headings** keep students focused on what they are learning throughout the unit.

- **New design with color photos** engages students and underscores graphically what students need to know, keeping them on track throughout the unit.

- **Expanded Pre-tests** give students the opportunity to discover what they already know about the error.

- **Expanded** *Improve Your Writing Style* sections give students guidance on style, encouraging them to think beyond error correction.

- **Updated exercises and text** reflect new trends in pedagogy.

- **All-new comprehensive Post-tests** enable students to check how much they have learned in each unit.

- **Updated writing topics** based on photos capture students' interest and give them the opportunity to practice writing and editing.

- **Revised and expanded charts** enable students to quickly find relevant grammar points.

- **Editing symbols** and example sentences in the appendix provide a quick reference to the editing symbols used in the units.

What are ways to use the text in a class?

The units can be used consecutively or selectively. In all cases, instructors should focus on global errors first, since these errors affect meaning the most. However, this does not preclude instructors from teaching a local error, such as subject-verb agreement or singular and plural of nouns, earlier in the course if students need work on it.

Each unit will take between four and six hours of class time. In classes with less time available, the instructor may select the material that is most appropriate or assign some material as homework. For example, the instructor could choose to spend less class time on *Review Grammar Solutions* and go over the *Practice What You Have Learned* exercises in class.

Section 3, *Beyond Grammar*, consists of five short parts which can be covered more quickly than a unit; alternatively, a part from Section 3 can be assigned for students to complete on their own outside of class.

In what contexts can *Writing Clearly: Grammar for Editing* be used?

Writing Clearly may be used as the main text in a writing course, or as a companion text to a writing or reading textbook. It can also be used as supplementary material for English language learners enrolled in a writing course geared toward native speakers of English. *Writing Clearly* is appropriate for tutoring or independent study in a writing center, or as a text for individual study and reference.

Supplementary Materials

- **Instructor Companion Website**, an online resource with an Instructor's Manual and Answer Key

- **Student Companion Website**, an online resource with a Glossary of Grammatical Terminology

TO THE STUDENT

As a language learner, even at the high intermediate or advanced level, you will make language errors when you write. Making errors is a natural part of learning another language. However, in formal writing, you will need to focus on reducing these errors because the readers' demands and expectations are very high at the academic and professional level. When your writing contains too many language errors, you risk either not getting your meaning across or causing the reader to be distracted from the content of what you have written.

Writing Clearly: Grammar for Editing will help you improve the grammar in your sentences so that what you are saying is clear to your reader. It is also designed to help you decide which errors to work on first.

With this textbook as a guide, you will learn

- Which grammar errors language learners most commonly make in their writing and which errors you commonly make when writing

- What each error is and which grammar guidelines apply to it

- How serious these errors are and which errors you should begin to work on first

- What steps you can take to reduce these errors in your writing

- How you can continue to improve your writing on your own

- How you can become more skilled at editing your own writing

With the knowledge you will gain from working with *Writing Clearly: Grammar for Editing,* you will increase not only your writing skills but also your level of confidence in your writing. We welcome you on this journey towards becoming a successful writer.

SECTION 1

GLOBAL ERRORS

This section contains nine units, each one addressing a global error that writers commonly have difficulty with. Each unit has an introduction to the error, examples of the kinds of problems writers frequently have with the error, grammar review with self-help strategies, exercises for practice, and writing assignments.

Global errors are more serious errors because they can significantly affect the reader's ability to comprehend what you have written. Just as we have chosen to put them first in this text, you will need to address these global errors first in order to make significant improvement in your writing.

Unit 1 · VERB TENSES

What are some of your favorite ways of relaxing? Which ones are most effective when you are feeling under stress?

GOALS

- Learn why mastering verb tenses is important in writing

- Understand two problems writers commonly encounter with verb tenses

- Form and use verb tenses correctly in exercises and writing assignments

LEARN WHAT THE ERROR IS

Errors with Verb Tenses

Verb tense refers to the time that a verb expresses. The form of the verb *ride* in the sentence *We rode our bicycles to campus* indicates that the action took place in the past, not in the present or future. Verb-tense errors are of two kinds: the incorrect choice of a verb tense in a sentence or the inappropriate shifting of verb tenses in a paragraph or a group of paragraphs. The editing symbol for an error with verb tense is *vt*.

Errors marked verb tense (*vt*) may also relate to aspect. The progressive and perfect tenses express aspect, which refers to that part of an event or action that goes beyond past, present, or future. For example, the following sentences both describe actions that take place in the present: *Matt studies in the library in the evening* and *Matt is studying in the library this evening.* However, the difference in meaning between the two actions is one of aspect. In the first sentence, *studies* indicates a habitual action. In the second sentence, *is studying* indicates a temporary action in progress. Aspect can also be used to show the duration of an action (*I worked* . . . vs. *I was working on my essay yesterday*) or the relationship of an action in the past to present and future time (*Alicia moved* . . . vs. *Alicia has moved to a new apartment*).

Verb-tense errors are global (more serious) errors and can make a piece of writing difficult for the reader to understand. Time is an important message expressed by the verb in English, so a writer must be able to control verb tenses in order for the reader to understand when actions and events take place. If you do not control verb tenses, your readers will have great difficulty following the sequence of events in your writing.

Suggestions for Reducing Errors

• Review the verb-tense chart in this unit to make sure you understand the uses of the 12 verb tenses in English. Carefully study the six most commonly used verb tenses: the simple present, the present progressive, the simple past, the past progressive, the future, and the present perfect. Pay special attention to the present perfect tense, one of the most difficult tenses to master for learners of English.

• Remember that in English, even when you have a stated time word or phrase (such as *last week, tomorrow,* or *yesterday*), the verb must also express time: *We went to the movies yesterday.*

- Be aware of how you move from one verb tense to another in a piece of writing (the sequencing of verbs). Avoid unnecessary shifts in tense, yet also be aware that you will often need to use several different verb tenses. The sample paragraphs in this unit will guide you in using different verb tenses in your writing.

- Examine the verb tenses in your academic, professional, and leisure-time reading material in order to become aware of the variety of verb tenses that can occur in a piece of writing. Note that when a writer shifts to a different verb tense, this shift is often signaled by a time-reference word or phrase, such as *when I was in high school, yesterday,* or *tomorrow.* These words alert the reader to a shift from one time frame to another.

Check Your Understanding

Write answers to the following questions. Share your answers with another student.

1. Why are verb-tense errors such serious errors?

2. Aside from time, what other kinds of information do some verb tenses convey?

GRAMMAR JOURNAL ENTRY 1   VERB TENSES

Respond to the following in your grammar journal.

1. Describe your week so far. What have you done? Overall, has this week been hectic, busy, routine, or slow?

2. Underline all of the verbs in this journal entry and notice what different verb tenses you have used. Do you think they are correct? If you are not sure, check with a classmate, a tutor, or your instructor.

UNDERSTAND COMMON PROBLEMS

This section presents two problems that writers commonly encounter with verb tenses. First, take the pre-test to see what you already know about verb tenses. When you finish, check your answers on page 350. Then, carefully study each problem and the examples that illustrate it. Pay particular attention to those problems that correspond to the pre-test questions you had difficulty with. Remember that becoming aware of the types of errors you most often make with verb tenses will increase your chances of avoiding these errors in your writing.

Pre-test

What Do You Already Know?

Test your ability to recognize and correct errors with verb tenses.

A Correct the marked verb-tense errors. These are examples of the two
common problems that are presented in this unit.

Problem 1 Since I moved to my new house 15 days ago, I <u>was</u> very busy. *vt*

Problem 2 Human beings make mistakes. Sometimes, we do things we *vt*
<u>regretted</u> later.

B Underline and correct the one error in each of the following items.
(The errors are not in any particular order.)

  1. Many students like to go abroad to study. Now I am in my second year
    of college, and I just find out yesterday that I have been accepted to go
    to Brazil.

  2. Last week, my parents sent me money for my tuition bill, and I pay it
    today.

Two Common Problems

Problem 1

An incorrect verb
tense has been used
in a sentence or
clause.

Incorrect: Alex <u>has sent out</u> several job applications last month. *vt*

Correct: Alex <u>sent out</u> several job applications last month.

Explanation: The action of sending out the applications has been completed.
Thus, the simple past tense is needed.

Incorrect: I <u>was</u> in the United States since last year. *vt*

Correct: I <u>have been</u> in the United States since last year.

Explanation: The action of being in the United States started in the past and is
continuing into the present. Thus, the present perfect tense is
needed.

Incorrect: At present, I live in the dormitory, but I <u>decided</u> to move out *vt*
next year.

Correct: At present, I live in the dormitory, but I <u>have decided</u> to move out
next year.

Explanation: Since no definite time has been given and since the decision to move into an apartment has probably been recently made, the present perfect tense is needed.

Incorrect: Students <u>pay</u> less tuition last year than this year. *(vt)*

Correct: Students <u>paid</u> less tuition last year than this year.

Explanation: Less tuition was paid by students last year. Thus, a past-tense verb is needed to agree with the time expression *last year*.

Incorrect: Yosemite <u>was</u> one of the most popular of all the national parks. *(vt)*

Correct: Yosemite <u>is</u> one of the most popular of all the national parks.

Explanation: The comment about Yosemite is a general statement that is true in the present. Thus, the present tense is needed.

Incorrect: Many students <u>participate</u> in the graduation ceremony next month. *(vt)*

Correct: Many students <u>will participate</u> (or <u>are participating</u>) in the graduation ceremony next month.

Explanation: The ceremony will take place next month. Thus, a verb that shows future time is needed to agree with the time expression *next month*.

SELF-HELP STRATEGY: Make sure that the verb tense you use fits the time you want to express. For example, if you are writing about something that will happen in the future, the verb should express future time. Also, remember that even when the time is indicated with a time word, such as *yesterday*, *today*, or *tomorrow*, the verb must still show the time of the action. When the time is not clearly stated, think carefully about the time you are trying to express. In the following sentence, the time is not stated in words, yet the writer is remembering a past action now. Thus, the verb *remember* is in the present tense even though the verb *had* and *went* are in the past tense.

         [right now]   [past]   [past]

EXAMPLE: I <u>remember</u> the fun we <u>had</u> when we all <u>went</u> to Disneyland.

Problem 2

The verb tenses shift inappropriately from one time frame to another within a piece of writing.

Incorrect: Although this is my first year in college, I have already found that there _were_ [vt] some differences between high school and college. One of the things I _learned_ [vt] in college is that a person has to be independent.

Explanation: Since the writer is in his or her first year of college, he or she appropriately started out in the present time frame (_is, have found_). However, the writer then inappropriately shifts to the past (_were, learned_) instead of staying in the present.

Correct: Although this is my first year in college, I have already found that there _are_ some differences between high school and college. One of the things I _have learned_ in college is that a person has to be independent.

Incorrect: Most students have many different expectations and ideas about college before they actually enter. Some of these expectations are similar to reality, yet some are quite different. Before I started college, I _have imagined_ [vt] how the classes and teachers would be and came to the conclusion that they _will_ [vt] not be any different from those in high school.

Explanation: The writer appropriately begins in the present with two general statements. However, the writer needs to shift to the past when writing about an experience that took place before she started college.

Correct: Most students have many different expectations and ideas about college before they actually enter. Some of these expectations are similar to reality, yet some are quite different. Before I started college, I _imagined_ (OR _had imagined_) how the classes and teachers would be and came to the conclusion that they _would_ not be any different from those in high school.

SELF-HELP STRATEGY: Remember that although you want to avoid unnecessary shifts in verb tense, it is often appropriate to shift tenses in a piece of writing. See the Review Grammar Solutions section for suggestions on how to master verb-tense sequencing.

REVIEW GRAMMAR SOLUTIONS

Forms and Uses of Verb Tenses

The following charts provide an explanation of the forms and uses of verb tenses. Begin by reviewing all of the tenses. Then, study more carefully those tenses that you find difficult.

SIMPLE PRESENT

USE	EXAMPLES
To express a habitual or repeated action in the present or to express a condition that is true at any time.	• Thuy <u>rides</u> her bicycle to school every day. • I <u>am</u> not a morning person. In fact, I usually <u>do not get up</u> until 10:00 AM.
To express general truths that are timeless (well-known laws or principles or even generally accepted truths about people, places, and customs).	• Water <u>boils</u> at 100°C. • Generally speaking, Spaniards <u>eat</u> dinner much later than Americans <u>do</u>. • College students often <u>do not get</u> enough sleep.
To report what appears in print. This use is common in academic writing when the writer is referring to texts and quotations. In the example, even though Norman Cousins wrote his article in the past, the writer has put the underlined verb in the present tense.	• In his article "The Communication Collapse," Norman Cousins <u>asserts</u> that schools encourage poor writing habits by forcing students to write under time pressure. (**Note:** The writer could also use the past tense, *asserted*.)
To describe past events as if they were happening now. This use is called the *historical present*. In the example, taken from a longer account of a visit to India, the writer has chosen to narrate his adventures using the present tense, even though the trip is over.	• My friend and I <u>arrive</u> at the Mumbai airport on February 25. Jim <u>meets</u> us with a taxi, and we <u>drive</u> to what is to be our apartment for nearly three weeks. The drive <u>is</u> culture shock number one.

FORMATION

Base form of the verb (infinitive without *to*). For third-person singular, add *-s* or *-es*.

Examples: I write, you write, we write, he/she/the student writes, they/the students write

PRESENT PROGRESSIVE

USE*	EXAMPLES
To express that an action or activity is happening right now (at this moment, today, this year); the action has begun and is still happening.	• Tammy <u>is working</u> on the first draft of her essay. • Monica <u>is majoring</u> in aeronautical engineering.
To express that an action or activity is happening at the present time and is temporary.	• Mark <u>is working</u> for his uncle. (allows for the possibility that Mark may not work for his uncle permanently)
To express that an action is already in progress at a specified point of time in the present.	• When my roommate gets home after class, I <u>am</u> usually <u>cooking</u>. • At 8:00 PM, Teresa <u>is</u> usually <u>studying</u> in the library.

FORMATION
am/is/are + present participle (*-ing*)   **Examples:** I am reading, you are reading, he/she/the student is reading, we are reading, they/the students are reading

*When a verb expresses a state of being (a stative verb), it cannot be used in the progressive tense. See "Stative Verbs" on page 15.

SIMPLE PAST

USE	EXAMPLES
To indicate that an action or event took place at a specific time in the past.	• I <u>visited</u> Korea last year. • Last night we <u>saw</u> a movie about India.
To indicate that an action or event occurred over a period of time in the past with the implication that it is no longer true in the present.	• I <u>lived</u> in Los Angeles for 15 years. • Barbara <u>was</u> on the volleyball team in college.

FORMATION

Regular verbs: base form + *-ed*
 	
    Examples: I walked, you walked, he/she/the student walked, we walked, they/the students walked
 	
    Note: Many verbs have irregular past-tense forms. Some common irregular past-tense forms include *took*, *ate*, and *came*. You can find irregular past-tense forms in the dictionary under the entry for the base form of the verb. Consult a learner's dictionary for a list of common verbs that have irregular past-tense forms.

PAST PROGRESSIVE

USE	EXAMPLES
To express that an activity was in progress at a specific point of time in the past, or was in progress and was interrupted.	• At 8:00 PM last night, I <u>was studying</u> in the library. • I <u>was cooking</u> when the phone rang.
To show that an activity lasted for a period of time in the past (emphasis on the duration).	• Gerald <u>was cooking</u> while you <u>were sleeping</u>.

FORMATION
was/were + present participle (-*ing*)

Examples: I was reading, you were reading, he/she/the student was reading, we were reading, they/the students were reading

PRESENT PERFECT

USE	EXAMPLES
To express that an action or state began in the past and continues in the present.	• Hiroaki <u>has lived</u> in Ohio for two years. • I <u>have known</u> Hiroaki since he came to Ohio.
To indicate that an action or event occurred some time in the past, although the exact time is not specified or important.	• Alex <u>has moved</u> back to France. • I <u>have</u> already <u>filed</u> my income taxes.
Note: This tense can also indicate that an event has very recently happened. The adverb *just* is often used in this case.	• I <u>have</u> just <u>completed</u> the application.
To indicate that an action or event has occurred more than once in the past (specific times are not given or important).	• Susan <u>has seen</u> the doctor several times about her allergy problem.

FORMATION
has/have + past participle

Examples: I have walked, you have walked, he/she/the student has walked, we have walked, they/the students have walked

Note: Many past-participle forms are irregular (for example, *known*, *seen*, *written*, *met*). Consult a learner's dictionary for a list of common irregular verbs.

PRESENT PERFECT PROGRESSIVE

USE	EXAMPLES
To emphasize the duration of an activity that started in the past and continues into the present.	• I <u>have been waiting</u> for you for an hour. • Abdul <u>has been living</u> here for two years.
To indicate that an activity has been in progress recently (the activity started in the past and is still going on).	• Ramon <u>has been reading</u> the book *War and Peace*. • I <u>have been thinking</u> about moving out of the dormitory.

FORMATION

has/have + *been* + present participle (*-ing*)

> **Examples:** I have been waiting, you have been waiting, he/she/the student has been waiting, we have been waiting, they/the students have been waiting

PAST PERFECT

USE	EXAMPLES
To indicate that an action was completed before another action began in the past or to indicate that an action was completed by a definite time in the past.	• I <u>had</u> never <u>read</u> anything by Jane Austen until last month. • In English class I suddenly realized that I <u>had forgotten</u> to bring my textbook.
Note: If the word *before* or *after* is in the sentence, the simple past may be used instead of the past perfect.	• After all my friends <u>left</u> (or <u>had left</u>), I cleaned up the apartment.

FORMATION

had + past participle

> **Examples:** I had called, you had called, he/she/the student had called, we had called, they/the students had called

> **Note:** Many past-participle forms are irregular (for example, *written*, *met*, *known*). Consult a learner's dictionary for a list of common verbs that have irregular past-participle forms.

PAST PERFECT PROGRESSIVE

USE	EXAMPLES
To emphasize the duration of an activity that was completed before another action or time in the past.	• I <u>had been waiting</u> for him for an hour when he finally arrived.

FORMATION
had + *been* + present participle (*-ing*)

Examples: I had been waiting, you had been waiting, he/she/the student had been waiting, we had been waiting, they/the students had been waiting

FUTURE

USE	EXAMPLES
To express that an action, event, or state will occur in the future.	• I <u>will drive</u> you to the airport tomorrow. • Terry <u>will graduate</u> next June.

FORMATION
will + base form

Examples: I will attend, you will attend, he/she/the student will attend, we will attend, they/the students will attend

Note: Do not use an *-s* on the base form of the verb in the third-person singular.

OTHER IMPORTANT INFORMATION ABOUT EXPRESSING FUTURE TIME

Future time can also be expressed in the following ways:

• *am/is/are going to* + base form

　　Examples: We <u>are going to take</u> the midterm on Friday.
　　　　　　　　The city <u>is going to have</u> a parade on July 4.

• simple present or present progressive (especially with verbs of arriving and departing)

　　Examples: The plane <u>leaves</u> at 8:00 PM this evening.
　　　　　　　　The plane <u>is leaving</u> at 8:00 PM this evening.

• *would* (when the future is expressed in a sentence that is in past time)

　　Examples:

　　1. **Present/future time:** The instructor <u>says</u> that the exam <u>will cover</u> the first five units of the textbook.

　　　　Past time: The instructor <u>said</u> that the exam <u>would cover</u> the first five units of the textbook.

　　2. **Present/future time:** Even though I plan to go to college next year, I <u>do not know</u> how demanding college classes <u>will be</u>.

　　　　Past time: When I <u>was</u> in high school, I <u>did not know</u> how demanding college classes <u>would be</u>.

FUTURE PROGRESSIVE

USE	EXAMPLES
To express that an action will be happening over a period of time at some specific point in the future.	• Even though I will be studying when you call, I will answer the phone.
To emphasize the duration of an action in the future.	• Lin will be working on this essay for the next week.

FORMATION

will + *be* + present participle (*-ing*)

Examples: I will be leaving, you will be leaving, he/she/the student will be leaving, we will be leaving, they/the students will be leaving

FUTURE PERFECT

USE	EXAMPLES
To indicate that an activity will be completed before another event or time in the future.	• Maria will have finished her Ph.D. by the time she leaves for France.
	• We will have written five essays by the end of the semester.

FORMATION

will + *have* + past participle

Examples: I will have gone, you will have gone, he/she/the student will have gone, we will have gone, they/the students will have gone

FUTURE PERFECT PROGRESSIVE

USE	EXAMPLES
To indicate that an action has been in progress for a period of time before another event or time in the future.	• Carlos will have been working on his dissertation for three years before he gets his Ph.D. degree.
	• By this time next year, I will have been living here for two years.

FORMATION

will + *have* + *been* + present participle (*-ing*)

Examples: I will have been practicing, you will have been practicing, he/she/the student will have been practicing, we will have been practicing, they/the students will have been practicing

Stative Verbs

Stative verbs describe a state rather than show an action. We don't use these verbs in the progressive tenses.

Examples:

Incorrect: You <u>are seeming</u> nervous. Do you have a test today?

Correct: You <u>seem</u> nervous. Do you have a test today?

Incorrect: That hamburger <u>was smelling</u> delicious!

Correct: That hamburger <u>smelled</u> delicious!

Incorrect: The students <u>will be appreciating</u> the fact that the test has been postponed.

Correct: The students <u>will appreciate</u> the fact that the test has been postponed.

Incorrect: James <u>has always been understanding</u> math better than chemistry.

Correct: James <u>has always understood</u> math better than chemistry.

Stative verbs are most commonly used to express the following states.

TO SHOW THOUGHTS OR GIVE OPINIONS	TO SHOW ATTITUDES	TO SHOW EMOTIONS	TO SHOW OWNERSHIP OR POSSESSION	TO REFLECT THE SENSES	TO DESCRIBE A STATE OF BEING
believe	appreciate	hate	belong to	feel	appear
feel (= think)	(dis)agree	(dis)like	have	hear	be
forget	hope	fear	owe	see	cost
know	mind	love	own	smell	look (like)
mean	need		possess	taste	seem
realize	prefer				sound (like)
remember	think				tend
suppose	want				weigh
think	wish				
understand					

Some verbs can be both stative and active. However, the meaning of the verb is different. As active verbs, they can be used in the progressive tense.

Examples:

Stative meaning: Arnold <u>looks</u> unhappy. (This describes Arnold's appearance.)

Active meaning: He <u>is looking</u> for his mother. (This means "He is searching for his mother.")

Stative meaning: I <u>think</u> she is wonderful. (This means "In my opinion, she is wonderful.")

Active meaning: I <u>am thinking</u> about Ana. (This means "My mind is focusing on Ana.")

Stative meaning: Hydrogen sulfide <u>smells</u> bad. (This means "It gives off a bad odor.")

Active meaning: He <u>is smelling</u> the soup. (This means "He is trying to see what the soup smells like.")

Stative meaning: Soap <u>feels</u> slippery. (This describes what the soap is like when you touch it.)

Active meaning: He <u>is feeling</u> the burner to see if it is hot. (This means "He is touching the burner.")

Stative meaning: The sample <u>weighs</u> 80 grams. (This describes how much the sample weighs.)

Active meaning: She <u>is weighing</u> the sample. (This means she is trying to determine its weight.)

The simple present with *have* means to "own" or "possess."

Correct: I <u>have</u> a car.

Incorrect: I <u>am having</u> a car.

Correct: She <u>has</u> a lot of free time.

Incorrect: She <u>is having</u> a lot of free time.

For stative verbs in the passive voice, see Unit 5, "Passive Voice."

In certain special expressions, you can use the progressive with *have*, such as *have a good time, have difficulty, have a problem,* and *have dinner.*

Frank <u>is having</u> a good time tonight.   (He is enjoying himself.)

Gloria <u>is having</u> trouble with her car.   (Her car is not working properly.)

Verb-Tense Sequencing

Verb-tense sequencing refers to the way a writer moves from one verb tense to another. Knowing how to do this is one of the most important keys to using verb tenses correctly.

Sometimes a shift in verb tenses is appropriate and sometimes it is not, as illustrated in the following paragraphs. In paragraph A, the underlined verb *were* shows where a shift occurs from present to past. This shift is **not** appropriate because the writer is still commenting in general about men in his or her country. General statements that are true in the present require the simple present tense, so the writer should have used *are* instead of *were.*

A.   Many men in my country do not encourage their wives to work outside the home because they think women should not do anything but housework and child care. However, these men <u>were</u> wrong. They will never know what their wives can do or who their wives might become.

In paragraph B, the underlined verbs also show a shift from present to past. However, this shift is appropriate because the writer has moved from a discussion of what is true in the present to a discussion of what it was like before computers. In this way, the comparison between present and past is immediately clear.

B.   Computers <u>are</u> an integral part of our modern lives. At home, we <u>use</u> them for writing letters, online banking or shopping, and doing income taxes, to name just a few examples. With the Internet, we <u>browse</u> for information, <u>read</u>, and <u>communicate</u>. In the workplace, we <u>use</u> computers for tasks ranging from simple word processing all the way up to designing airplanes. Before homes and offices <u>had</u> computers, our world <u>was</u> very different. Letters <u>had</u> to be typed on a typewriter and it <u>was</u> difficult to correct mistakes. Engineers <u>drafted</u> and <u>designed</u> projects using pens, paper, and drawing boards. Students and researchers <u>went</u> to the library to manually search for materials they <u>needed</u>. From writing to designing to communicating, computers <u>have made</u> our lives easier and more enjoyable both in the home and at the workplace.

How Verb Tenses Work Together

A writer usually uses several different verb tenses in a piece of writing and must be able to switch back and forth between tenses automatically. The two passages that follow, along with the notes for each one, will show you how various verb tenses work together in a text to show time.

Passage 1

In this student paragraph, the writer explains why a certain class is hard for first-year college students. Each verb or verb phrase is underlined and explained.

> A difficult class for first-year students at my college is (*general truth*) Introduction to Psychology (Psychology 1). One reason why it is (*general truth*) so hard is that most students have had (*began in the past and continues in the present*) insufficient preparation for the demands of the class. Back in high school, for most of their classes, students did not do (*past fact*) much reading and preparation before each lecture. Students in Psychology 1 must complete (*modal; present time*) long reading assignments to understand the lectures and to do well on the exams. I took (*past action*) Psychology 1 last quarter, and we were assigned (*past action in passive voice*) hundreds of pages each week. Not only did I have to finish (*modal; past action*) the readings before class in order to really understand the lecture but also I had to review (*modal; past action*) them before exams. In high school, we simply brought (*past action*) our books to class where we read (*past action*) a page and then discussed (*past action*) it. Another reason this class is (*general truth*) hard is that psychology consists (*general truth*) of many difficult concepts such as how the brain works, how infants develop, and how humans learn (*general truths*). Many of the concepts sound the same but are, in reality, different (*general truths*). What made (*past action*) them particularly hard in this class was (*past action*) that we had to apply (*modal; past fact*) these concepts to problem-solving on the tests. It is (*general truth*) clear that first-year students are justified (*general truth, stative passive*) when they label (*general truth*) Psychology 1 as hard, but if they devote (*conditional; real*) time to studying, go (*conditional; real*) to all the classes and discussion sections, and seek (*conditional; real*) help when needed, they will do (*conditional; future result*) well in the class.

Passage 2

In this introduction to a longer essay, the writer summarizes an article by the American author, Eudora Welty (1909–2001).

The writer uses three tenses: the simple present, the simple past, and the present perfect. An explanation for why these three verb tenses are used is given at the end of the passage.

> In her article, "Listening," Eudora Welty tells how she became committed to reading and writing through listening. Welty was first introduced to the world of books when she was three years old. She reports that her mother

<u>read</u> to her all day long, in every room of the house. Because of her mother's reading to her, Welty <u>developed</u> a love of books, and she also <u>learned</u> to listen to what she <u>heard</u> and what she <u>read</u>. She <u>says</u>, "Ever since I <u>was</u> first <u>read</u> to, then <u>started</u> reading to myself, there <u>has</u> never <u>been</u> a line read that I <u>didn't</u> *hear*." She <u>feels</u> that her ability to listen to words <u>has influenced</u> her in her desire to write and her ability to write, as she <u>has</u> "always <u>trusted</u> this voice." Although Welty <u>does</u> not <u>say</u> it directly, it <u>is</u> clear that her mother <u>served</u> as an excellent role model because she <u>taught</u> her the love of reading.

Explanation of Verb-Tense Use

1. The writer uses simple present tense to report what Welty wrote in her article. The writer can choose either the simple present or simple past in this case, but the writer must be consistent. Note the use of *tells, reports, says,* and *feels* to relate what Welty wrote in her article.

2. The writer uses the simple past to refer to Welty's childhood experience because all this happened when Welty was a child.

3. In the quotation from the article, the writer uses the tenses used by Welty. Of course, Welty was still alive at the time of her article and the use of the present perfect ("*there has never been a line …*") is appropriate.

4. The writer uses the present perfect to indicate that the action began in the past and is still true at the present time. In this paragraph, the present time includes the present time of the article, when Welty was still alive.

IMPROVE YOUR WRITING STYLE
CHOOSING THE MOST APPROPRIATE VERB TENSE

Writers often have a choice of verb tenses that are similar but not exactly the same in meaning. Sometimes you may want to choose one tense over another for a specific reason. At other times, you may have options, with your choice of tense creating little difference in meaning. For you, as advanced writers, what is important is to be aware of the differences that can be created by the use of one verb tense over another. The sentences that follow illustrate some of the differences you should become aware of.

Continued on page 20.

IMPROVE YOUR WRITING STYLE (*CONT.*)
CHOOSING THE MOST APPROPRIATE VERB TENSE

Examples:

a. We <u>decided</u> to go to the movies. (simple past tense)

b. We <u>have decided</u> to go to the movies. (present perfect tense)

Explanation of difference: In both sentences above, the decision to go to the movies has already been made. The present perfect tense in sentence b makes it clear that the decision has either just been made or has been made recently. Also, with sentence a, the meaning could be that we decided to go to the movies and <u>already went</u>. *However, in sentence b, the action of going to the movies has not yet been completed.*

Examples:

a. It <u>rained</u> yesterday. (simple past tense)

b. It <u>was raining</u> yesterday. (past progressive tense)

Explanation of difference: The use of the past progressive tense was raining *in sentence b emphasizes the duration of time that it rained yesterday: it rained over a period of time. In sentence a, in contrast, the verb in the simple past tense does not indicate whether or not it rained briefly or over a period of time. A time reference word, such as* all day (It rained all day) *or* briefly (It rained briefly) *would have to be used with the verb to indicate how long it rained.*

Examples:

a. We <u>had eaten</u> dinner when you came over to visit. (past perfect tense)

b. We <u>ate</u> dinner when you came over to visit. (past tense)

c. We <u>had eaten</u> dinner before you came over to visit. (past perfect tense)

d. We <u>ate</u> dinner before you came over to visit. (past tense)

Explanation of difference: In sentences a and b, the time that the eating took place in relation to the action of coming over to visit is different. In sentence a, the past perfect tense indicates that the action of eating had already happened before the action of coming over to visit. In sentence b, in contrast, the action of eating occurred at the same time or even slightly after the action of coming over happened. Note, however, that in sentences c and d, the action of eating in both cases was finished before the action of coming over to visit happened. The subordinating conjunction before *in sentences c and d clearly indicates that the action of eating comes first in both cases.*

Examples:

a. I <u>am studying</u> in the library. (present progressive tense)
b. I <u>study</u> in the library. (simple present tense)

Explanation of difference: Although both verbs are in the present, their meanings are different. In sentence a, the present progressive tense shows that the action of studying is happening either exactly at the moment of speaking or for a temporary period of time in the present. In other words, the studying in the library is happening right now or for a period of time in the present (such as this week*) that is considered temporary. In contrast, the simple present tense in sentence b indicates that the action of studying in the library is done on a regular basis (for example,* every night*).*

PRACTICE WHAT YOU HAVE LEARNED

EXERCISE 1

Directions: Decide whether each of the following sentences is correct (C) or incorrect (I). If it is incorrect, make the correction. Be prepared to explain why your choice of verb tense is correct.

Example: *I*   Since I have been a college student, I m̶a̶d̶e̶ *have made* many new friends.

_____ 1. I was interested in physics since high school.

_____ 2. Having good social skills is essential for my job, and I decide to take a class in personal communication.

_____ 3. Since she was a child, she likes sports, especially water sports, such as swimming and waterskiing.

_____ 4. Mario graduate as a veterinarian in January of last year.

_____ 5. Hector speaks Spanish and comes from Costa Rica.

_____ 6. First, we went to Italy. Then, we travel to Austria and Germany. Finally, we visit Spain.

_____ 7. The professor had given an introduction to the course yesterday, the first day of class.

_____ 8. There are rumors that college tuition is higher next year.

_____ 9. By the time of the presidential election, the candidates will have campaigned in most, if not all, of the 50 states.

_____ 10. In my opinion, voting in elections was very important.

EXERCISE 2

Directions: Fill in each blank with the correct tense of the verb in parentheses. For some blanks, more than one verb tense is possible.

One quality that _____*helps*_____ (help) students succeed in their studies is
(1)
self-discipline. Self-discipline _____ (be) particularly important in
(2)
college. I _____ (learn) a great deal about self-discipline by observing
(3)
two of my friends. I have noted that my roommate Betsy _____
(4)
(plan) her time every night before she _____ (go) to bed. She
(5)
_____ (write) down what she _____ (have) to do the
(6)   (7)
next day and how much time she _____ (spend) doing each
(8)
activity. First, she _____ (schedule) time for attending classes
(9)
and working. She also _____ (set) aside time for socializing,
(10)
running, studying, and eating. By having a timetable and sticking to it, Betsy
_____ (be) always able to accomplish a lot more than I can.
(11)
Another friend, Jo, _____ (discipline) herself by not doing anything
(12)
unless she _____ (complete) all of her homework and reading.
(13)
One night last semester, I _____ (invite) her to go out to dinner, but
(14)
she _____ (refuse) because she _____ (not finish) her
(15)   (16)
physics homework. I wish I could be as disciplined as these two friends of
mine are. I _____ (know) that self-discipline is important if I want to
(17)
be successful in college. Thus, next term I _____ (make) an effort to
(18)
discipline myself.

EXERCISE 3

Directions: Fill in each blank with the correct form of the verb given in parentheses. Pay particular attention to the sequence of tenses you use. For some blanks, more than one verb tense is possible.

October 31, 2012

Internship Office
Mighty Corporation
Hometown, CA 90001

Dear Dr. Martinez:

I _____ (read) your advertisement in our campus newspaper
(1)
yesterday and _____ (write) to apply for a summer internship
(2)
position. I _____ (hear) many wonderful things about your company
(3)
and would be very interested in working for you.

I _____ (graduate) last June from the University of Michigan with a
(4)
B.S. in electrical engineering. After graduating from college, I _____
(5)
(fulfill) a lifelong dream of traveling to Japan, the country of my parents' origin.

Currently, I _____ (work) on my M.S. degree in electrical and
(6)
computer engineering at Stanford University. I _____ (complete) my
(7)
degree next June, at which time I would like to work full time for a company

such as yours.

As you can imagine, the summer internships you offer are exactly what

I _____ (look) for. The internship will not only be valuable to
(8)
me in terms of professional experience, but, I believe, will also help me

focus my studies in my second year of the M.S. program to reflect what I

_____ (need) when I am working for the computer industry in the
(9)
future. Because of its proximity to my university, Stanford, I _____
(10)
(visit) your company's Hometown branch a number of times. I am especially

interested in working at this site because of its focus on research and

development. In addition, as someone who is bilingual and bicultural (English

and Japanese), I _____ (find) the idea of an internship with a
(11)
multinational company such as yours particularly appealing.

I _____ (enclose) a copy of my résumé for your consideration. Please
                (12)
do not hesitate to contact me if you have any questions or wish to set up an
interview.

Sincerely,

Peter E. Engineer

Peter E. Engineer

EXERCISE 4

Directions: The following student paragraph has 11 verb-tense errors.
Cross out each incorrect verb and write the correct verb above
it. For some verbs, more than one option is possible. The first
error has been corrected for you.

    I have a positive attitude toward writing in English. When I first ~~come~~ to *(came)*
the United States, I am very confused about using English, a new and strange
language. But as time go by, my feeling toward the language begin to change.
I force myself to write even though it was hard at first. I write a lot, and I become
more confident each time I write. Now, although I am more confident about writing,
I still have many problems to overcome. I find that writing takes a great deal of
time, and one has to be patient and disciplined in order to be good at it. At times,
I was frustrated and impatient with my writing. In fact, sometimes I sat for hours
and cannot write even a word. Nevertheless, despite my frustration and long hours
of work, I tend to have a positive attitude toward writing in English. Even though
English was not my native language, I have found that I simply like to write.

EXERCISE 5

Directions: The following student paragraph has eight verb-tense errors.
Cross out each incorrect verb and write the correct verb above
it. In some cases, more than one option is possible. The first
error has been corrected for you.

    Children of immigrants who do not speak English often ~~functioned~~ more like *(function)*
adults than children. As a child of immigrant parents myself, I have often had
to act as an adult. Ever since my family arrived here five years ago, I take care

of them in many ways. I have had to pay the rent, the utilities, the telephone, and any other bills. I translated letters from English to Vietnamese for the whole family. When a family member was sick, I had gone along to the doctor to explain the problem and to translate the doctor's suggestions. I believe it has been good for me to do all these things because it prepared me for what I face when I am living on my own. Having adult responsibilities gave me the chance to understand what the world is like outside of my home. It provides me with hands-on training and has been beneficial for me.

EXERCISE 6

Directions: The following student paragraph has nine verb-tense errors. Cross out each incorrect verb and make the correction above it. The first error has been corrected for you.

Luckily for me, at the very end of my first semester here at college, my grades changed for the better. My Chemistry 1A class last semester is one example. At the start of the semester, I did not understand the materials or the problems. I was confused when I read and ~~try~~ *tried* to solve problems. Even though I did the homework and go to all the laboratory sessions, my understanding did not seem to improve. In fact, on my first and second tests, I receive a D and an F. After receiving those two grades, I start to realize that I had to change the way I was studying. I decide to put myself on a strict schedule and to go to the library every day after dinner. I continue to follow this plan until the end of the semester. Even now, I still cannot believe how well I had done on my final. I received a B on the final and a C for the semester. This is what I think happen: When I reviewed all the materials systematically, I am able to understand principles of chemistry that I did not understand before.

EXERCISE 7

Directions: Choose a news article to read. Underline all the verbs in one or two paragraphs. Can you explain why the different verb tenses were used? If you are unsure of any of them, ask a classmate, a tutor, or your instructor.

Post-test   **What Do You Know Now?**

A   Decide whether the underlined verb tense in each of the following sentences is correct (C) or incorrect (I). If it is incorrect, make the correction.

_____ 1. My high school teacher <u>used</u> the same textbook for algebra since 2009.

_____ 2. When they <u>will begin</u> taking a Chinese language class, many students are nervous about learning the writing system.

_____ 3. After he <u>had studied</u> three hours for his Spanish quiz, my roommate decided to go to bed and get a good night's sleep.

_____ 4. It <u>is seeming</u> very cold in the classroom, and most students are wearing jackets.

_____ 5. World War I <u>lasts</u> from 1914–1918.

_____ 6. Access to higher education <u>means</u> that even though a college education can be expensive, most students can still go to college.

_____ 7. The instructor <u>wrote</u> the grammar exam last Friday when she suddenly realized she had forgotten to teach a particular point.

_____ 8. An article in today's paper focuses on 20 inventions that <u>have changed</u> our lives.

_____ 9. In a recent article, Lawrence Thomas, a teacher in Kansas, says that he never votes. He also <u>said</u> that he is against paying taxes.

_____10. Yesterday we celebrated Thanksgiving and most of us ate turkey; many of us also <u>eat</u> pumpkin pie.

B   Check (✓) the sentence that has the correct verb tense for the meaning indicated.

1. Habitual action

_____ a. Mark is riding the bus to school because it is raining.

_____ b. Mark rides the bus to school when it is raining.

2. An action that is happening right now

_____ a. Many students at my school major in communications.

_____ b. Many students at my school are majoring in communications.

3. An action that began in the past and continues into the present

_____ a. Women have made great progress in closing the gender gap in salaries.

_____ b. Women made great progress in closing the gender gap in salaries.

C Find and underline the inappropriate tense shift in each paragraph and correct it.

1. In 1849, many people came to Northern California to hunt for gold. They soon found that looking for it was hard and dangerous work. Many then decide to open up businesses to sell equipment and supplies to the miners. Some became very wealthy because they had struck gold above ground.

2. Although there are many different routes to obtaining an education, going to college is not the only path. In her article, "Where Learning Takes Place," retired English professor Patricia Harrelson shares her philosophy that attending college is not the only means of getting an education. Harrelson sees self-directed learning as learning that does not occur in a classroom. She listed such activities as cooking, gardening, and parenting as self-directed education. Although Harrelson views self-directed learning as something that cannot be achieved in a formal college setting, it is my belief that self-directed learning and traditional college learning can be combined.

D Correct the underlined errors in verb tense.

Finals week is a time of great pressure for college students. In many courses, a big percentage of the final grade is based on the final exam, and the final itself <u>covered</u> an entire semester of material taught. Also, all final exams are taken during just one week. Some students study for three or four, maybe even five, finals during finals week. This can really be exhausting, especially for first-year students who <u>have experienced</u> finals week for the first time. What students find the most difficult of all <u>was</u> to have two final exams on the same day. Last quarter was my first experience of finals week. I had never thought that I would ever spend so much time studying. In fact, the night before my math final, I slept for only two hours. I <u>stay up</u> all night trying to memorize all of the equations for the final. After the math final, I <u>come</u> home and went straight to bed. I think having a week of no classes before finals week would ease the pressure and help students perform better because they would have more time to study.

E   **Fill in each blank with the correct tense of the verb in parentheses.**

American English is spoken in the United States, and British English is spoken in the United Kingdom. Americans and British can easily understand each other, but American English has distinctive features of its own. For example, since the 1600s it _____ (borrow) words from other

(1)
languages, such as *canyon* from Spanish and *squash* and *igloo* from native American languages.

Another interesting feature of American English is its accents and dialects. Many of our accents today reflect where the early immigrants _____ (come) from or the languages they _____

(2)   (3)
(speak), such as German, or their English accents, such as Scotch Irish. The most well-known dialect, African American Vernacular English (AAVE), began with the slave trade in the early 1700s. Without a common language to communicate with each other, the slaves _____ (begin)

(4)
to speak their own form of English, learned from traders and plantation owners. That language _____ (become) a dialect with its own

(5)
grammatical rules.

APPLY WHAT YOU HAVE LEARNED TO WRITING

Select a writing topic and follow the steps in Appendix A on page 337.

Topic 1:

In our fast-paced lives, it is more important than ever to build in time for relaxation. Different individuals find different activities relaxing. While some people find it relaxing to do yoga, others might find relaxation in taking a leisurely walk, watching a new movie, or reading a good book. Describe several activities you personally find relaxing and comment on how each is beneficial or enjoyable.

Topic 2:

Explain what different kinds of jobs are available for people in your field of study. Then, explain either what you do as a career or what your career goals are (i.e., what kind of work you would like to do in the future). If you do not have a specific goal, suggest what you might be interested in considering. Finally, comment on what the current job market is like for those in your field.

Topic 3:

Write about a historical event that had or is continuing to have major effects, either positive or negative, on your country. First, explain the event. Then, analyze its effects, making it clear whether you consider these effects to be positive or negative.

VERB FORMS

GOALS

- Learn why mastering verb forms is important in writing

- Understand seven problems writers commonly encounter with verb forms

- Form and use verb forms correctly in exercises and writing assignments

What sports do you participate in or enjoy watching? How important is it to you to exercise regularly?

LEARN WHAT THE ERROR IS

Errors with Verb Forms

A verb-form error is an error in the formation of the main verb, any part of a verb phrase, or with a gerund, an infinitive, or participle. For example, the verb form in the following sentence is incorrect: *We have not yet <u>estimate</u> the cost of the trip.* Here, the past participle *estimated* is needed instead of the base form *estimate.* In the sentence *Mona has decided <u>enrolling</u> in three courses,* the verb following *decide* must be *to enroll* (an infinitive) instead of *enrolling,* a gerund. The editing symbol for a verb-form error is *vf.*

In the sentence *The students <u>confuse</u> about the assignment,* a main verb has been incorrectly used instead of *be* + the past participle. The sentence should read *The students <u>are confused</u> about the assignment.*

Note that verb-form errors with modals and the conditional are not covered in this unit but rather in Units 3 and 4, respectively. Also, present and past participles used as adjectives are covered in Unit 14, "Word Forms."

Verb-form errors are global (more serious) errors and will usually significantly affect the reader's ability to understand the meaning of a text. Furthermore, such errors distract the reader because verbs are important content words that often convey action in English sentences. Because readers in the academic and professional worlds expect verb formation to be correct, incorrect verb forms make a piece of writing appear flawed to the reader, no matter how strong the content is.

Suggestions for Reducing Errors

- Learn the following terminology to understand verb forms.
  an infinitive
  > to walk, to study, to speak

  a base form (the infinitive without *to*)
  > walk, study, speak

  a gerund or a present participle (the base form + -*ing*)
  > walking, studying, speaking

  a past participle
  > walked, studied, spoken

  a simple past form
  > walked, studied, spoke

  a verb phrase (a main verb with any auxiliary verbs)
  > has been speaking, has spoken, am speaking, will have spoken

- Study grammar rules to avoid verb-form errors due to incorrect formation of part of a verb phrase. For example, in the sentence *He has send out several resumes,* the writer needs to learn that the present perfect is formed with the past participle (in this case, *sent*), not the base form. If you are making such errors, study the rules for verb-phrase formation given in this unit.

- Memorize verb forms that are not governed by rules, such as those involving verbals following verbs. For example, you might have to memorize the fact that certain verbs, such as *dislike,* are always followed by a gerund (the *-ing* form), as in *I dislike running,* while other verbs, such as *hope,* are followed by an infinitive, as in *I hope to run.* Still others, such as *like,* can be followed by either a gerund or an infinitive, as in *I like running* or *I like to run.* Use the guidelines for forming verbals in this unit to help you recognize and master these verb forms.

- Do not depend upon your ear to help you master verb formation because, in spoken English, it is often difficult to hear exactly how a verb is formed. For example, it is difficult to hear the difference between *talk* and *talked* in spoken English because the *-ed* ending is not stressed in speaking. Likewise, because auxiliary verbs are most often unstressed (not said loudly, or clearly, or are contracted) in spoken English, your ear will probably not help you distinguish between the correct *I am going* and the incorrect *I going.*

- Become aware of gerunds, infinitives, participles, main verbs, and verb phrases when you read. Written material—such as newspapers, magazines, journals, web sites, and textbooks—is an excellent resource for examples of correct verb formation.

Check Your Understanding

Write answers to the following questions. Share your answers with another student.

1. How is a verb-form error different from a verb-tense error?

2. Why is it necessary to memorize the use of some verb forms?

GRAMMAR JOURNAL ENTRY 2   VERB FORMS

Respond to the following in your grammar journal.

1. Write about your most recent vacation from school or work. What did you do? Did you travel? If so, where? Overall, did you enjoy your vacation?

2. Underline all the verbs and verb phrases in the journal entry you have written. Look at the verb forms you have used and check to see if the formation is correct. If you have questions about any of them, put a question mark above them and check them with a classmate, a tutor, or your instructor.

UNDERSTAND COMMON PROBLEMS

This section presents seven problems that writers commonly encounter with verb forms. First, take the pre-test to see what you already know about verb forms. When you finish, check your answers on page 350. Then, carefully study each problem and the examples that illustrate it. Pay particular attention to those problems that correspond to the pre-test questions you had difficulty with. Remember that becoming aware of the types of errors you most often make with verb forms will increase your chances of avoiding these errors in your writing.

Pre-test

What Do You Already Know?

Test your ability to recognize and correct errors with verb forms.

A   Correct the marked verb-form errors. These are examples of the seven common problems that are presented in this unit.

Problem 1   Mario <u>chosed</u> to live in the dormitory rather than in an apartment.

Problem 2   The hikers <u>had walk</u> two miles before they realized their mistake.

Problem 3   Sometimes <u>I totally confuse</u> about English grammar.

Problem 4   The company <u>did clearly deserved</u> to win the award for their research.

Problem 5   An effective speaker tries <u>look</u> directly at his or her audience.

Problem 6   I hope <u>to presenting</u> a convincing argument during my presentation.

Problem 7   After <u>finish</u> work, Margarita likes to work out in the gym for at least an hour.

B   Underline and correct the one error in each of the following sentences. (The errors are not in any particular order).

1.   Gwen does spends too much time texting her friends.

2.   My former roommate wants me call her when I am in Washington, D.C.

3.   I interested in seeing this new play.

4.   My sister teached me how to write my name when I was four years old.

5. After the game was over, we wanted going to a restaurant.

6. We planned to took the TV back to the store because it wasn't working properly.

7. Most of the students had finish their homework before class began.

Seven Common Problems

Problem 1

The main verb or verb phrase has been incorrectly formed.

Incorrect: My comment $\overset{vf}{\underline{\text{hurted}}}$ my roommate's feelings.

Correct: My comment <u>hurt</u> my roommate's feelings.

Incorrect: She $\overset{vf}{\underline{\text{flied}}}$ to Los Angeles for the Chinese New Year.

Correct: She <u>flew</u> to Los Angeles for the Chinese New Year.

Incorrect: I $\overset{vf}{\underline{\text{been studying}}}$ hard lately.

Incorrect: I $\overset{vf}{\underline{\text{studying}}}$ hard lately.

Correct: I <u>have been studying</u> hard lately.

> SELF-HELP STRATEGY: If you find you do not know the forms of irregular verbs in English, study a list of the most common irregular verb forms in a learner's dictionary. You can also look up the base form of a particular verb in a dictionary. Even though software grammar-check programs can help you pick up some of these errors, you should know irregular verb forms.

Problem 2

The past participle in a verb phrase has been incorrectly formed.

Incorrect: Ben did not want the teacher to know that he had not $\overset{vf}{\underline{\text{study}}}$ for the quiz.

Correct: Ben did not want the teacher to know that he had not <u>studied</u> for the quiz.

Incorrect:	One of my colleagues was <u>fire</u> [vf] from his job.
Correct:	One of my colleagues was <u>fired</u> from his job.

Incorrect:	The choir had already <u>sang</u> [vf] their last song before I got there.
Correct:	The choir had already <u>sung</u> their last song before I got there.

> **SELF-HELP STRATEGY:** Do not omit the *-ed* ending of a past participle. The majority of verbs have past participles that end in *-ed*. This *-ed* ending is hard to hear in spoken English because it is not stressed and often is not a separate syllable. It is easier to hear the *-ed* in verbs like *wanted* and *needed* because the ending is clearly pronounced as a separate syllable after verbs ending in the sounds *d* or *t*.

Problem 3

A main verb or an adjective has been incorrectly used instead of *be* + past participle.

Incorrect:	I <u>confuse</u> [vf] about what you just said.
Incorrect:	I <u>confused</u> [vf] about what you just said.
Correct:	I <u>am confused</u> about what you just said.

Incorrect:	The store is <u>close</u> [vf] on Sundays.
Correct:	The store is <u>closed</u> on Sundays.

Incorrect:	I <u>concerned</u> [vf] about getting a good grade on my chemistry midterm.
Incorrect:	I <u>am concern</u> [vf] about getting a good grade on my chemistry midterm.
Correct:	I <u>am concerned</u> about getting a good grade on my chemistry midterm.

Incorrect:	San Francisco <u>located</u> [vf] on the northern coast of California.
Correct:	San Francisco <u>is located</u> on the northern coast of California.

SELF-HELP STRATEGY: Note that this type of construction is a form of the passive voice and is sometimes called the **stative passive.** Some stative passive constructions can be made active by changing the word order, while some cannot be made active. See Unit 5, p. 110, for more information on the stative passive.

- I am confused about what you just said. (stative passive)
  What you just said confuses me. (active voice)

- I am greatly concerned about getting a good grade on my chemistry midterm. (stative passive)
  Getting a good grade on my chemistry midterm concerns me greatly. (active voice)

- The store is located on First Street. (stative passive)
  (No active-voice construction is possible.)

Problem 4

An auxiliary verb and a main verb that do not go together have been used in a verb phrase.

Incorrect: John failed the test because he <u>did not studied</u> enough. [vf]

Correct: John failed the test because he <u>did not study</u> enough.

Incorrect: Tina was discouraged because she <u>was not progressed</u> very quickly. [vf]

Correct: Tina was discouraged because she <u>had not progressed</u> very quickly.

Correct: Tina was discouraged because she <u>was not progressing</u> very quickly.

Incorrect: The employment office <u>does accepts</u> applications year round. [vf]

Correct: The employment office <u>accepts</u> applications year round.

Correct: The employment office <u>does accept</u> applications year round.
(special emphatic use)

Incorrect: The company <u>did received</u> my application for employment. [vf]

Correct: The company <u>received</u> my application for employment.

Correct: The company <u>did receive</u> my application for employment.
(special emphatic use)

SELF-HELP STRATEGY: Make it a point to memorize the information in Rules for Verb-Phrase Formation, pp. 39–40.

Problem 5
The form of a verbal following a verb is incorrect.

Incorrect: He decided <u>going</u> *vf* to the library tonight.

Incorrect: He decided <u>go</u> *vf* to the library tonight.

Correct: He decided <u>to go</u> to the library tonight.

Incorrect: Matthew avoided <u>to discuss</u> *vf* that issue.

Incorrect: Matthew avoided <u>discuss</u> *vf* that issue.

Correct: Matthew avoided <u>discussing</u> that issue.

Incorrect: The bystander helped me <u>pushed</u> *vf* my car to the side of the road.

Correct: The bystander helped me <u>push</u> my car to the side of the road.

> SELF-HELP STRATEGY: Keep in mind that the form of a verbal that follows a verb is not rule-based. Instead, you will need to memorize which forms of the verbal follow each verb on a case-by-case basis. You will find lists of the most common verbs and the verbals that follow them in the Review Grammar Solutions section in this unit, starting on page 39.

Problem 6
The infinitive has been incorrectly formed.

Incorrect: It was hard for Naomi to <u>admitted</u> *vf* to me that she was wrong.

Incorrect: It was hard for Naomi <u>admitted</u> *vf* to me that she was wrong.

Correct: It was hard for Naomi <u>to admit</u> to me that she was wrong.

Correct: It was hard for Naomi <u>to have admitted</u> to me that she was wrong.

Incorrect: Mike often forgets <u>to checks</u> *vf* his mail on Saturdays.

Correct: Mike often forgets <u>to check</u> his mail on Saturdays.

> SELF-HELP STRATEGY: Remember that infinitives consist of either *to* + base form (as in *to admit*) or *to* + *have* + past participle (as in *to have admitted*) for the past infinitive. Do not add an *-s* ending to an infinitive form.

Problem 7

The base form of a verb has been used instead of a gerund, an infinitive, or a participle.

Incorrect: He says that <u>discuss</u> *vf* his problem would be too painful.

Correct: He says that <u>discussing</u> his problem would be too painful.

Correct: He says that <u>to discuss</u> his problem would be too painful.

Incorrect: <u>Study</u> *vf* all night does not usually improve your test grade.

Correct: <u>Studying</u> all night does not usually improve your test grade.

Incorrect: It is easy <u>communicate</u> *vf* with him.

Correct: It is easy <u>to communicate</u> with him.

Incorrect: He changed his way of <u>look</u> *vf* at senior citizens.

Correct: He changed his way of <u>looking</u> at senior citizens.

Incorrect: By <u>study,</u> *vf* we can learn these formulas.

Correct: By <u>studying,</u> we can learn these formulas.

Incorrect: My sister just saw a girl <u>wear</u> *vf* a dress she really liked.

Correct: My sister just saw a girl <u>wearing</u> a dress she really liked.

REVIEW GRAMMAR SOLUTIONS

Rules for Verb-Phrase Formation

By learning the following rules for verb-phrase formation, you will increase your chances of avoiding verb-form errors when you write.

1. ***Do (not)* + base form**

   Examples:

   I <u>do</u> not <u>know</u> the answer.

   She <u>does</u> not <u>know</u> the answer.

   She <u>did</u> not <u>know</u> the answer.

2. *Have* (*not*) + **past participle (base form + *-ed* or irregular form)**

   Examples:

   > I <u>have</u> not left yet.
   >
   > She <u>has left</u>.
   >
   > She <u>had</u> already <u>left</u> when I arrived.

   Note: The form for *to have* is *have + had*. (She <u>has</u> already <u>had</u> breakfast.)

3. *Be* (*not*) + **present participle (base form of verb + *-ing*)**

   Examples:

   > I <u>am sleeping</u>.
   >
   > She <u>is</u> not <u>sleeping</u>.
   >
   > We <u>are sleeping</u>.
   >
   > She <u>was sleeping</u>.
   >
   > We <u>were sleeping</u>.
   >
   > We <u>have been sleeping</u> for an hour.
   >
   > She <u>has been sleeping</u> for an hour.
   >
   > She <u>had been sleeping</u> for an hour when I arrived.

Emphatic Use of Auxiliary Verbs in Verb Phrases

Sometimes, in order to make a sentence emphatic, an auxiliary verb is used in a verb phrase where it normally would not be needed. Although found in writing, emphatic sentences tend to be more common in speaking than in writing.

   Examples:

   > I wonder whether the employment office accepts applications year round. (in response) Yes, it <u>does accept</u> them year round.
   >
   > I discovered that the employment office <u>does accept</u> applications year round. (This sentence is emphatic because at some point previous to this statement, the writer did not know that the employment office accepted applications year round, and the writer is emphasizing that he or she <u>does know</u> that information now.)
   >
   > I do not think the company received your application for employment. (in response) Yes, the company <u>did receive</u> my application.

Guidelines for Choosing Verbals

In English, a verb can be followed by a verb form called a *verbal*. For example, in the sentence *He <u>decided to go</u> to the library*, the verb *decided* is followed by the verbal *to go*. A verbal following a verb may be an infinitive, a gerund, or occasionally a base form. There is no grammar rule, however, that will tell you which form of the verb will follow another verb. Some verbs are followed by a gerund, other verbs are followed by an infinitive, while still others can be followed by either, and a few can be followed by the base form. Thus, you will need to learn, on a case-by-case basis, which verbal should be used after a given verb.

Study these rules for adding verbals. Then, study the lists of commonly used verbs and the verbals that follow them.

1. Some verbs must be followed by an infinitive.

Incorrect: Paul agreed <u>going</u> to Sacramento tomorrow.

Incorrect: Paul agreed <u>go</u> to Sacramento tomorrow.

Correct: Paul agreed <u>to go</u> to Sacramento tomorrow.

> **Note:** Some verbs, such as *ask, choose, want,* or *expect,* can be followed by a noun or pronoun before the infinitive. In the following example, the noun *Isabel* functions both as the direct object of *wants* and as the subject of the infinitive.

Example:

IBM wants *Isabel* <u>to fly</u> to New York for an interview.

2. Some verbs must be followed by a gerund.

Incorrect: Bill gave up <u>to study</u> for the exam.

Incorrect: Bill gave up <u>study</u> for the exam.

Incorrect: Bill gave up <u>studies</u> for the exam.

Correct: Bill gave up <u>studying</u> for the exam.

3. Some verbs can be followed by either a gerund or an infinitive.

Incorrect: Mia likes <u>sail</u> on Folsom Lake.

Correct: Mia likes <u>to sail</u> on Folsom Lake.

Correct: Mia likes <u>sailing</u> on Folsom Lake.

4. A small, commonly used group of verbs (*make, let, help, have*) must be followed by a base form (the infinitive without *to*). These verbs always have a noun or pronoun between them.

Incorrect: Please make the children <u>to go</u> upstairs.

Incorrect: Please make the children <u>going</u> upstairs.

Correct: Please make the children <u>go</u> upstairs.

Incorrect: Joseph let me *to carry* his suitcase.

Correct: Joseph let me <u>carry</u> his suitcase.

Note: The verb *help* may be followed by either a base form or an infinitive in current usage.

Example:

Hien helped the elderly woman <u>cross</u> the street.

Hien helped the elderly woman <u>to cross</u> the street.

Gerunds, Infinitives, or Base Forms

VERBS FOLLOWED BY A GERUND

admit	dislike	postpone	resent
avoid	enjoy	quit	resume
consider	finish	recall	risk
deny	imagine	recommend	suggest
discuss	miss	regret	

Examples:

I miss <u>seeing</u> you.
Barbara cannot risk <u>going</u>.

VERBS FOLLOWED BY AN INFINITIVE

agree	deserve	need	seem
appear	endeavor	offer	tend
attempt	fail	plan	volunteer
consent	hesitate	prepare	wish
decide	hope	promise	
demand	intend	refuse	

Examples:

He hesitated <u>to call</u> me.
She promised <u>to write</u> soon.
We will attempt <u>to finish</u> the task by tomorrow.

Note: The following verbs **can** take a noun or pronoun before the infinitive.

ask	expect	need	promise
beg	intend	prepare	want
choose			

Examples:

I asked *him* <u>to go</u>.
I need *the children* <u>to help</u>.

Note: Except in the passive voice, the following verbs **must** have a noun or pronoun before the infinitive.

advise	command	instruct	select
allow	convince	invite	teach
appoint	encourage	order	tell
authorize	forbid	permit	tempt
cause	force	remind	trust
challenge	hire	require	

Examples:

> He challenged *me* <u>to participate</u> in the contest.
> I will remind *you* <u>to get up</u> early.
> She was advised <u>to leave</u> by the security guard. (passive voice)

VERBS FOLLOWED BY A GERUND OR AN INFINITIVE

begin	like	remember	stop
continue	love	start	try
hate	prefer		

Examples:

> I like to <u>hike</u>.
> I like <u>hiking</u>.

VERBS FOLLOWED BY A BASE FORM

Note: Since these four verbs are very commonly used, memorize them along with the form of the verbal that must follow them. *Help* can also be followed by an infinitive.

have	help	let	make

Examples:

> I will let you <u>know</u>.
> Could you help me <u>carry</u> these boxes?

Guidelines for Using Gerunds and Infinitives

The following guidelines for using gerunds and infinitives in a variety of situations will help you use them correctly in the majority of cases. However, all of the rules for using gerunds and infinitives are not fully treated in this text. If you want to know a particular rule in more detail, you may wish to consult an advanced ESL grammar textbook.

1. Use an infinitive or gerund, not a base form, when a verbal functions as a subject or an object.

Examples:

To win (not *Win*) the election is what he wants.

Reading (not *Read*) is one of her hobbies.

We have benefited greatly from listening (not *listen*) to her lectures.

2. Use a gerund, not a base form, as the object of a preposition.

Examples:

Pedro helped me forget my bad grade by coming over to visit.

Martha talked me into helping her.

3. Use an infinitive, not a base form, after many adjectives.

Examples:

I am sorry to see you so unhappy.

I am eager to get my driver's license.

Note: Some adjectives that are followed by infinitives include the following: *afraid, amazed, anxious, ashamed, careful, certain, content, delighted, determined, disappointed, eager, fortunate, glad, happy, hesitant, likely, pleased, proud, ready, reluctant, sad, shocked, sorry, surprised, upset.*

4. Use an infinitive, not a base form, to express a purpose.

Examples:

He went to the teaching assistant's office to ask a question.

(The *to* is a shortened form of *in order to*.)

5. Use a past infinitive (*to* + *have* + past participle) in cases in which the event or condition expressed by the infinitive is in the past.

Examples:

To have won the election fulfilled all his dreams. (He already won the election.)

I am sorry to have seen Mike so unhappy at the last meeting. (I saw that Mike was unhappy at the last meeting, and I am sorry about this fact.)

It was thoughtful of you to have done that. (You already did something thoughtful, and the speaker is acknowledging it now.)

Forming Gerunds, Infinitives, and Participles

By knowing how to form infinitives, gerunds, and participles correctly, you will increase your mastery of verb forms. These verb forms are also called *verbals*.

1. **Gerunds**

   a. Present (base form of the verb + *-ing*)

   Example:

   <u>Taking</u> the bus to school saves students money.

   b. Perfect (or past) (*having* + past participle)

   Example:

   After <u>having gone</u> to the opera once, Melissa decided to go again.

   Note: Gerunds can be made negative by adding *not* before the gerund.

2. **Infinitives**

   a. Present (*to* + base form of the verb)

   Example:

   We need <u>to buy</u> some milk.

   b. Progressive (*to* + *be* + present participle)

   Example:

   He is happy <u>to be moving</u> to a new apartment.

   c. Perfect (or past) (*to* + *have* + past participle)

   Example:

   Jerome seems <u>to have recovered</u> from his accident.

   d. Perfect (or past) progressive (*to* + *have* + *been* + present participle)

   Example:

   We were lucky <u>to have been sitting</u> on the porch when it began to rain.

   Note: Infinitives can be made negative by adding *not* before the infinitive.

See Unit 5, "Passive Voice," page 110 for forming the passive of gerunds, infinitives, and participles.

3. Participles

a. Present (base form of the verb + -ing)

Examples:

This is a very <u>challenging</u> class.

Our teacher, <u>understanding</u> the problems we were having with it, revised parts of the handout.

b. Past (base form of the verb + -ed or an irregular form)

Examples:

When my teacher read my <u>revised</u> paper, she gave it an A.

The campus has a newly-<u>built</u> recreation center.

c. Perfect (having + past participle)

Examples:

<u>Having finished</u> the exam early, Melinda went to get some coffee.

<u>Not having eaten</u> breakfast, she was hungry.

IMPROVE YOUR WRITING STYLE
KNOWING WHETHER TO USE A GERUND OR AN INFINITIVE

Sometimes either a gerund or an infinitive form of a verb can be used. In some cases, the choice of one or the other will not change the meaning of the sentence, as in the examples below, which have equivalent meanings.

Examples:

<u>Riding</u> a bicycle without a helmet is not advisable.

<u>To ride</u> a bicycle without a helmet is not advisable.

However, with certain verbs, the meaning can change. The difference in meaning can be either very significant or minor, depending on the verb. With the verb remember, *a significant difference in meaning results, depending on whether a gerund or infinitive follows it.*

Examples:

The customer remembered <u>to ask</u> about the store's return policy. (The meaning is that the customer remembered that she needed to ask about the return policy and that she <u>did</u> ask about it.)

The customer remembered <u>asking</u> about the store's return policy. (The meaning is that the customer asked about the store's return policy when she was in the store and at present the customer remembers having done the action.)

The choice of a gerund or infinitive after the verb stop *can also affect the meaning of a sentence. Note that an infinitive after the verb* stop *shows <u>the purpose</u> for stopping.*

Examples:

John stopped <u>smoking</u>. (The meaning is that he does not smoke anymore.)

John stopped <u>to smoke</u>. (The meaning is that the reason he stopped was to smoke a cigarette. It was his purpose to do so.)

The choice of a gerund or infinitive after the verb prefer *can indicate whether or not an event is happening, has already happened, or could potentially happen.*

Examples:

David prefers <u>doing</u> research over teaching. (The meaning is that David *is currently doing* research and that he prefers it over teaching.)

David preferred <u>doing</u> research over teaching. (The meaning is that David <u>was doing research</u> at some time in the past and that he preferred it over teaching.)

David prefers <u>to do</u> research next semester. (The meaning is that David's preference for <u>the future</u> would be to do research rather than teach.)

Generally speaking, gerunds are used when an action is already completed or in progress, while infinitives are more commonly used to show future time or the intention to do something. This fact is illustrated in the following newspaper headlines.

Examples:

Man <u>to Sue</u> Reckless Driver (The infinitive is a short form of *is going to sue* or *will sue* and shows a future intention.)

Man <u>Suing</u> Reckless Driver (The gerund shows that the *suing* is already in progress, as in *is suing*.)

Continued on page 48.

IMPROVE YOUR WRITING STYLE (*CONT.*)
USE OF THE POSSESSIVE WITH A GERUND

When a noun or a pronoun modifies a gerund, the possessive form should be used. However, if the sentence sounds awkward, it should be reworded. In less formal English, the noun is often not used in the possessive form.

Examples:

> <u>Jim's asking</u> the teacher so many questions annoyed the class.
>
> Less formal: <u>Jim asking</u> the teacher so many questions annoyed the class.
>
> <u>Her</u> suddenly <u>deciding</u> to listen to classical music was a surprise.
>
> Reworded: <u>Her sudden decision</u> to listen to classical music was a surprise.

The possessive is not used with a participle.

Examples:

> We saw a <u>cat sleeping</u> in the window.
>
> My mother got mad when she caught <u>us eating</u> candy.

PRACTICE WHAT YOU HAVE LEARNED

EXERCISE 1

Directions: Decide whether the verb form in the following sentences is correct (C) or incorrect (I). If it is incorrect, correct the error.

Example: __*I*__ Everyone should know where he or she ~~are came~~ from.   *(comes)*

_____ 1. I have live in the United States for two years.

_____ 2. By exercise on a regular basis, an athlete can maintain muscle flexibility and strength.

_____ 3. My instructor does not please with my lack of participation in class.

_____ 4. I believe that I have a good chance of getting into medical school.

_____ 5. Scientists are currently try to find a cure for AIDS.

_____ 6. Elizabeth has decided postpone taking her driving test until next month.

_____ 7. I did not expect you to call me so soon.

_____ 8. Skip breakfast is not good for one's health.

_____ 9. My best friend asked me to take a vacation and to come to Florida for a visit.

_____10. The government greatly concern about the high inflation rate.

EXERCISE 2

Directions: Fill in each blank with the correct form (gerund, infinitive, or base form) of a verb of your choice. Use a verb form even if other parts of speech are possible. If necessary, add words in addition to the verb to correct (or improve) the sentence grammatically.

Example: Jack plans _____*to go*_____ to the movies tonight after he finishes studying.

1. I avoided _____ my friend last night because I am angry at him.

2. Many students prefer _____ late at night rather than during the day.

3. By _____ to each other, we can work out our problems.

4. These boxes are too heavy for me. Could you help me _____ them?

5. The coach encouraged the team _____.

6. One of my goals is _____.

7. Many employees dislike _____.

8. _____ is one of my hobbies.

9. I consider myself good at _____.

10. A colleague let me _____ his notes when I was not able to attend the seminar.

11. It is easy _____ to the southern part of the country by train.

EXERCISE 3

Directions: Fill in each blank with the correct form of the verb in parentheses. If more than one verb form is possible, give both options.

One of my very favorite activities is ___*to walk/walking*___ (walk) through the
                                            (1)
arboretum near my dormitory. After a stressful day of classes, I go there

_____ (relax) and _____ (enjoy) the sight and the smell of
        (2)   (3)
the trees. As I stroll along the path next to a small creek, I pass numerous tall

trees including redwoods, oaks, and pines. I also pass a lake with ducks on

it. The natural beauty and quiet of the area helps me _____ (relax).
                                                                (4)
I love _____ (walk) through the arboretum any time of the year,
            (5)
but on a hot summer day it is especially refreshing. The shade from the trees

keeps the area cool no matter how hot it is. I am always refreshed and ready

_____ (continue) studying after a walk through the arboretum.
        (6)

EXERCISE 4

Directions: Use each of the following verbs in a sentence in the form *be* + past participle. Pay special attention to the form of the verb. Follow the model.

Example: to be confused

The voters were confused about several of the proposals on the ballot.

1. to be concerned

_____

2. to be located

_____

3. to be closed

_____

EXERCISE 5

Directions: Complete each blank with the perfect infinitive of the verb in parentheses.

Example: When I was in Yosemite National Park, I would have liked
_____*to have seen*_____ (see) Nevada Falls, but it was too far to hike in one day.

1. Mathias is thrilled _____ (complete) his bachelor's degree and _____ (find) a job immediately.

2. A bystander claimed _____ (witness) the accident that occurred last night.

3. The Smiths are happy _____ (move) to a new and bigger house.

4. _____ (swim) ten miles was a great accomplishment for Janice.

5. I would have loved _____ (see) Bill Clinton speak when he was president of the United States.

EXERCISE 6

Directions: The following is a job application cover letter. Correct the underlined verb-form errors.

Dear Dr. Wong:

I am writing <u>for applying</u> *to apply* for your internship position. I <u>am very interesting</u> in this position. I am a graduate student in the master's degree program in the Department of Biological and Agricultural Engineering. This department has a good reputation for its high level of research and the high quality of its students. <u>I am major</u> in food engineering, and my research project deals with nuclear magnetic resonance imaging (NMRI) <u>for study</u> bruises in apples. I <u>have take</u> NMRI classes, read many papers about NMRI, and <u>do</u> a variety of experiments using this technique. I hope <u>expand</u> my practical experience in this area by <u>get</u> this internship with your company.

I <u>have include</u> my résumé for your review. I hope <u>hearing</u> from you soon.

Sincerely,

Cheryl Young

Cheryl Young

EXERCISE 7

Directions: The following student paragraph has eight verb-form errors. Find and correct them. The first one has been done for you.

It takes a great deal of courage for a person to leave his or her family and
start
~~starts~~ life all over again in another country. The person must not only face many changes alone but also separate from friends and rely on phone calls and e-mail messages as a means of share thoughts. The new environment and the new setting make even the bravest individual feels scared as he or she encounters many sudden changes and undergoes many kinds of struggles in a short period of time. Despite these difficulties, go abroad has many benefits, for it gives a person the chance to see the world, to face new challenges, to make new friends, and gaining more knowledge about people and places. Before I came to the United States, I had many expectations. I thought that life in this country would be similar to life in my country. However, after be here for five months, I have came to the conclusion that life in the United States is entirely different from what I had expect.

EXERCISE 8

Directions: Choose a short news article to read. Underline all the verbs (for example, main verbs, verb phrases, gerunds, infinitives) in two paragraphs. Can you understand why the different verb forms are used? If you are unsure about any of them, ask a classmate, a tutor, or your instructor.

Post-test   **What Do You Know Now?**

A   Fill in the blanks with the correct form of the verb *finish*.

Base form   _____

Infinitive   _____

Gerund   _____

Present participle   _____

Past participle   _____

B   Decide whether the verb forms in the following sentences are correct (C) or incorrect (I). If a verb form is incorrect, make the correction.

_____ 1. At school, English is speaking all around me.

_____ 2. Entomologists concern with insects.

_____ 3. Economists try to understand the economy and prevent any crisis from happen.

_____ 4. Many elderly people feel that practicing Tai Chi enhances their ability to maintain balance.

_____ 5. A study that is being conducted at a well-known university aims to examining the effects of Tai Chi on the elderly.

_____ 6. One of my dreams is to move to another country at some point in my life.

_____ 7. I believe that come to the U.S. to study will broaden my life.

_____ 8. Being a teaching assistant is the most difficult challenge I have ever face.

_____ 9. My research is progressing according to schedule.

_____10. People live in some cities in California feel earthquakes more than people in other cities.

C Correct the underlined verb-form errors in this student paragraph.

The service at our university's bookstore continues to be poor. To begin with, the manager has not learned <u>hiring</u> the right number of clerks. Every semester during registration and the first week of classes, a lot of students <u>are try</u> to buy their books, but the manager only schedules three or four clerks to <u>checks</u> out customers. Unless you enjoy standing in a long line for hours, you should avoid going to the bookstore at this time. However, after a couple of weeks, when the initial rush <u>be</u> over, the manager will <u>starts</u> to hire more clerks. Of course, because they are not busy, they waste a lot of time by standing around and <u>talk</u> to each other. As a result, asking the clerks to help you is never easy.

D Fill in each blank with the correct form of the verb in parentheses.

Last week at the bookstore, I noticed a new student _____ (1) (ask) a clerk where to find a particular book. Even though the new student was _____ (2) (speak) directly to her, the clerk didn't even look at him. The poor student just kept on searching for the book by himself. Perhaps the worst incident I have _____ (3) (experience) there happened one day when I asked the assistant manager _____ (4) (cash) a check for me. He enjoyed _____ (5) (tell) me that the bookstore does not cash personal checks for students. He made me _____ (6) (feel) so frustrated that I have now quit going to the bookstore entirely.

APPLY WHAT YOU HAVE LEARNED TO WRITING

Select a writing topic and follow the steps in Appendix A on page 337.

Topic 1:

Choose a sport that you enjoy either watching or participating in. Describe how it is played or done. Tell why you enjoy this sport. Conclude by suggesting ways a person could benefit from participating in this sport or activity.

Topic 2:

Discuss one of your goals, either short term or long term. Explain what the goal is and why you want to accomplish it.

Topic 3:

Both the pace of life and how people view time and punctuality can vary from culture to culture. Compare the pace of life and people's attention to time in your culture of origin and U.S. culture in order to show to what extent they are similar or different. Then, comment on which pace of life you are most comfortable with and why.

Unit 3

MODALS

Unit 3

Have you ever done any volunteer work in your community or at your school? If so, what kind? If not, what volunteer or community service work would you be interested in doing?

GOALS

- Learn why mastering modals is important in writing

- Understand three problems writers commonly encounter with modals

- Form and use modals correctly in exercises and writing assignments

LEARN WHAT THE ERROR IS

Errors with Modals

Modals are auxiliaries—such as *may, might, should, must, can,* and *could*—that add a specific meaning to a verb. In the sentences below, notice how the modal adds a specific meaning to the verb *exercise.*

Examples:

I <u>exercise</u> at the gym regularly. (a fact)

I <u>might exercise</u> at the gym tonight. (a possibility)

I <u>should</u> exercise at the gym more often. (advice to myself)

I <u>could have exercised</u> at the gym yesterday. (a past opportunity that I did not take advantage of)

A modal error is an error that involves the wrong choice of a modal, the wrong form of any part of a modal verb phrase, or the wrong time reference of a modal verb phrase. A modal verb phrase consists of a modal and all the verbs that appear with it, including the main verb.

Example:

    modal verb phrase
I <u>should have exercised</u> at the gym last night.

Errors with modals involve verbs and are thus global (more serious) errors that can affect a reader's ability to understand a text. Writers who are unable to use modals correctly will have limited ability to show the difference between facts, assumptions, and possibilities in English—distinctions frequently made in academic and professional writing. The editing symbol for a modal error is ***modal.***

The following examples illustrate how modals can be used to show assumptions and possibilities.

Examples:

Someone I know has lived in the dorm for four years. (a fact) Because most students stay in the dorm for only one or two years, the person I know <u>must like</u> the dorm very much. (a logical conclusion based on the information given)

My roommate did not eat much at dinner last night. (a fact) She <u>might be trying</u> to lose weight, or she <u>might not have been</u> very hungry. (logical assumptions marked as possibilities by the modal *might*)

Another important function of modals is that they serve to qualify statements or adjust their degree of certainty. Compare the following three statements and notice how the underlined modal serves to lessen the degree of certainty of the statement.

Examples:

This method <u>will</u> simplify the analysis of the data. (statement of fact)

This method <u>should</u> simplify the analysis of the data. (probability or expectation)

This method <u>may</u> simplify the analysis of the data. (possibility)

Thus, modals have specific and important functions in English, and being able to use them correctly increases a writer's ability to express his or her ideas clearly and precisely.

Suggestions for Reducing Errors

- Study the meaning and use of the different modals using the chart in this unit. Learn and understand what meaning each modal adds to the verb it accompanies. Learn the time reference of each form also.

- Be aware that some modals, like *must, can,* and *could,* have more than one meaning, depending on the context in which they are used. For example, the modal *must* can indicate a <u>requirement</u> as in the sentence *Passengers must fasten their seat belts during takeoff and landing.* Or it can indicate a <u>logical assumption</u> as in the sentence *Pat was not at an important meeting today. She must have forgotten.* You will find all of the different meanings for modals listed in the chart in this unit.

- Pay attention to how modals are used in what you read. As you read books, articles, and other material in English, notice how writers use modals to add meaning to verbs.

Check Your Understanding

Write answers to these questions. Share your answers with another student.

1. What are some examples of modals?

2. What makes modals important in academic and professional writing? What meanings can modals add to a sentence?

GRAMMAR JOURNAL ENTRY 3   MODALS

Respond to the following in your grammar journal.

1. What is something you feel you should have done recently but did not? Why weren't you able to do it?

2. Write two sentences with modals and underline the modal verb phrase. Explain what meaning the modal gives to the verb.

UNDERSTAND COMMON PROBLEMS

This section presents three problems that writers commonly encounter with modals. First, take the pre-test to see what you already know about modals. When you finish, check your answers on page 350. Then, carefully study each problem and the examples that illustrate it. Pay particular attention to those problems that correspond to the pre-test questions you had difficulty with. Remember that becoming aware of the types of errors you most often make with modals will increase your chances of avoiding these errors in your writing.

Pre-test

What Do You Already Know?

Test your ability to recognize and correct errors with modals.

A   Correct the marked modal errors. These are examples of the three common problems that are presented in this unit.

          modal

Problem 1 I have not seen my next-door neighbor for a week. She <u>can be</u> out of town.

          modal

Problem 2 In order to be successful, a person <u>must has</u> the determination to achieve goals.

          modal

Problem 3 I cannot find my favorite pen. I <u>must leave</u> it at home.

B   Underline and correct the one error in each of the following items. (The errors are not in any particular order.)

   1.   When we arrived, Lili was not at the station. She must had forgotten that we were coming at 3:00 PM.

   2.   My e-mail did not go through. I should have forgotten to press "send."

   3.   Juan told me he can play the flute at age five.

Three Common Problems

Problem 1

The wrong modal has been chosen to express the writer's intended meaning.

          modal

Incorrect: I <u>must have gone</u> to see my instructor on Monday, but I did not have time.

Correct: I <u>should have gone</u> to see my instructor on Monday, but I did not have time.

Note: *Should have gone* is correct because it shows <u>advisability after the fact</u>. *Must have gone* is incorrect because it shows that an <u>assumption</u> has been made <u>about the past</u> and this is not what the writer wishes to express.

Problem 2

The modal verb phrase has been incorrectly formed.

Incorrect: She <u>might studies</u> at the library tonight.

modal (vf)

Incorrect: She <u>might to study</u> at the library tonight.

modal (vf)

Correct: She <u>might study</u> at the library tonight.

Note: Your instructor may mark this kind of modal error *modal (vf)* to indicate that the error is a <u>modal verb-form</u> error.

modal (vf)

Incorrect: I <u>could had submitted</u> the proposal, but I wanted to do some

additional editing.

Correct: I <u>could have submitted</u> the proposal, but I wanted to do some

additional editing.

modal (vf)

Incorrect: Marina <u>can be able to</u> return the book tonight.

Correct: Marina <u>can return</u> the book tonight.

Correct: Marina <u>is able to</u> return the book tonight.

Note: Do not use the modals *can* or *could* and *be able to* together.

SELF-HELP STRATEGY: Remember not to add an -s to a third-person singular verb following a present modal. Instead, use the base form after a modal as in the sentence *John may <u>give</u>* (not *gives*) *a short presentation.* Also, carefully check the formation of past modals, making sure you use the modal + <u>have</u> + past participle as shown in the sentence *John may <u>have</u>* (not *had*) *given a short presentation.*

Problem 3

The time reference of the modal verb phrase is incorrect.

modal (vt)

Incorrect: My muscles are sore. I <u>should not exercise</u> so hard yesterday.

Correct: My muscles are sore. I <u>should not have exercised</u> so hard yesterday.

Note: Your instructor may mark this kind of modal error *modal (vt)* to indicate that the error is a <u>modal verb-tense</u> error.

REVIEW GRAMMAR SOLUTIONS

Formation of Modal Verb Phrases

1. Present time

a. modal + base form

Examples:

Why does Chris look so pale?

He <u>might be</u> sick. (present)

What does he usually do for exercise?

He <u>might exercise</u> at the gym, but I am not sure. (present habitual)

b. modal + *be* + present participle (*-ing* form)

Example:

What is he doing right now?

He <u>might be exercising</u> at the gym. (present; happening now)

2. Future time

a. modal + base form

Example:

What is she going to do tomorrow night?

She <u>might exercise</u> at the gym. (future)

b. modal + *be* + present participle (*-ing* form)

Example:

She <u>should be studying</u> tomorrow night. (future; happening over a period of time)

See Unit 5 for information on using modals in the passive voice.

3. Past time

a. modal + *have* + past participle

Example:

What did he do last night?

He <u>might have exercised</u> at the gym. (past)

b. modal + *have* + been + present participle (*-ing* form)

Example:

What was he doing when you called last night?

He <u>might have been exercising</u> at the gym. (past; happening over a period of time)

4. *Ought to* and *have to*

The modals *ought to* and *have to* in the present and in the past are formed with <u>ought</u> and <u>have</u> + the infinitive.

Examples:

We <u>ought to study</u> before the test. (present)

We <u>have to study</u> before the test. (present)

We <u>ought to have studied</u> more than we did. (past)

We <u>had to study</u> hard before the test. (past)

5. Negatives

Modals are generally made negative by putting *not* after the modal and before the verb. One exception is the negative of *have to*.

Examples:

The library might <u>not</u> be open right now.

You had better <u>not</u> be late.

We might <u>not</u> have remembered to lock the door.

We do <u>not</u> have to go to the meeting tonight.

Meaning and Use of Modals

The following Dictionary of Modals shows the different meanings that modals can have. For example, modals can express ability, necessity, and advisability. The meanings are listed alphabetically, with the present and past forms. Note that some modals have more than one meaning.

DICTIONARY OF MODALS

ABILITY: *can, could*

- To show that a person or a thing has the ability or capacity to do something

- To show potential ability

Present	Past
can + base form	*could* + base form
Miranda <u>can play</u> the piano very well. (She has the ability.)	When he was younger, my father <u>could understand</u> German. (He had the ability to understand German.)
I <u>cannot use</u> the new software because my computer does not have enough memory. (I am not able to use the new software.)	I <u>could not use</u> the new software because my computer did not have enough memory. (I was not able to use the software.)
Exercise <u>can reduce</u> high blood pressure. (It has the potential ability to reduce high blood pressure.)	Researchers found that lowering salt intake <u>could reduce</u> high blood pressure.

ADVISABILITY: *should, ought to, had better*

- To show that something is advisable or to give a piece of advice

- To make a strong suggestion

- To show regret after something happened or was done

- To give instructions

Present	Past
should + base form *ought to* + base form *had better* + base form (*stronger*)	*should have* + past participle *ought to have* + past participle *had better have* + past participle
Diana <u>should stop</u> smoking.	Diana <u>should have stopped</u> smoking last year (but she didn't).
You <u>should pay</u> your bills on time to avoid late penalties.	My sister feels she <u>should not have bought</u> that expensive car because now she is having difficulty paying for it.
People <u>should not drink</u> too much coffee.	You <u>had better have turned</u> off the stove when you left the house.
You <u>had better study</u> as the test is going to be difficult.	
You <u>ought to</u> exercise daily.	

ASSUMPTION: *must*

- To indicate that something is probable based on information believed to be true

- To come to a logical conclusion or inference based on information believed to be true

Present	Past
must + be	*must have* + past participle
must + be + present participle	The movie <u>must have finished</u> as people are coming out of the theater. (I am quite sure that I am correct.)
That store <u>must be</u> new because I have never seen it before.	
Janine is absent today; she <u>must not be feeling</u> well.	My friend did not know about the test today. He <u>must not have attended</u> class the day the test was announced.

CHOICE: See Option

DESIRE: *would like*

- To express a desire

- To express a desire that was not realized (negative)

Present	Past
would like + infinitive	*would have liked* + past infinitive (OR infinitive)
I <u>would like to go</u> to medical school.	I <u>would have liked to have seen</u> (OR <u>to see</u>) that show but it was sold out.

EXPECTATION: *should, ought to*

- To show that something is expected to happen or to have happened

Present	Past
should, ought to + base form	*should have* + past participle *ought to have* + past participle
According to the weather report, it <u>should rain</u> tonight. (It is probable because of the weather conditions.)	The express letter <u>should have reached</u> her by noon on Saturday according to the post office. (OR: <u>ought to have reached</u>) (It is expected that this has happened.)
The flight <u>should arrive</u> soon (OR: <u>ought to arrive</u>). (It is expected to be on schedule.)	

Continued on page 66.

Dictionary of Modals (*cont.*)

GENERAL TRUTH: *will*	
• To state a general truth	
Present	
will + base form When water is heated to a high temperature, it <u>will boil</u>. My new car <u>will run</u> on either gas or electricity.	

INFERENCE: See Assumption	

NECESSITY: *must, have to*	
• To show that it is absolutely necessary to do something	
• To indicate a requirement or an obligation	
Note: *must* is stronger than *have to*	
Present	**Past**
must, have to + base form All students <u>must attend</u> the orientation. (This is a requirement.) We <u>must start</u> our final project soon. (It is absolutely necessary.) Members <u>do not have to pay</u> the entrance fee. (It is not necessary.)	*had to* + base form Alexander <u>had to make up</u> the exam yesterday. (This was a requirement and Alexander was obliged to do it.) We <u>did not have to buy</u> trip insurance. (It was not necessary.)

OBLIGATION: See Necessity	

OPPORTUNITY: *can, could have*	
• To show an opportunity for something to happen or to be done	
• To show an opportunity that was not taken advantage of	
Present	**Past**
can + base form We <u>can pick up</u> our new puppy tomorrow. (We have the opportunity to do this tomorrow.)	*could have* + past participle The instructor <u>could have given</u> us more time to write the paper. (He had the opportunity to do so, but he didn't.) Erika <u>could have gone</u> home this weekend, but she stayed on campus.

OPTION: *can, could*	
• To show an option or indicate a choice	
Present	**Past**
can + base form Students <u>can</u> either <u>register</u> online or in the office.	*could* + base form I <u>could register</u> online when I was at my previous school, but here I cannot.

PERMISSION: *can, could, may*

- To ask for or give permission

Present

can, could, may + base form

<u>Could</u> I make an appointment?

<u>May</u> I make an appointment? (more formal)

You <u>can leave</u> when you have finished your exam.

You <u>may leave</u> when you have finished your exam. (more formal)

POLITE QUESTION: *could, would*

- To ask a polite question

Present

could, would + base form

<u>Could</u> you <u>tell</u> me where the nearest post office is?

<u>Would</u> you <u>have</u> time to meet with me tomorrow?

POSSIBILITY: *may, might, could*

- To express the possibility that something will happen or has happened

Present	Past
may, might, could + base form	*may have, might have, could have* + past participle
It <u>might rain</u> tomorrow.	George, rather than Ted, <u>may have picked up</u> the parcel from the post office.
The snowstorm <u>could develop</u> into a blizzard if a strong wind comes up.	Arthur <u>could not have been</u> in class today because he had to go to the dentist. (impossibility)
Melissa <u>may come</u> this afternoon after she gets off work.	

PREDICTION: *will*

- To predict that something will happen or will have happened

Time: Future

will + base form

will have + past participle

I think our team <u>will win</u> the game.

We all think that when the results are in, our candidate <u>will have won</u> the election.

Continued on page 68.

DICTIONARY OF MODALS (*CONT.*)

PREFERENCE: *would rather*

• To show a definite preference

Present	Past
would rather + base form	*would rather have* + past participle
Sejin <u>would rather play</u> video games than study.	Sejin <u>would rather have played</u> video games than study last night.

PROBABILITY: See Assumption and Expectation

PROHIBITION: *must not*

• To show prohibition

Present	
must not + base form	
You <u>must not smoke</u> in the classroom.	

PROMISE: *will, would*

• To make a promise

Present	Past
will + base form	*would* + base form
The federal government <u>will provide</u> assistance to the flood victims.	The federal government stated yesterday that it <u>would provide</u> assistance to the flood victims.

REPEATED ACTION IN THE PAST: *would*

• To show an action that took place over a period of time in the past

	Past
	would + base form
	When I lived in Los Angeles, I <u>would go</u> to the beach every weekend.

SUGGESTION: *should, could, might*

• To strongly suggest that something should happen or be done, use *should*

• To make a weak suggestion, use *could* or *might*

Note: A strong suggestion is similar to advice. See Advisability.

Present	Past
should, could, might + base form	*should have, could have, might have* + past participle
Everyone <u>should come</u> to class on time. (This is a strong suggestion that this behavior is preferred.)	We <u>should have bought</u> a faster computer. (This is a strong suggestion after the fact; it indicates that we didn't do it but that it would have been a good idea.)
Brenda <u>could try</u> speaking more loudly. (weak suggestion)	
Jim <u>might consider</u> political science for his major as he does not like math. (weak suggestion)	Helen <u>could have saved</u> herself time by flying instead of driving to St. Louis. (This is a weaker suggestion after the fact.)

IMPROVE YOUR WRITING STYLE
ADJUSTING THE DEGREE OF CERTAINTY OR NECESSITY

Modals are frequently used to adjust the degree of certainty or necessity. These functions are important because they allow the writer to be precise and accurate in making assertions. Note how the degree of certainty or necessity changes in the lists below.

	DEGREE OF CERTAINTY	MODAL	EXAMPLE
Certain	Assertion of fact	(none)	Aspirin <u>reduces</u> pain.
	Prediction showing certainty	will	Aspirin <u>will reduce</u> the pain.
	Assertion showing capability	can	Aspirin <u>can reduce</u> pain.
Probable	Prediction showing probability	should	Aspirin <u>should reduce</u> the pain.
Possible	Prediction showing possibility	may	Aspirin <u>may reduce</u> the pain.
	Prediction showing possibility	might	Aspirin <u>might reduce</u> the pain.
	Prediction showing possibility	could	Aspirin <u>could reduce</u> the pain.

	DEGREE OF NECESSITY	MODAL	EXAMPLE
Fact	Assertion of fact	(none)	Students <u>use</u> the library.
Requirement	Requirement or obligation	must	Students <u>must use</u> the library for this project.
Recommendation	Strong recommendation/ advice	should	Students <u>should use</u> the library as much as possible.
	Opportunity or option	can	Students <u>can use</u> the library if they wish.
Suggestion	Suggestion	could	Students <u>could use</u> the library for their meeting.

PRACTICE WHAT YOU HAVE LEARNED

EXERCISE 1

Directions: Change the following sentences from present to past time.
For some of the sentences, you will need to change time
words and phrases.

Example: I do not see Monica at the reception, but she might arrive
later.

Past: *I did not see Monica at the reception, but she might have arrived later.*

1. Bob might be joking about his decision to quit school.

   Past: Bob might have been joking about his decision to quit
   school.

2. Lian could be finished by 3:00 PM this afternoon.

   Past: Lian could have been finished by 3:00pm yesterday

3. Max, who is on the track team, can run a mile in 4 minutes,
   30 seconds.

   Past: When he was on the track team, Max could have run a mile in
   4 min and 3 sec.

4. Jill must be full after eating at that restaurant.

   Past: ~ must have been full ~ ~ eating at that restaurant

5. Because Lydia needs to get a good grade on her exam, she must
   study this evening.

   Past: Lydia must have studied   because she
   needs to get a good grade on her exam.

6. I should exercise regularly to get into shape for the backpacking trip.

   Past: I should have exercised regularly to get into shape

7. You ought to send your roommate's parents a thank-you card when
   you get home.

   Past: You ought to have sent your roomates ~ ~ ~
   ~ when you get home.

8. My supervisor must be sick since she did not attend the office party this afternoon.

   Past: _My Supervisor must have been sick, becase she didn't attend the office party this afternoon_

9. Mary may not have time to call her parents tonight.

   Past: _mary may not have time to call her parents last night_

10. My roommate has to do the shopping this week.

    Past: _my roommate has to have done the shopping this week._

EXERCISE 2

Directions: For each sentence, write down what the meaning or function of the modal is, as well as the time frame of the statement.

Example: I really **should** exercise more often. *(advisability; present or future)*

1. In most states, drivers **must** carry proof of car insurance. _obligation_

2. Analyzing your data in a different way **may** give you better results. _possiblity_

3. You **must** be tired after working at the office for ten straight hours. _Assumption_

4. Tom is looking for someone who **can** translate a document from Japanese to English. _Ability_

5. The study **could** have a considerable impact on the field of molecular biology. _Possiblity_

6. When I was young, I **could** speak French, but I have forgotten most of it. _Past ability_

7. What a beautiful new sports car! It **must have** cost a lot of money. _assuption_

8. I **should not have** spent so much time on the proposal because now I am behind on other important tasks. _regret_

9. Both of these factors **may** be important in explaining the recurrence of the disease. _Possiblity_

10. Students **can** request a book either in person or online. _option_

EXERCISE 3

Directions: Use a modal to express the underlined part of each of the following ideas.

I might have missed him.

Example: I didn't see Bob at the library. It's possible that I missed him.

1. I didn't see Judy at the library after 10:00 PM. She probably left early.

   she might have left

2. The sky is getting cloudy. There is a chance of rain. *it might rain tomorrow*

3. Elena didn't come to class yesterday. It was necessary for her to go to Chicago.   *she had to go to chicago*

4. Linda received a gift from her aunt. It is advisable for her to send a thank-you note. *she had better send her aunt a Thank-You not*

5. We don't have much work today. It is possible that our supervisor will allow us to leave early. *our supervisor may allow us to learn eerly.*

6. My brother-in-law just bought a nice house in an expensive section of town. I assume the house cost a lot of money. *The house must have cost a lot of money*

7. Jose was available to help over the weekend. In retrospect, I realize that it would have been a good idea to have asked him to help. *(regret)* *In retrospect, I should have aske him to help*

8. When I was young, I knew how to play the piano, but I have forgotten how since I have not played in many years. *I could play the piano.*

9. My roommate had time to wash the dishes last night, but she went out instead. *my roomate could have washed the dishes last night*

10. One option that we have is to camp out on our way to the Grand Canyon. *we can camp out on our way to the Grand canyon*

EXERCISE 4

Directions: Decide whether each of the following sentences is correct (C) or incorrect (I). If it is incorrect, correct the error and note the meaning that the modal gives to the verb.

have (advisability)

Example: __*I*__ I should not ~~had~~ told you about my problem because now you are worried.

__I__ 1. My brother must had forgotten to call me.
                    ed

__I__ 2. My brother could have call me while I was at the library.

__I__ 3. My brother may calls late tonight.

__I__ 4. I did not have time to stop at the store because I must have *had*
            stayed late at the office to finish my work. *it is past*

__C__ 5. Susan felt she could have worked out longer in the gym, but
            her coach advised her not to do so.
                                        been
__I__ 6. I got a speeding ticket! I should not have be driving over the
            speed limit on the freeway.

__C__ 7. My roommate is in Hawaii interviewing for a job. It should
            be warm there even though it is winter here.

__C__ 8. Most people now realize that we must take action soon to
            save endangered species.

EXERCISE 5

Directions: Underline each modal verb phrase in the following paragraph. Then, below the paragraph, write each modal or modal verb phrase and the meaning. The first two have been done for you.

Grand Canyon National Park in Arizona is a paradise for nature lovers and outdoor enthusiasts. Visitors <u>will be awed</u> by the fabulous view of the canyon— its vast depth and beautifully colored walls. The National Park Headquarters and Visitor Center is at the South Rim where visitors <u>can pick up</u> information about the park. Visitors who have only a little time to spend can view the canyon from either the North Rim or the South Rim. People who have more time may want to see more of the Grand Canyon than just the North or South Rim. Such visitors can drive along parts of the rim or hike down into the canyon on various trails. In fact, hikers can walk or ride a mule all the way to the bottom of the canyon to the Colorado River. However, hikers must be sure to drink plenty of water to avoid dehydration, as the weather can be extremely hot and dry. At the bottom, hikers can stay at either Phantom Ranch, which consists of cabins or dormitories, or at an adjacent campground. Perhaps the best way to see the canyon, however, is to float down the Colorado River either on a rubber raft or in a wooden dory. Seeing the canyon from this perspective is spectacular, but people who are afraid of white water should not take this trip since some of the Colorado River rapids are among the largest in the world. For most visitors, a trip to the Grand Canyon should be a truly unforgettable experience.

1. _will be awed: shows future tense_

2. _can pick up: shows an option_

3. _can view / present / option_

4. _may want / present / possibility / option_

5. _can drive / present / option_

6. _can walk / p / option_

7. _must be / p / necessity_

8. _can be extremely / prediction_

9. _can stay / option_

10. _Should not take / Advisa..._

11. _should be a truly / expectation_

EXERCISE 6

Directions: Fill in each blank with the correct modal verb phrase in this student paragraph. The main verb and modal meaning are indicated in parentheses.

Writing a term paper last semester was very challenging for me. At the beginning of the term, I was looking forward to doing the research and writing the paper. But, unfortunately, I waited longer than I *should have waited* (wait / (1) advisability) to get started. I Could have started (start / opportunity) earlier, but (2) for some reason I just kept waiting. I found myself working right up until the last minute. I know I Should have (proofread / advisability) the paper more (3) carefully. I also Could have (add / opportunity) some illustrations if I had (4) ed had more time. Because I started so late, I not only had to submit a less than satisfactory paper, but I also had to stay (stay up / necessity) all night to (5) up finish it.

EXERCISE 7

Directions: Choose a short news article to read. Underline every modal verb phrase and identify the meaning the modal verb phrase gives to the sentence.

Post-test

What Do You Know Now?

A Decide whether the use of the modal is correct (C) or incorrect (I). If it is incorrect, cross out the error and make the correction.

_____ 1. He believes he can pass his exam even though he has not studied much.

_____ 2. The students standing outside the library looked upset.
The library door must had been locked.

_____ 3. I did very poorly on my chemistry test yesterday. I realize that
I must have studied more before taking it.

_____ 4. She must forget our meeting yesterday because she never showed up.

_____ 5. Zhang Wei is not in class today. He could oversleep and miss the bus.

B Restate these sentences by filling in an appropriate modal or modal verb phrase.

1. Students are required to complete all of their essays to pass the class.

Students _____ complete all of their essays to pass the class.

2. Mike will be able to complete all his classes for graduation next semester.

Mike _____ complete all his classes for graduation next semester.

3. I was supposed to buy a present for my brother's birthday, but I forgot.

I _____ a present for my brother's birthday, but I forgot.

4. My teacher expects that I will pass this class if I do well on the final exam.

I _____ pass this class if I do well on the final exam.

5. I did not do well in school last semester. My parents are demanding
that I _____ do better in school this semester.

My parents informed me that I _____ do better in school this semester.

6. When Ana calls, I will tell her that I prefer to see a movie rather than eat out.

I _____ rather go to a movie than eat out.

C Correct the marked modal errors in this student paragraph.

I faced many challenges when I first came to college. Among the greatest

had to live

was the discovery that I <u>must live</u> in a dorm room with a complete stranger.
 (1)

have

Originally, I had hoped to room with my high school friend, but I <u>must had</u>
 (2)

<u>waited</u> too long to mail in my housing request, and so I was assigned a

different roommate. During the first couple of weeks of school, my new

must

roommate <u>would have thought</u> that I was an extremely unfriendly and
 (3)

unkind person since I seldom responded to her with much warmth. I know

have

that I <u>could adjusted</u> to the situation and <u>approach</u> my roommate in a more
 (4)   (5) *ed*

positive way. Unfortunately, I was so focused on my own concerns that I

was not able to

<u>could not be able to</u> think about things from my roommate's perspective.
 (6)

D Complete the paragraph by using the correct modal with the verb in parentheses.

When my aunt was a student at the University of Arizona, all students

_____ (fulfill / necessity) a language requirement. She thought
 (1)

that she _____ (take / advisability) Russian as that seemed to be
 (2)

an important language at the time because of the Cold War. However, she

found out it was very difficult because students _____ (learn /
 (3)

necessity) the Cyrillic alphabet. Therefore, she dropped the class. Now

she feels that she _____ (continue / advisability after the fact)
 (4)

with the Russian class because next summer she _____ (take /
 (5)

possibility) a trip to Russia.

APPLY WHAT YOU HAVE LEARNED TO WRITING

Select a writing topic and follow the steps in Appendix A on page 337.

Topic 1:

Describe any volunteer or community service work you have done in your school, your community, or your country. To what extent do you feel it is important for each person to do some volunteer or community service work at some point in his or her life?

Topic 2:

You have been asked to give some advice to people who would like to visit your country of origin for the first time for a two-week period. What suggestions do you have for them? For example, what do you think they might like to see and do? Should they go to one city or several? What should they take with them? How should they prepare for the trip?

Topic 3:

Write about a situation that you feel you did not handle as well as you could have. First, describe the situation. Then, explain what you think you could have done differently.

Unit 4

CONDITIONAL SENTENCES

If you could travel anywhere in the world, where would you go? Why would you like to go there?

GOALS

- Learn the importance of mastering conditional sentences

- Understand four problems writers commonly encounter with conditional sentences

- Form and use the conditional correctly in exercises and writing assignments

LEARN WHAT THE ERROR IS

Errors with Conditional Sentences

An error with the conditional occurs when a conditional sentence has been incorrectly formed or has not been used when it is needed. A conditional sentence usually consists of an *if*-clause that states a condition and a result clause that shows the effect of that condition. Here is an example of a conditional sentence: *If our school had more money for equipment* (the condition), *we would have a better computer lab* (the result).

Conditional sentences can express two types of conditions: factual (sometimes called *real*) and hypothetical (sometimes called *unreal*). A factual conditional sentence expresses a real or predictable situation. *If he goes to the gym* (condition), *he relaxes* (result). A hypothetical conditional sentence expresses an unreal, untrue, or imagined situation. *If she were here* (condition, meaning she is not here), *we could leave* (result).

Errors with conditional sentences are global (more serious) and affect the meaning of individual sentences, parts of a paragraph, and whole paragraphs. The editing symbol for an error with the conditional is *cond*. The conditional has many important uses in academic and professional writing. Here are some examples.

1. To show cause-effect relationships

Example:

If prices increase (condition), spending drops (result).

2. To speculate about a past event

Example:

If ticket prices had dropped (condition), more people would have traveled (result).

3. To show a future possibility

Example:

If oil prices continue to increase (condition), the airlines will increase ticket prices (result).

To be able to show such relationships, writers need to master conditional sentences.

Suggestions for Reducing Errors

- Because both clauses must function together, learn the correct formation of the verb or verb phrase for both the *if*-clause (the condition) and the result clause of a conditional sentence.

- Check **both** clauses when revising to make sure that the verb or verb phrase is correct in each.

- Be aware that native speakers often do not form the conditional correctly when they are speaking.

  Examples:

  Incorrect: The hurricane <u>could of</u> (*for* <u>could have</u>) done major damage if it had lasted longer.

  Incorrect: James would not have taken French if the university <u>did not require</u> (*for* <u>had not required</u>) it.

- Notice conditional sentences when you read; try to understand what they mean from the context.

- Memorize a set of your own hypothetical conditional sentences to use as a guide in your own writing. (See the Grammar Journal Entry in this unit.)

- Remember that, in a conditional sentence, a past verb form does not always mean past time, but may indicate a hypothetical condition.

  Example:

  If people used less water, we could conserve this precious resource.
  (The time expressed in this conditional sentence is the present, but the past tense is used to show the writer is hypothesizing.)

Check Your Understanding

Write answers to the following questions. Share your answers with another student.

1. Write a sample conditional sentence and identify the condition clause and the result clause.

2. What are the two types of conditional sentences?

— cause-effect

If prices increase, spending drops

future: —if oil prices continue to increase, the airlines will increase ticket prices.

GRAMMAR JOURNAL ENTRY 4   CONDITIONAL SENTENCES

Respond to the following in your grammar journal.

1. If you were given the chance to change your life today, what would you do?

2. Write two example conditional sentences: one for the present/future hypothetical and the other for the past hypothetical. Check them with your instructor. Once you know they are correct, memorize them to use as guides for forming the hypothetical conditional when you are writing.

UNDERSTAND COMMON PROBLEMS

This section presents four problems that writers commonly encounter with conditional sentences. First, take the pre-test to see what you already know about conditional sentences. When you finish, check your answers on page 350. Then, carefully study each problem and the examples that illustrate it. Pay particular attention to the problems that correspond to the pre-test questions you had difficulty with.

Remember that becoming aware of the types of errors you most often make with conditional sentences will increase your chances of avoiding these errors in your writing.

Pre-test   **What Do You Already Know?**

Test your ability to recognize and correct errors with conditional sentences.

A   Correct the marked conditional errors. These are examples of the four common problems that are presented in this unit.

                                                        cond

Problem 1 If the weather improves, I <u>would play</u> tennis after finishing my
                                                   will

                 homework.

                                                cond

Problem 2 The flight attendant <u>would never have fix</u> the problem if we had
                                                  ✓

                 not brought it to her attention.

Problem 3 I am sorry I can't join you because I moved to New York last
                         cond   *cond*

                 month. If I <u>am</u> still in Chicago, I <u>will go</u> to the meeting with you.
                         were   *would have*

Problem 4 If she had not brought her ATM card with her, Sheila would have

been without any money soon after she arrived in San Diego.

cond

After a few days of not eating much, she <u>will feel</u> very hungry.

would have left

B Underline and correct the error(s) in each of the following sentences.
(The errors are not in any particular order.)

were

1. If her apartment <u>was</u> closer to the university, she could walk to class

instead of taking the bus or riding her bike.

2. The teaching assistant for my math class has very strict rules. If we do

not turn in our homework on time, he deducts points. He also <u>refused</u>

to accept papers that are not stapled together.   *refuses*

burned

3. The house would have <u>burn down</u> had the firefighters not arrived so

quickly.

4. Last week, my teacher brought some candy bars containing peanuts to

class to reward us for our hard work and good attendance. If she knows   *if she had*

that two students are allergic to peanuts, she will not bring the candy.   *known*

would have not brought

Four Common Problems

Problem 1

The wrong verb or verb phrase has been used in either the condition or the result clause of a conditional sentence.

	cond ⟶ *cond*
Incorrect:	If I <u>study</u> hard for my anthropology exam, I <u>would pass</u> it.
Correct:	If I <u>study</u> hard for my anthropology exam, I <u>will pass</u> it. (factual)
Correct:	If I <u>studied</u> hard for my anthropology exam, I <u>would pass</u> it. (hypothetical)
	cond ⟶
Incorrect:	I <u>would have gotten</u> to class earlier if the bus <u>did not come</u> late.
Correct:	I <u>would have gotten</u> to class earlier if the bus <u>had not come</u> late. (past hypothetical)

SELF-HELP STRATEGY: If you are unsure about which verb form to use in the verb phrase, ask yourself if you are making a factual statement or hypothesizing. See Review Grammar Solutions on page 85.

Problem 2
The verb phrase in the conditional sentence has a verb-form error.

Incorrect: If Christi <u>had not come</u> to class, she <u>would never had known</u> an outline was due.

cond

Correct: If Christi <u>had not come</u> to class, she <u>would never have known</u> an outline was due.

Incorrect: They <u>would have cook</u> dinner for us if we <u>had ask</u> them.

cond   *cond*

Correct: They <u>would have cooked</u> dinner for us if we <u>had asked</u> them.

Incorrect: If she <u>had called</u> earlier, I <u>could of answered</u> her question.

cond

Correct: If she <u>had called</u> earlier, I <u>could have answered</u> her question.

Note: *Have* often sounds like *of* in speaking, which is why writers sometimes make this mistake.

SELF-HELP STRATEGY: Check the verb phrase in **both** clauses. Make sure that you have not only chosen the correct verb for the conditional but also have not made any errors in the verb form.

Problem 3
A hypothetical conditional sentence has not been used where one is needed.

Incorrect: I am a very disorganized person. For instance, I often cannot find my English homework because I have put it in my math notebook. If I <u>am</u> more organized (condition), I <u>will have</u> a separate color-coded folder for each class (result).

cond   *cond*

Correct: I am a very disorganized person. For instance, I often cannot find my English homework because I have put it in my math notebook. If I <u>were</u> more organized (condition), I <u>would have</u> a separate color-coded folder for each class (result).

(The writer is referring to a hypothetical situation, not a real situation.)

Problem 4
A conditional form has not been used in a later sentence to show an additional result of a condition that was stated in an earlier sentence.

Incorrect: If our instructor gave us a test today (condition), she would find

that we have not yet mastered the conditional (result). We <u>will</u>

probably all <u>fail</u>.

Correct: If our instructor gave us a test today, she would find that we have

not yet mastered the conditional. We <u>would</u> probably all <u>fail</u>.

(The conditional form must be used in the second sentence because it, too, is a result based on the condition in the preceding sentence. That is, *We would probably all fail if our instructor gave us a test today.*)

> SELF-HELP STRATEGY: Use a conditional verb or verb phrase in all the result clauses that are based on a particular condition, whether or not the *if*-clause is repeated.

REVIEW GRAMMAR SOLUTIONS

A conditional sentence can either express a real or a hypothetical (contrary-to-fact) condition and gives the result of that condition.

Factual Conditional Sentences: Meaning and Use

In a factual conditional sentence, a real situation by definition exists or has a strong possibility of existing. Factual conditional sentences allow the writer to do the following:

1. To make predictions or express future possibilities

Examples:

If we use this method, we will probably get better results.

If my neighbor plays loud music, I will complain to the manager.

2. To express facts or habitual actions

Examples:

If sugar is mixed with water, it dissolves. (general fact)

If the elderly exercise regularly, they are generally happier.
(habitual action)

Note: *When* or *whenever* can be substituted for *if* in these sentences.

3. To make inferences

Examples:

> If this compound contains carbon, it is organic material.

> If that book is the latest edition, I bought the wrong one.

Note: *When* or *whenever* cannot be substituted for *if* in these sentences.

4. To give commands or instructions

Example:

> If your laboratory experiment fails, do it again tomorrow.

Hypothetical Conditional Sentences: Meaning and Use

In a hypothetical conditional sentence, a situation does not exist or is not likely to exist. Hypothetical conditional sentences allow the writer to do the following:

1. To hypothesize or imagine what might happen in the present or future as the result of a given condition

In the writer's mind, it is not very likely that the situation will exist or the event will happen.

Example:

> If my neighbor started to play loud rock music, I would complain to the apartment manager. (I do not think that she will start playing rock music, but I would take this action if she did.)

What is confusing about the hypothetical is that often the writer could use the factual conditional for the same sentence and simply make a prediction. What differentiates the two is how certain the writer feels about the action or event. Consider, for example: *If my neighbor starts to play rock music, I will complain to the apartment manager.* With the factual conditional, the sentence now has a different meaning. The writer knows that this neighbor often plays rock music, so she can safely predict the event will happen.

2. To express an impossible or counterfactual condition and the result of that condition

Examples:

> If I were you, I would move out of that apartment. (I am not you, but this is what I would do in this situation.)

> If Thomas Jefferson saw the White House today, he would not recognize it. (Thomas Jefferson cannot return to life to see the White House today, and since he was president, the White House has completely changed.)

Note: The factual conditional cannot be used in the example sentences
above because these conditions cannot be made possible or true.

3. To imagine what could have happened in a past situation but never did

Example:

If Sang had not reviewed conditional sentences before the quiz,
he would have lost ten points. (Sang did review them and he did
not lose ten points.)

4. To evaluate or critique

Examples:

The article on carbon footprints would be more convincing if
further information were presented.

The data would be easier to read if the author had presented it in
table form.

The presentation would have been clearer if the presenter had
shown us her data on slides.

Factual Conditional Sentences: Forming the Verb and Verb Phrase

In factual conditional sentences, the sequence of tenses varies according
to the meaning of the conditional sentence and the time the writer
wants to express.

1. To make predictions or talk about future possibilities

CONDITION CLAUSE	RESULT CLAUSE
present tense	*will, can, should, could, may, might* + base form
present progressive tense	OR
present perfect tense	*will, can, should, could, may, might* + *be* + base form + *-ing*

Examples:

If we <u>go</u> to Philadelphia, we <u>can see</u> the Liberty Bell.

If Andreas <u>is trying</u> to get online right now, he <u>will discover</u> that the server
is down.

If the committee <u>has reached</u> a decision, we <u>can continue</u> the meeting.

If her flight <u>has not yet taken off</u>, Emiliana <u>might be arriving</u> after midnight.

The conditional sentence with *will* in the result clause on page 87 expresses the strongest possibility, a prediction. The other modals in the example sentences indicate a lesser degree of possibility.

The future tense is not used in an *if*-clause.

Examples:

If you <u>have not bought</u> your ticket, you <u>may not get</u> a seat.

If Mina <u>is not attending</u> class regularly, she <u>could fail</u> the course.

If the letter <u>has not come</u> by now, it <u>might not arrive</u> at all.

2. To express facts or habitual actions

CONDITION CLAUSE	RESULT CLAUSE
same tense (present or past)	same tense (present or past)

Examples:

If the alarm <u>rings</u>, it <u>is</u> time to get up. (fact)

Whenever my roommate <u>studied</u> late, I <u>stayed up</u>, too. (habitual action)

Note: *When* and *whenever* are often used instead of *if* to express a habitual action.

3. To make inferences

CONDITION CLAUSE	RESULT CLAUSE
present tense	*must* or *should* + base form
past tense	*must have* + past participle

Examples:

If the store <u>is</u> already <u>closed</u>, it <u>must be</u> later than we thought.

If Nam <u>forgot</u> his identification card, he <u>must have gone</u> to the security office.

4. To give commands or instructions

CONDITION CLAUSE	RESULT CLAUSE
present tense	imperative
past tense	
present perfect tense	

Examples:

If you <u>miss</u> the lecture, <u>go</u> to see the teacher.

If you <u>missed</u> the lecture, <u>go</u> to see the teacher.

If you <u>have missed</u> your plane, <u>go</u> to the ticket counter.

Hypothetical Conditional Sentences

When forming the verb or verb phrase in hypothetical conditional sentences, note that the time of the sentence is not related to the verb tense used. For example, in the sentence *If I were you* (condition), *I would go* (result), *were* does not signal past time but, instead, a condition that is contrary to fact. The same is true for the sentence *If I had been there* (condition), *she would not have won* (result). In this sentence, *had been* does not signal an event that happened before another in the past, but rather it is used to indicate that the writer is speculating about an event that has already taken place in the past.

1. **To express a present or future hypothetical or contrary-to-fact situation**

   Note: In the condition clause, *were* is used for all forms of *be*.

CONDITION CLAUSE	RESULT CLAUSE
simple past tense	*would, could, might* + base form
	would, could, might + *be* + *-ing* form

   Examples:

   If I <u>were</u> you, I <u>would save</u> more money.

   If Tran <u>lived</u> at home instead of in the dormitory, she <u>would have</u> a quiet place to study.

   If Abdul <u>washed</u> his car every week, he <u>would not always be complaining</u> about how dirty it is.

CONDITION CLAUSE	RESULT CLAUSE
past progressive tense	*would, could, might* + base form
	would, could, might + *be* + *-ing* form

   Examples:

   If Sheila <u>were not working</u> in the dining hall, she <u>could not afford</u> college.

   If Ara <u>were working</u> in town, he <u>would not be spending</u> so much time driving to work.

CONDITION CLAUSE	RESULT CLAUSE
could, would + base form	*would, could, might* + base form
	would, could, might + *be* + *-ing* form

Example:

If Mike <u>could think</u> of a good topic, he <u>would start</u> his term paper.

2. To express a hypothetical situation in the past

CONDITION CLAUSE	RESULT CLAUSE
past perfect tense	*would, could, might* + *have* + past participle
	would, could, might + *have* + *been* + *-ing* form

Examples:

If Gail <u>had turned</u> her lab report in on time, she <u>would have received</u> the full ten points on it.

If Lan <u>had not refused</u> to loan us his car, we <u>could have been driving</u> to the beach right now.

CONDITION CLAUSE	RESULT CLAUSE
past perfect progressive tense	*would, could, might* + *have* + past participle
	would, could, might + *have been* + *-ing* form

Examples:

Natasha <u>might have enjoyed</u> the movie if she <u>had not been feeling sick</u>.

If Matt <u>had been paying</u> attention in class, he <u>would not have been asking</u> his friends about the assignment last night.

Note: It is often helpful to understand hypotheticals by mentally inserting a "but" clause after the condition.

Examples:

If I had studied harder last night [*but I did not*], I would have done better on my midterm this morning.

If the Olympic Committee had not chosen Salt Lake City for the Winter Games [*but they did*], the United States would have been disappointed.

IMPROVE YOUR WRITING STYLE

MIXING CONDITIONAL TYPES

It may sometimes be necessary to mix conditional types. The most common combination involves a past condition and a present result.

Example:

> If I had eaten breakfast this morning, my stomach would not be growling.
>   (I did not eat breakfast this morning, so my stomach is growling now.)

VARIATIONS IN CONDITIONAL SENTENCES

You can use conjunctions other than if. *Although* if *is the most commonly used conjunction to express the conditional, other conjunctions—such as* even if, when, whenever, whether, *and* unless *(meaning "if . . . not")—can also be used.*

Examples:

> Whether it rains or not, I will still go to the movies.
>   (I will go [result] regardless of the weather [condition].)

> Unless I find my keys, I cannot unlock my bike.
>   (I must have my keys [condition] to unlock my bike [result].)
>   (If I do not find my keys, I cannot unlock my bike.)

You can write conditional sentences without if *by reversing the subject and the verb in the* if-*clause. This formation is most commonly used with* had *and* should *but may also be used with* were.

Examples:

> Had I known the test was today, I would have studied the chapter.

> Should the telephone ring while I am out, please answer it.

> Were I closer to the front, I could hear the speaker better.

Continued on page 92.

IMPROVE YOUR WRITING STYLE (CONT.)

CONDITIONAL SENTENCES WITHOUT AN *IF*-CLAUSE

Be aware that sometimes the if-*clause is not stated with the past hypothetical.*

Examples:

> That experiment would not work.
>> (Implied statement: even if the researcher tried it)

> Most students would prefer a night class to an 8:00 AM class.
>> (Implied statement: if they had the opportunity to choose)

IF MEANING *WHETHER*

Know that if *does not always signal a conditional clause. It can also be used to replace "whether" (whether . . . or not) in a noun clause.*

Example:

> The instructor has not yet decided *if* she will offer a review session.

COMMON USES OF THE HYPOTHETICAL

Know these common uses of the hypothetical, which are found in both written and spoken English.

1. To give advice

Examples:

> If I were you, I would ask Professor Jones if he would be your advisor.

> If I were you, I wouldn't choose Professor Smith as an advisor.

> Do you think I should take the job? If I were you, I would.

2. To express a wish

Examples:

> I wish the spring quarter were over.

> I wish I had a car.

> I wish I had passed the English examination.

> I wish I hadn't had to disagree with my professor (but I felt he was wrong).

PRACTICE WHAT YOU HAVE LEARNED

EXERCISE 1

Directions: Read each sentence and then answer the questions to
test your understanding of the structure and meaning
of conditional sentences.

1. If Lucia has enough money, she will go to Hawaii for a vacation.

   a. Does Lucia have enough money yet? _____*no*_____

   b. Will she go to Hawaii for a vacation? __*yes, when she has enough money*__

   c. What is the time expressed in the statement? _____*future*_____

2. If Jim were 16 years old, he would be able to drive.

   a. Is Jim 16 yet? _____NO_____

   b. Can he drive? _____NO_____   *second cond*

   c. What is the time expressed in the statement? __Past Simple / present modal__

3. If Mary had asked Jim to keep the news a secret, he would not have

   told you that she had received an award.

   a. Did Mary ask to have the news kept a secret? _____NO_____

   b. Did Jim tell you the news? _____Yes_____

   c. What is the time expressed in the statement? __past perfect / past modal__

EXERCISE 2

Directions: Test your understanding of the time frame of the conditional
by reading the following conditional sentences. Check (✓)
which time you think is expressed in each sentence.

1. If I have time, I work out at the gym.

☑ present   ☐ past   ☐ future

2. If I have time, I will work out at the gym.

☐ present   ☐ past   ☑ future

3. If I had time, I would work out at the gym.   *Second*

present modal

☐ present   ☑ past   ☐ future

4. If I had had time, I would have worked out at the gym. *Third*

Past perfect   *past modal*

☐ present   ☑ past   ☐ future

5. If I hadn't worked out at the gym, I would not be so far behind on
my paper.   *P·P*   *P.M.P*

3/2

☐ present   ☑ past   ☐ future

6. If I had been smart, I would have started my paper earlier.

P·P   *Past Modal*

third

☐ present   ☑ past   ☐ future

EXERCISE 3

Directions: Test your understanding of the meaning and formation of
conditional sentences. Decide whether each of the following
sentences is correct (C) or incorrect (I). If a sentence is
incorrect, make the correction.

have

Examples: __I__ If the teacher had not been ill, he would ~~had~~ come to class.

__C__ Bob would have received a better grade if he had
attended class regularly.

had

__I__ 1. If I have a car, I would not ask my friends to take me

past simple   *present modal*

shopping.

___ 2. If Margaret had slept more, she would not have trouble staying awake during the chemistry lecture yesterday.

___ 3. If the teacher had not stopped us at 10 o'clock, I would have been able to finish the test.

___ 4. If I will go to Los Angeles next week, I will see all my friends.

___ 5. If Peter went to the bookstore later today, he can buy two notebooks for the price of one.

___ 6. If Edith had not had to turn in her paper today, she would had skipped class.

___ 7. If the weather is nice, Marcella always took a walk after dinner.

___ 8. If I could found a ride home this weekend, I would give my parents a surprise visit.

___ 9. When it is hot outside, I drink plenty of water.

___ 10. If I were going to a community college, I would be living at my parents' home.

EXERCISE 4

Directions: Complete each sentence with the correct form of the verb in parentheses.

Example: If the weather is nice tomorrow, the teacher _____*will hold*_____ (hold) class outside.

1. If the city __had expanded__ (expand) the parking space downtown, we would not have had to park so far away from the movie theater.

2. When my roommate ____Snores____ (snore) loudly, I cannot sleep.

3. Some celebrities get depressed if their names _____do_____ not ____appear____ (appear) in the news.

[handwritten: Past perfect]

[handwritten: unreal third] 4. If we _____ had _____ not _____ had _____ (have) to take an exam

on the conditional, we might not have learned it.

[handwritten: Past Modal]

[handwritten: real] *[handwritten: first]* 5. Maya _____ will _____ not _____ pass _____ (pass) her driving test

unless she calms down.

[handwritten: s.m]

[handwritten: unreal Second] 6. If it _____ was _____ (be) winter, all these trees would be covered

with snow. *[handwritten: Present Modal]*

[handwritten: would]

[handwritten: third] 7. Had it not rained, the farmers _____ have lost _____ (lose) their crops.

8. If the airplane had not had a mechanical problem, we

___ would have ___ probably _ have arrived _ (arrive) in Tucson by now.

[handwritten: would be laying]

9. We _____ (lie) on the beach in Mexico right now if we

had been able to get our visas on time.

[handwritten: would try]

10. I _____ (try) to find more opportunities to speak English

if I were you.

EXERCISE 5

Directions: In this student paragraph, fill in the blanks with the correct
form of the conditional.

　　In April, I had difficulty deciding whether to go home and get a job for

the summer or to attend summer school at my university. I decided that if

I _____ *talked* _____ (talk) to my friend, who is already a senior, I would get
　　　　　　(1)

some useful advice. He told me that he wished he _ would not stay _ (not stay)
　　　　　　　　　　　　　　　　　　　　　　　(2)

on campus the summer after his first year of college. He thinks that if he

[handwritten: Past perfect] had spent his first summer at home recovering from an intense first year of

college, he _____ would have felt _____ (feel) refreshed and ready to return to studying
　　　　　　　　(3)

as a sophomore. I have decided he is right. Although I will miss my friends on

campus, I know it is important for me to make money this summer and to take

a break from school. Moreover, if I _ don't make _ (not make) any money, I am
　　　　　　　　　　　　　　　　　(4)

afraid that I will have to take out a loan to pay my tuition fees in the fall.

EXERCISE 6

Directions: Complete the following sentences.

Example: If I were the instructor of this class,
            I would let the students out early today. _____.

   1. If Jennifer did not have to be in class right now, _____
   _____.

   2. I would have gotten to class earlier if _____
   _____.

   3. If I had gotten enough sleep last night, _____
   _____.

   4. I would complain about this class if _____
   _____.

   5. If Vincent has time later, _____
   _____.

   6. If I had had time during the weekend, _____
   _____.

   7. If I had a little extra money, _____
   _____.

   8. If students are given too much to learn, _____
   _____.

   9. If the tuition were lowered, _____
   _____.

  10. Even if we could have raised the money to buy George a gift,
   _____.

EXERCISE 7

Directions: Write answers to the following questions.

1. If you have a problem, whom do you usually share it with?

    _____

    _____

2. If today were Saturday, where would you probably be right now?

    _____

    _____

3. Given the chance to make the decision again, would you choose to attend the same school you are attending or to accept the same job?

    _____

    _____

EXERCISE 8

Directions: The following student paragraph contains errors in the use of the conditional. Correct these errors. The first one has been done for you. There is more than one way to revise the paragraph, and the number of errors will vary depending on how you choose to revise it.

Last year, I lived in a dormitory on campus. It was, unfortunately, always noisy. If I ~~did not live~~ *had not lived* there, I would certainly have had more time to study for my classes, and I would have eaten better food. On the other hand, I would *have made* make fewer friends last year. For next year, I have decided I want to live off campus in an apartment. Soon I will have to start thinking about choosing a roommate and getting an apartment. On the one hand, I would prefer to live with my best friend, Joan. However, if I pick my best friend, I *will* would have no one to turn to when my roommate and I have an argument. On the other hand, if I decided to live with one of my new friends from the dorm, then I *will* hurt Joan's feelings. Perhaps, when I talk to Joan next week, we *will* would figure out together what to do.

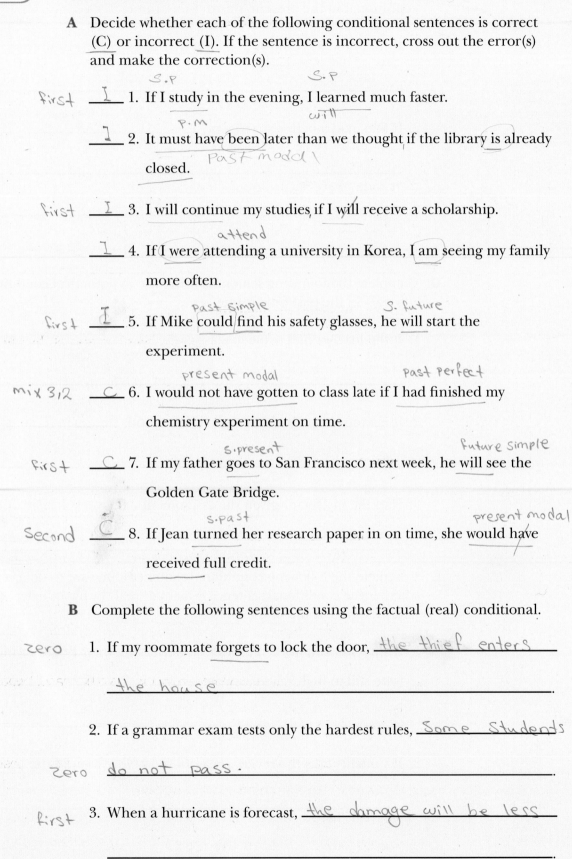

Post-test   **What Do You Know Now?**

A Decide whether each of the following conditional sentences is correct (C) or incorrect (I). If the sentence is incorrect, cross out the error(s) and make the correction(s).

first ___I___ 1. If I study in the evening, I learned much faster.

___I___ 2. It must have been later than we thought if the library is already closed.

first ___I___ 3. I will continue my studies, if I will receive a scholarship.

___I___ 4. If I were attending a university in Korea, I am seeing my family more often.

first ___I___ 5. If Mike could find his safety glasses, he will start the experiment.

mix 3,2 ___C___ 6. I would not have gotten to class late if I had finished my chemistry experiment on time.

first ___C___ 7. If my father goes to San Francisco next week, he will see the Golden Gate Bridge.

Second ___C___ 8. If Jean turned her research paper in on time, she would have received full credit.

B Complete the following sentences using the factual (real) conditional.

zero   1. If my roommate forgets to lock the door, _the thief enters the house_.

2. If a grammar exam tests only the hardest rules, _Some Students_

zero _do not pass._

first   3. When a hurricane is forecast, _the damage will be less_

Past Simple/past modal

C Complete the following sentences using the hypothetical (unreal) conditional in the present/future time frame.

Two Three Mix

Past Simple

1. If the students could vote on whether to take a test or not,

two they would passed their exam   .

mix 2,3 *Past Simple* 2. If Max had a better apartment, he would have lived easier *present modal*

_____.

mix 2/3 3. If Francis bought a brand-new car, *simple past* she would have driven

more safely   .

Past Time **D** Complete the following sentences using the hypothetical conditional (unreal) in the past time frame.

Past Perfect

1. If the teacher had come to class early, all the exercises

mix 3/2 would have been done   .

Third 2. If my roommate had not eaten all the food, *past perfect* I would had

eaten too   .

3. Had the instructor given the assignment next week instead of today,

If the students would have finished on next .

Freedom **E** Complete the following conditional sentences. Be sure to determine whether the conditional sentence is factual (real) or hypothetical (unreal) and what time frame it is expressing.

Past Perfect

1. If students had worked harder on improving their English while they

were still in high school, they would had passed their

final exam.

2. If students take the review class offered before a midterm, they

will do their best   .

3. Many students will be on the waiting list for advanced calculus unless

_____.

4. Janice felt that she would have passed the writing test last spring if

she _____.

past, present future

F Correct the underlined errors marked *cond.*   "wrong"

Yesterday we had our last midterm in Psychology 1A before the final

cond   second
exam. It was a difficult exam. The teacher told us that if we study all the
studied

chapters, the exam would be easy. However, it was extraordinarily difficult,

for it tested us on what we did not know rather than on what we did know.

cond
I honestly feel, in looking back, that even if I studied more, I would not have
had studied

mix 3/2   done any better on the test. My friend thinks that if she had had more time,
Past perfect

cond
she would do better. She insists that if she plans her time better, she will do
would have done

cond
well on the final exam, which is in two weeks. If the last midterm was not so

difficult, I would believe her. However, based on that exam, I think that even

cond
if I study the chapters and have plenty of time, I would pass, but I will not
will

get an A. In fact, I think that if I studied for a whole year, I still would not get

an A on that exam.

APPLY WHAT YOU HAVE LEARNED TO WRITING

Select a writing topic and follow the steps in Appendix A on page 337.

Topic 1:

If you could take an all-expense-paid trip to any place in the world for two weeks, where would you most like to go and why? Write about what type of transportation you would probably use the most on this trip and what kinds of activities you would most like to do at this place.

Topic 2:

If you had the power to change anything in your country or in the United States, what would you most like to change and why? (Alternatively, you could choose to change something in your school or workplace.)

Topic 3:

Think about the growth in online education. What are some of the advantages and disadvantages of this type of education, in which the student does not go to class but rather sits in front of a computer or uses other electronic equipment to learn?

PASSIVE VOICE

GOALS

- Learn why mastering the passive voice is important in writing

- Understand three problems writers commonly encounter with the passive voice

- Form and use the passive voice correctly in exercises and writing assignments

What are some of the most pressing environmental problems facing your city, your country, or the world today? Are there any obvious solutions?

LEARN WHAT THE ERROR IS

Errors with the Passive Voice

In English, most verbs can be used in either the active voice or the passive voice. In the sentence *The bookstore sells computer supplies,* the verb is in the active voice because the subject is doing the action. In the sentence *Our teachers will be moved to temporary offices this spring,* the verb is in the passive voice because the subject is being acted upon. The doer of the action is not named; "by someone" is understood. However, in the sentence *Our Spanish textbook was written by my teacher,* the doer of the action—"my teacher"—is mentioned. The writer chooses whether or not to name the doer of the action depending on how important it is for the reader to have that information.

An error with the passive voice occurs when a verb in the passive voice has been incorrectly formed or when the passive voice has been used where the active voice is needed. The editing symbol for an error with the passive is *pass.*

A problem with the passive voice may occur when the active voice is preferable to the passive voice in a sentence. In that case, your instructor may use an alternative symbol, *wk pass* (for weak passive).

The verb *be* + the past participle, as in the sentence *The lake is situated halfway between the two towns,* is sometimes considered a passive construction (called the stative passive). Errors in this type of formation are treated in this unit and in Unit 2, "Verb Forms."

Errors with the passive voice are global (more serious) errors and can affect the meaning of individual sentences, parts of a paragraph, and whole paragraphs. In formal writing, knowing how to use the passive voice correctly is very important. Although a sentence in the passive voice may be grammatically correct, it may not be the best choice in a piece of writing. Rather, the decision of whether or not to use the passive voice should be based upon whether the subject of the sentence is doing the action or being acted upon.

Knowing how to form the passive voice correctly is very important. If the passive voice is incorrectly formed in a sentence, the reader will try to supply its correct form but may be confused about whether the writer intended to use the active or passive voice.

In academic and professional writing, the writer uses both active and passive voice; therefore, it is essential that writers master the use and formation of the passive voice.

Suggestions for Reducing Errors

- Memorize how to form the passive voice so that you can do so automatically. (Consult the charts in the Review Grammar Solutions section of this unit.)

- Make sure the verb you have chosen can be used in the passive voice by checking your dictionary to find out whether or not the verb is transitive (takes a direct object and can be made passive, like the verbs *collect, teach,* or *follow*) or intransitive (does not take a direct object and cannot be made passive, like the verbs *arrive, exist,* or *stay*).

- Compare the way the two voices are used when you are reading textbooks, the newspaper, or magazine articles. In particular, try to determine why the author used the passive instead of the active voice and whether you think its use is effective.

- If you need to write a scientific paper or a laboratory report, examine similar papers in that field or any sample papers the instructor has provided so that you can see the balance of active and passive voice. If you are in doubt, ask your instructor for help.

Check Your Understanding

Write answers to the following questions. Share your answers with another student.

   1. What two voices can verbs have in English?

   2. What kinds of verbs cannot be made passive and why?

GRAMMAR JOURNAL ENTRY 5   THE PASSIVE VOICE

Respond to the following in your grammar journal.

1. What is the best gift that has ever been given to you and why?

2. Write two sample sentences, one in the active voice and the other in the passive voice. Label each one correctly.

UNDERSTAND COMMON PROBLEMS

This section presents three problems that writers commonly encounter with the passive voice. First, take the pre-test to see what you already know about the passive voice. When you finish, check your answers on page 351. Then, carefully study each problem and the examples that illustrate it. Pay particular attention to those problems that correspond to the pre-test questions you had difficulty with. Remember that becoming aware of the types of errors you most often make with the passive voice will increase your chances of avoiding these errors in your writing.

Pre-test

What Do You Already Know?

Test your ability to recognize and correct errors with the passive voice.

A   Correct the marked passive-voice errors. These are examples of the three common problems that are presented in this unit.

pass
Problem 1 Some math problems <u>can be solve</u> very easily.

pass
Problem 2 The speaker's question <u>directed</u> at the younger members of the audience.

pass
Problem 3 While in New York City last month, we <u>were stayed</u> in a hotel near Wall Street.

B   Underline and correct the one error in each of the following sentences. (The errors are not in any particular order.)

1.   My friends had already been arrived when I got to the airport.

2.   The textbook send to him yesterday by priority mail.

3.   Many of the books I want have already been check out from the library.

Three Common Problems

Problem 1

The passive voice has been incorrectly formed.

pass
Incorrect: Some pronunciation problems <u>can be fix</u> easily.

Correct: Some pronunciation problems <u>can be fixed</u> easily.

Note: Some instructors may choose to mark this error as

vf (verb form).

Incorrect: Your grades <u>will sent</u> next week. *pass*

Incorrect: Your grades <u>will being sent</u> next week. *pass*

Correct: Your grades <u>will be sent</u> next week.

Problem 2

The passive voice is needed instead of the active voice.

Incorrect: A new air conditioner <u>will install</u> next week. *pass*

Correct: A new air conditioner <u>will be installed</u> next week. (The air conditioner cannot install itself; it must be installed by someone.)

Problem 3

The passive voice has been used with a verb that cannot be made passive.

Incorrect: It is possible that life <u>is existed</u> on planets other than ours. *pass*

Correct: It is possible that life <u>exists</u> on planets other than ours.

Incorrect: A power failure <u>was occurred</u> last month. *pass*

Correct: A power failure <u>occurred</u> last month.

> SELF-HELP STRATEGY: If you are unsure whether a verb is transitive or intransitive, check the verb in a dictionary.

REVIEW GRAMMAR SOLUTIONS

A proficient writer knows when to choose the active or the passive voice. In expository writing, the active voice is generally a better choice than the passive voice except in cases where the writer wants to emphasize what has happened rather than who or what caused the action. In scientific and technical writing, the passive voice is often preferred so that the emphasis is on the experiment or the phenomenon, not on the researcher(s).

Remember that while a sentence with the passive voice may be grammatically correct, the writer must choose either the active or passive voice to effectively express what he or she wants to say. The following guidelines can help you learn how to form and decide when to use the passive voice in expository writing.

Passive Voice of Verb Tenses

The passive voice is formed by using *to be* in whatever tense the writer selects and then adding the past participle. To form the negative of the passive, use *not*.

Examples:

The Internet connection <u>has not been fixed</u> at my apartment.
The bottles <u>are not sealed</u> at the factory.

The present and past perfect progressive, the future progressive, and the future perfect progressive are not used in the passive voice.

VERB-TENSE FORMATION IN PASSIVE VOICE	
PRESENT	**EXAMPLES**
am, is, are + past participle	Mail <u>is delivered</u> every day except Sunday.
PRESENT PROGRESSIVE	
am being, is being, are being + past participle	A new addition <u>is being added</u> to the library.
PAST	
was, were + past participle	The grades <u>were posted</u> by the teaching assistant at 3:00 PM.
PAST PROGRESSIVE	
was being, were being + past participle	When I arrived, the corrected quizzes <u>were</u> just <u>being distributed.</u>
PRESENT PERFECT	
has been, have been + past participle	The money <u>has</u> already <u>been sent</u> electronically by the bank.
PAST PERFECT	
had been + past participle	All the food <u>had been eaten</u> when I arrived at the potluck dinner.
FUTURE	
will be + past participle	The tests <u>will be given back</u> on Thursday.
FUTURE PERFECT	
will have been + past participle	By the time we arrive at the concert hall, all the free tickets <u>will have been given out</u>.

Passive Voice of Modal Verb Phrases

In a modal verb phrase, the passive is formed by adding *be* + the past participle after the modal for the present tense and *have been* + the past participle after the modal for the past tense.

PRESENT	EXAMPLES
modal + *be* + past participle	Spelling <u>can be checked</u> on a computer. Backpacks <u>should not be left</u> unattended in the library.
PAST	**EXAMPLES**
modal + *have been* + past participle	It is possible that the train <u>could have been delayed</u>. She <u>should not have been elected</u> chair of the committee.

Passive Voice of Conditional Verb Phrases

In a conditional sentence, the passive voice can be used in the condition clause, the result clause, or both. To correctly form the passive voice in a conditional sentence, use the guidelines for forming the passive voice of verb tenses and modal verb phrases in this section. The chart below shows examples of the passive voice in conditional sentences.

	EXAMPLES
Factual conditional	If Ben makes a mistake, he <u>is corrected</u> by his friend.
Hypothetical conditional (present or future)	If the computer software <u>were shipped</u> tonight, it would arrive tomorrow. (<u>was</u> becomes <u>were</u> in the *if* clause)
Hypothetical conditional (past)	If the dam <u>had</u> not <u>been repaired</u>, we would have had a flood last spring.

Passive of Infinitives, Gerunds, and Participles

1. Infinitives in the passive voice

PRESENT	EXAMPLE
to + be + past participle	She arranged for the test <u>to be given</u> Monday.
PERFECT (OR PAST)	**EXAMPLE**
to + have been + past participle	The results were supposed <u>to have been sent</u> yesterday.

2. Gerunds in the passive voice

PRESENT	EXAMPLES
being + past participle	He did not like <u>being called</u> Jim instead of James. <u>Being awakened</u> in the middle of the night by a telephone call upset George.
PERFECT (OR PAST)	**EXAMPLE**
having + been + past participle	After <u>having been told</u> to go from one office to another, Phil finally found where to turn in his application.

3. Participial phrases in the passive voice

PRESENT	EXAMPLE
base form + -ing + past participle	<u>Being surrounded</u> by all her friends and <u>feeling supported</u> by them, Janice no longer felt nervous about giving the speech.
PERFECT (OR PAST)	**EXAMPLE**
having been + past participle	<u>Having been rejected</u> for the position, my cousin decided to apply for a different job.

The Stative Passive

Another form of the passive is the stative passive. It is formed by the verb *to be* (or verbs like *seem, appear,* or *feel*) + the past participle. This formation expresses a state of being. Some grammar books treat it as a passive without an agent while others consider it as a verb + adjective. The verbs used to form this type of passive are called stative verbs.

Examples:

Peter <u>is finished</u> with his paper and <u>is satisfied</u> with his work.

Kirsten <u>has been exhausted</u> ever since she finished her dissertation.

My roommate <u>felt discouraged</u> after she received her scores.

For information on stative verbs, see Unit 1, page 15. For additional information on the stative passive, see Unit 2, Problem 3, Self-Help Strategy.

The following are two common errors that occur with the stative passive formation.

Incorrect: My brother <u>confined</u> to his apartment because he has the flu.

   (The verb *is* has been left out.)

Incorrect: My brother <u>is confine</u> to his apartment because he has the flu.

   (The past participle is incorrectly formed.)

Correct: My brother <u>is confined</u> to his apartment because he has the flu.

Common Uses of the Passive Voice

1. To express something that happened to the subject

Example:

The new bridge <u>was completed</u> last week.

Note: The agent, or doer of the action, may or may not be mentioned, depending upon whether the agent is known or how important it is to know the agent.

2. To explain how something was done or what methodology was used

Examples:

The data <u>were analyzed</u> and the results <u>were recorded</u>.

The forms <u>were completed</u> and <u>sent</u> to the physician yesterday.

3. To describe a process

Examples:

Water <u>can be purified</u> by boiling it for a period of time.

Each letter <u>should be drafted, typed</u>, and <u>proofread</u> before it <u>is sent</u> out.

4. To express a state

Examples:

Brendan <u>was relieved</u> to see his sister at the airport.

The library <u>is located</u> near the administration building.

IMPROVE YOUR WRITING STYLE

AVOIDING WORDINESS

You can use the active voice to avoid wordiness. A passive construction can sometimes make a sentence wordy—which, of course, will negatively affect the writer's style.

Examples:

It <u>is stated by the author</u> that Mondays are depressing. (passive voice, ten words)

<u>The author states</u> that Mondays are depressing. (active voice, seven words)

You can reduce the passive verb phrase to avoid wordiness as well as vary your style.

Examples:

The air samples <u>were analyzed</u> and the results <u>were recorded</u>.

The air samples <u>were analyzed</u> and the results <u>recorded</u>.

USING PASSIVE VOICE IN SCIENTIFIC AND TECHNICAL WRITING AND FACTUAL REPORTING

In scientific and technical writing, the passive voice is often preferred so that the emphasis is on the experiment or the situation itself, not on the researcher(s).

Examples:

The dragonflies <u>were collected</u> and then <u>kept</u> at 2°C for four hours.

The software <u>should be updated</u> regularly.

In reporting, the passive voice is also preferred in some cases as in the examples below.

Examples:

More thunderstorms <u>are expected</u> to hit the Southland late Sunday, but the rainfall <u>is expected</u> to be considerably less than that of last week's storm. More showers and thunderstorms <u>are predicted</u> through Wednesday, with a heavy surf advisory until 10:00 AM today. A 48-year-old man <u>was rescued</u> early Saturday morning after high waves knocked him off his surfboard and he <u>was swept</u> under.

The president <u>was reported</u> to have suffered a fall last night at the hotel where he was staying. At this time, no details <u>have been released</u> to the press. The president <u>will be transported</u> by helicopter to a military hospital later this morning for an examination. At that time, his press secretary will hold a press conference.

In the above examples, the passive voice has been used to keep the focus on the subject or to keep the source of the information confidential.

INEFFECTIVE USE OF THE PASSIVE VOICE

It is important for writers to be aware of ineffective use of the passive voice. The symbol for such use is wk pass—*weak passive.*

In the following short paragraph, the passive voice has been used ineffectively. There is no focus on who performed the actions.

Listing my ideas in a disorganized way is a second weakness of mine in writing. Organization was not adequately taught in my high school. My thoughts <u>were scribbled</u> in list form and <u>were accepted</u> by my instructors.

In the revised paragraph below, the writer uses the active voice, and the paragraph now focuses on the writer doing the action.

Listing my ideas in a disorganized way is a second weakness of mine in writing. Organization was not adequately taught in my high school. I merely scribbled out my thoughts in list form and my instructors accepted them.

While the sentences in the first paragraph are grammatically correct, the use of the active voice in the revised paragraph in the last sentence makes the paragraph flow better.

PRACTICE WHAT YOU HAVE LEARNED

EXERCISE 1

Directions: Fill in the correct form of the passive voice. Use the verb tense indicated.

1. **Present**

   All of the participants in the race _____ (invite) to the awards ceremony.

2. **Present progressive**

   Applications for part-time jobs _____ (accept) from now until the end of the month.

3. **Past**

   Volkan told me that the concert _____ (cancel), so I did not go.

4. **Present perfect**

   Do you know whether or not the package _____ (send)?

5. **Past perfect**

   The officer announced that the suspects _____ (arrest) for the crime.

6. **Future**

   Stanley does not have to buy a plane ticket; it _____ (take care of) by his assistant.

7. **Future perfect**

   By the time I get home, I hope that the dishes _____ (wash) by my roommates.

8. **Infinitive**

Johnson expects _____ (lay off) next month because the store is experiencing financial problems. (present)

The building was expected _____ (complete) by now, but only the foundation has been laid. (perfect or past)

9. **Gerund**

Marilyn did not anticipate _____ (charge) a late fee for the library book. (present)

_____ (accept) by Yale should have pleased Kim, but she really wanted to go to Harvard. (perfect or past)

10. **Modal**

I am afraid that the date _____ (might, change). (present time)

Do you think this box _____ (might, deliver) to my house by mistake? (past time)

11. **Conditional**

If the English test _____ (can, postpone), I would be very relieved.

12. **Participial phrases**

1. _____ (applaud) so warmly by the audience, the piano player began to play even more enthusiastically. (present)

2. _____ (win) the lottery, the recipient announced that he was going to buy a new house. (perfect).

EXERCISE 2

Directions: Change the underlined verbs or infinitives in the following sentences from the active voice to the passive voice, if possible. Make other changes in the sentences as necessary. Be particularly careful to use the correct formation of the passive voice for the verb tense you are using.

Example: The Red Cross <u>collected</u> canned food and clothes for the earthquake victims. (active)

Canned food and clothes <u>were collected</u> for the earthquake victims by the Red

Cross. (passive)

1. Most restaurants <u>accept</u> credit cards.

   _____

2. They <u>must have torn</u> down the bookstore since I was there in March.

   _____

3. The teacher expects the students <u>to do</u> the assignment before class.

   _____

4. If the temperature <u>had dropped</u> last night, snow <u>would have fallen</u>

   _____

5. The reporter <u>interrupted</u> the program for a special bulletin on the approaching storm.

   _____

6. By the time I get home, the letter carrier <u>will have delivered</u> the mail.

   _____

7. At the end of the school year, teachers and students <u>are ready</u> for summer vacation.

   _____

8. The university press <u>has published</u> Dr. Robertson's book.

_____

9. If they <u>cannot change</u> the meeting location, they should reschedule the meeting.

_____

10. Although I <u>had invited</u> six people for dinner, only three came.

_____

11. I would have taken advantage of the field trip if the instructor <u>had announced</u> it earlier.

_____

12. Tom <u>must have broken</u> his foot in the accident as he is wearing a cast.

_____

EXERCISE 3

Directions: Correct the passive voice formation error by writing in the correct answer above the sentence.

Example: When I was walking in the streets of Taiwan, Chinese
was being spoken
~~was speaking~~ all around me.

1. We constantly being asked by the government to pay in taxes.

2. My conversation with her conducted in Vietnamese.

3. Are you sure that the bakery is still existed?

4. Juan has the honor of having awarded the prize for the best attendance.

5. A solid friendship create between them because of their common interest in soccer.

6. My fear about speaking English in public was contributed to my shyness.

7. This English class offer only to nonnative speakers.

8. When the announcement was been made, some students were not there.

9. Many English words derived from Latin.

EXERCISE 4

Directions: The writer of this paragraph has elected to use some verbs in the passive voice. Underline each passive construction. With your classmate, identify two passive constructions that you might change from the passive to the active voice.

Although riding the train <u>has been</u> negatively <u>labeled</u> as nostalgic in our car-dependent society and many trains have long ceased to exist, a short commuter train ride can be a unique trip into the past—and a beautiful ride. On a recent short train trip, I was thrilled by the variety of bird life in the salt marsh the train passed through. In fact, the train was virtually ignored by the stately white egrets, shiny red-winged blackbirds, and plump mallard ducks. As we moved out of the marsh and glided along the water's edge, we were greeted by fishermen out to try their luck for the day. Farther from shore lay the oil tankers, and behind them, in the distance, the bay was decorated with white sails. As we approached the city, I wondered whether there was anything left to be seen. To my surprise, I found myself looking into people's backyards, catching glimpses of downtown streets, and, best of all, being treated to a panoramic view of the highway. There cars were creeping along, bumper to bumper, while out on the tracks, we peacefully glided by, rocking gently on the rails. I like to think that as our whistle tooted, it may have been heard by a driver out there who wished he or she were riding on the train.

Post-test   ## What Do You Know Now?

A   Fill in each blank with the correct passive voice of the verb in parentheses.

1.   **Present**

Hurricane Katrina _____ (view) by many Americans as one of the worst natural disasters in the history of the United States.

2. **Present progressive**

   Today is July 4th. All over the United States, the holiday _____ (celebrate) with parades and fireworks.

3. **Future**

   Next week, flu shots _____ (give) at the clinic. I recommend that you get one.

4. **Future perfect**

   By next week, all of the popular classes _____ (fill).

5. **Past tense**

   My roommate _____ (assign) to a study group by her professor, but she has never attended it.

6. **Past progressive**

   When I went home last weekend, I was surprised to see that a new house _____ (build) on my street.

7. **Present perfect**

   It _____ (point) out that writing clearly is important in all academic disciplines.

8. **Past perfect**

   During high school, she _____ (introduce) to several computer programming languages and that has helped her greatly in college.

9. **Infinitive**

   My professor hopes _____ (recognize) as a prominent researcher in genetics after her next publication comes out.

10. **Gerund**

    _____ (name) the most valuable player on his soccer team was a great honor for my brother.

B Rewrite each sentence, changing the underlined verbs or verbals to passive, if possible. Make any other necessary changes in the sentence, but do not change the verb tense.

1. Scientists often <u>announce</u> their new discoveries in *Science* magazine.

   _____

2. Scientists <u>have</u> recently <u>announced</u> the discovery of a new kind of eye cell.

   _____

3. Dr. David Berson <u>described</u> this discovery in last week's issue of *Science*.

   _____

4. These eye cells <u>may control</u> the body's internal clock.

   _____

5. Before this discovery, scientists believed that the eye <u>had</u> only two types of light-sensitive cells.

   _____

6. Now scientists have a new way of understanding how the nervous system <u>interprets</u> light.

   _____

7. Researchers <u>are</u> currently <u>studying</u> these cells in mice and expect to find similar cells in humans.

   _____

8. Scientists expect <u>to apply</u> the new information to disorders, such as jet lag.

   _____

C Decide whether the use of the passive voice in the following sentences is correct (C) or incorrect (I). If it is incorrect, make the correction.

_____ 1. His attitude towards doing homework is concerned his parents.

_____ 2. An announcement is being made right now about a flight delay, so we need to listen carefully.

_____ 3. Tom is telling the truth. That is exactly what is happened.

_____ 4. The new building was design and construct two years ago.

_____ 5. Jennifer has just been offered the job.

D Correct the underlined errors in the following paragraph.

As the end of fall semester approaches, students often feel very <u>stress</u>.
                                                                      (1)

One reason is that many of them could not do much schoolwork over the

Thanksgiving break because they were visiting family and friends. Another

reason is that the semester is not yet over, and there are tests to be taken,

end-of-the-quarter papers <u>to be finish</u>, and other deadlines to be met.
                           (2)

Also, some <u>feel confuse</u> because they cannot remember what <u>was cover</u>
            (3)   (4)

in class the last few weeks. Although holidays are wonderful, getting back

into the rhythm of classes again is difficult. Because stress can interfere

with academic success, places <u>have be set up</u> on many campuses where
                              (5)

students <u>can be relax</u>. Research has even shown that a 20-minute nap
         (6)

can significantly reduce stress. Most important for students, however, is to

realize that stress <u>is existed</u> as a part of student life and that they can learn
                     (7)

skills to manage it so that it does not interfere with their academic success.

APPLY WHAT YOU HAVE LEARNED TO WRITING

Select a writing topic and follow the steps in Appendix A on page 337.

Topic 1:

Identify a serious environmental problem facing the world—or a specific part of the world—today. First, explain the problem, giving some of the major causes and/or effects. Then, suggest possible ways of addressing the problem.

Topic 2:

What is one of the most important discoveries that has been made and how, in your opinion, have humans benefited from it?

Topic 3:

In recent years, public art—art that is displayed in public places, such as airports or parks—has become increasingly popular. What, in your opinion, is the value of such art to society?

Unit 6

RELATIVE, ADVERBIAL, AND NOUN CLAUSES

GOALS

- Learn why mastering relative, adverbial, and noun clauses is important in writing

- Understand problems writers commonly encounter with relative, adverbial, and noun clauses

- Form and use relative, adverbial, and noun clauses correctly in exercises and writing assignments

Exercising regularly is one important aspect of good health and fitness. Do you get enough exercise in your life at present? What other factors are important in maintaining good health and fitness?

LEARN WHAT THE ERROR IS

Errors with Relative, Adverbial, and Noun Clauses

A clause error is an error in which the formation of a relative, adverbial, or noun clause is incorrect. These three dependent clauses are treated in this unit. The editing symbol for an error in a dependent clause is *cl*.

Types of Clauses and Their Definitions

All clauses, whether dependent or independent, must have a subject and a verb.

An **independent** or **main clause** can stand alone as a sentence because its meaning is complete.

Example:

> Last year, my university had an enrollment of 15,000 students.

A **dependent** or **subordinate clause** cannot stand alone but must work together with an independent clause to complete its meaning.

Example:

> Although last year my university had an enrollment of 15,000 students [dependent clause], this year the number of students has increased by ten percent [independent clause].

There are three types of dependent clauses: relative clauses, adverbial clauses, and noun clauses.

Examples:

> The student who came late [relative clause] missed an important quiz.
>
> Although living in a foreign country is interesting [adverbial clause], I want to return to Korea after I get my degree.
>
> Melissa thought that she had missed the deadline for her paper [noun clause].

Although sentences marked clause (*cl*) may also have other errors, your instructor may choose not to mark them. In the sentence *There is questions concerning the possible dangers of this machines may cause*, a relative clause is needed after *dangers* (*dangers that this machines may cause*). In addition, the sentence contains a subject-verb agreement error (*there is questions*) and a singular/plural error (*this machines*). However, the most serious problem is the relative-clause error.

The dependent-clause errors covered in this unit are global (more serious) errors. In the sentence *Although my parents expect me to do well in school, but I am not always dedicated to my studies,* the reader mentally has to delete *but* in order to understand the sentence. The coordinating conjunction *but* is not used after an adverbial clause that starts with the subordinating conjunction *although* or *even though*.

Meaning may also be highly affected by dependent clause errors as in the following sentence: *The doctor examined the patient had a bad headache.* Because the relative pronoun *who* is missing from the dependent clause, the reader is unsure who had the headache, the patient or the doctor.

Readers of formal written English expect writers in the academic and professional worlds to have good control of clauses. Having this control enables the writer to show a relationship between the independent and dependent clause, thus allowing him or her to express complex ideas, such as cause and effect or relationships of time. Therefore, writers who are having difficulty with relative, adverbial, or noun clauses will want to give high priority to reducing these errors in their writing.

Suggestions for Reducing Errors

• Determine whether your errors are with relative, adverbial, or noun clauses by examining your essays or by asking your instructor or a tutor.

• Study specific rules in this unit once you know what your clause errors are.

• Consult an advanced grammar textbook to find a more detailed analysis of dependent clauses if you need a more detailed explanation than this unit provides.

• Read extensively in English. Although you may not notice it at first, reading will help you become more familiar with both independent and dependent clauses and improve your ability to use them correctly in your own writing.

Check Your Understanding

Write answers to the following questions. Share your answers with another student.

1. What are three types of dependent clause errors that writers may make?

2. Why should writers pay particular attention to dependent clause errors?

GRAMMAR JOURNAL ENTRY 6 RELATIVE, ADVERBIAL, AND NOUN CLAUSES

Respond to the following in your grammar journal.

1. What has been your most embarrassing moment? Describe it and explain what made it so painful for you.

2. Scan a magazine or book that you are currently reading. See if you can pick out three dependent clauses on a page. Write them in your grammar journal.

Part A: Relative Clauses

UNDERSTAND COMMON PROBLEMS

This section presents problems that writers commonly encounter with relative clauses. As you study Part A, first take the pre-test to see what you already know. When you finish, check your answers on page 351. Then, carefully study each problem and the examples that illustrate it. Pay particular attention to those problems that correspond to the pre-test questions you had difficulty with. Remember that becoming aware of the types of errors you most often make with relative clauses will increase your chances of avoiding these errors in your writing.

Note: Your instructor may mark this error *rel cl*. Relative clauses are also called adjective clauses.

Pre-test **What Do You Already Know?**

Test your ability to recognize and correct errors with relative clauses.

A Correct the marked relative-clause errors. These are examples of the four common problems that are presented in Part A of this unit.

Problem 1 <ins>People live</ins> *rel cl* in Florida are used to warm, sunny weather for much of the year.

Problem 2 The students <ins>who their cars</ins> *rel cl* were illegally parked will get a ticket.

Problem 3 After college, David wants to find a <ins>job which</ins> *rel cl* he will need to use math.

Problem 4 A chemistry experiment <u>that I did it</u> in high school gave me the
idea that I might want to major in chemistry in college.

B Underline and correct the one error in each of the following sentences.
(The errors are not in any particular order.)

1. The calculus student who her test scores were the highest won a prize.

2. When the semester started, most students did not know the buildings
    which their classes were located.

3. Students transfer from a two-year college to a university say that it
    takes time to adjust.

4. One problem that the instructor solved it ended up having several
    possible answers.

Four Common Problems With Relative Clauses

Problem 1

The relative clause
is missing.

Incorrect: Feelings of isolation are common among people <u>live in new</u>
<u>language and cultural environments</u>.

Correct: Feelings of isolation are common among people <u>who</u> (or <u>that</u>)
live in new language and cultural environments.

Incorrect: <u>There are more than one in three marriages will end</u> in divorce.

Correct: There are more than one in three marriages <u>that</u> (or <u>which</u>) will
end in divorce.

Correct: More than one in three marriages will end in divorce.
(No relative clause is needed here.)

Problem 2

The wrong relative
pronoun or the
wrong form of it
has been used in
the relative clause.

Incorrect: I just met the people <u>who their house</u> I am planning to rent for
the summer.

Correct: I just met the people <u>whose house</u> I am planning to rent for the
summer.

Incorrect: Cases have been found *that*^{rel cl} even good students resort to cheating in college due to the pressure to get good grades.

Correct: Cases have been found <u>in which</u> even good students resort to cheating in college due to the pressure to get good grades.

Problem 3

The preposition is missing in a relative clause.

Incorrect: Whenever I get into <u>a situation which it is hard</u>^{rel cl} to make a decision, I try to look at it from different perspectives.

Correct: Whenever I get into a situation <u>in which it is</u> hard to make a decision, I try to look at it from different perspectives.

Correct: Whenever I get into a situation <u>which it is hard to make a decision in</u>, I try to look at it from different perspectives.

Incorrect: The person <u>whom</u>^{rel cl} I was supposed to return the key is not home.

Correct: The person <u>to whom</u> I was supposed to return the key is not home.

Correct: The person <u>whom</u> I was supposed to return the key <u>to</u> is not home.

Problem 4

A noun or a pronoun has been unnecessarily repeated in a relative clause.

Incorrect: The people <u>whom I have met them</u>^{rel cl} in my class are very friendly.

Correct: The people <u>whom I have met</u> in my class are very friendly.

Incorrect: The schedule <u>which I read it online</u>^{rel cl} said the train would leave at 8:15.

Correct: The schedule <u>which I read online</u> said the train would leave at 8:15.

REVIEW GRAMMAR SOLUTIONS FOR RELATIVE CLAUSE ERRORS

Relative clauses are adjective clauses formed with the relative pronouns *who, whom, whose, which,* or *that* or with the relative adverbs *when, where,* or *why.* To use relative pronouns correctly, you need to be aware of how they function in a relative clause.

1. ***Who, that,* and *which* can function as the subject of a relative clause.** *Who* refers to people, *that* refers to people and things, and *which* refers only to things.

Examples:

> The teacher called out the names of those students <u>who</u> (or that) were absent. (*Who* [or *that*] refers to students and is the subject of the relative clause.)
>
> The book <u>that</u> (or <u>which</u>) was left on the table is no longer there. (*That* [or *which*] refers to the book and is the subject of the relative clause.)

2. *Whom, that,* **and** *which* **can function as a direct object in a relative clause.** *Whom* refers to people, *that* refers to people and things, and *which* refers only to things.

Examples:

> The student <u>whom</u> (or <u>that</u>) they have chosen to be editor of the class newspaper does not want the job. (*Whom* [or *that*] refers to the student and is the direct object of *have chosen* in the relative clause. In spoken English, *who* can be used, but it should not be used in formal, written English.)
>
> The gift <u>that</u> (or <u>which</u>) I found will please Samuel. (*That* [or *which*] is the object of *found* and refers to the gift.)

Notes:

- *Whom, that,* and *which* may be omitted when they function as direct objects if the writer wishes to do so. (The gift I found will please Samuel.)

- In the relative clauses in rules 1 and 2 above, *that* is preferable to *which* in current American English.

3. *Whom* **and** *which* **can function as the object of a preposition in a relative clause.** *Whom* refers to persons and *which* refers to things.

Examples:

> The person for <u>whom</u> these theater tickets were reserved never picked them up. (*Whom* is the object of the preposition *for* and refers to the person.)
>
> The history class in <u>which</u> Adela is enrolled requires a term paper. (*Which* is the object of the preposition *in* and refers to the history class.)

4. *Whose* **functions as a possessive pronoun in a relative clause and refers to people or things.**

Examples:

> The person <u>whose</u> books are on the table will be back soon. (*Whose* shows that the books belong to the person.)
>
> Eric fixed my car as well as the car <u>whose</u> transmission was broken. (*Whose* shows that the transmission belongs to the car.)

5. Relative clauses can also be connected to the nouns they modify with the relative adverbs *when, where,* and *why.*

Examples:

The restaurant <u>where</u> we ate is only open for dinner.

Tell me the reason <u>why</u> you had so much difficulty with the exam.

I will never forget the time <u>when</u> the teacher got mad at us in class.

In the example sentences given so far in this section, the information added to the sentence by the relative clause is essential, meaning that it is necessary to identify the noun or to distinguish the noun from others of the same type. However, if the relative clause adds additional or extra information to the sentence, it is set off by commas. The first is called a **restrictive** relative clause and the second a **nonrestrictive** relative clause. The sentences below contain nonrestrictive relative clauses. In nonrestrictive relative clauses, *that* is not interchangeable with *who, whom,* or *which.* Note that sometimes a restrictive relative clause is called *essential,* and a nonrestrictive relative clause is called *nonessential.*

Examples:

My mother, <u>who</u> is 91 years old, lives in a retirement community.

The University of California, <u>which</u> is a public school, has ten campuses.

My math professor, <u>who</u> loves to cook, invited us all to dinner at his house.

Thomas Jefferson, <u>whose</u> home was in Virginia, always loved to return there.

Pepe's restaurant, <u>where</u> we often eat, has an excellent buffet.

My fall schedule, <u>which</u> I arranged very carefully, is not working.

IMPROVE YOUR WRITING STYLE
REDUCING RELATIVE CLAUSES

In rule 2 in this section, you learned that whom, that, *and* which *can be omitted if they function as direct objects. If* who, that, *or* which *is a subject and the main verb is* to be, *the relative clause can be reduced as follows:*

1. To a past participle

Long form: The book <u>that was left on the table</u> is no longer there.

Reduced: The book <u>left on the table</u> is no longer there.

2. **To a noun**

   Long form: My math professor, <u>who is a Harvard graduate</u>, is a very strict teacher.

   Reduced: My math professor, <u>a Harvard graduate</u>, is a very strict teacher.

3. **To a prepositional phrase**

   Long form: The woman <u>who is in the red car</u> is not wearing a seat belt.

   Reduced: The woman <u>in the red car</u> is not wearing a seat belt.

4. **To an infinitive**

   Long form: The packages <u>that are to be sent</u> are on the table.

   Reduced: The packages <u>to be sent</u> are on the table.

5. **To a participial phrase**

   Long form: The revised lab manual, <u>which includes six new experiments</u>, has come in.

   Reduced: The revised lab manual, <u>including six new experiments</u>, has come in.

Part B: Adverbial Clauses

UNDERSTAND COMMON PROBLEMS

This section presents problems that writers commonly encounter with adverbial clauses. As you study Part B, first take the pre-test to see what you already know. When you finish, check your answers on page 351. Then, carefully study each problem and the examples that illustrate it. Pay particular attention to those problems that correspond to the pre-test questions you had difficulty with. Remember that becoming aware of the types of errors you most often make with adverbial clauses will increase your chances of avoiding these errors in your writing.

Note: Your instructor may mark this error **adv cl**.

Pre-test

What Do You Already Know?

Test your ability to recognize and correct errors with adverbial clauses.

A Correct the marked adverbial-clause errors. These are examples of the seven common problems that are presented in Part B of this unit.

Problem 1 Although Henry hates grammar, *adv cl* but he studies it anyway.

Problem 2 We have purchased one of those pens *adv cl* while we like them.

Problem 3 *adv cl* Because of the rain has stopped, we can go on our picnic.

Problem 4 *adv cl* Especially I see shoes, I want to buy them.

Problem 5 *adv cl* While you were at the movies. Alexander called to ask about the weekend.

Problem 6 Some travelers fly business class, *adv cl* because they like the wider seats.

Problem 7 *adv cl* While he will be working in Australia, we will visit him.

B Underline and correct the one error in each of the following sentences. (The errors are not in any particular order.)

1. While children do not exercise enough, obesity in children has increased.

2. We will text you as soon as we will arrive in town.

3. The man was not allowed to board the plane because of his passport had expired.

4. Matthew promised to complete his part of the group project. As soon as he could.

5. Even though Ron is not a vegetarian, but he prefers not to eat meat.

6. Although the weather has been cool in the past few days hotter weather is expected.

7. Especially Alison enjoys the outdoors, she goes hiking frequently.

Seven Common Problems with Adverbial Clauses

Problem 1

An adverbial clause is connected to an independent clause with both a subordinating conjunction and a coordinating conjunction.

Incorrect:
adv cl
<u>Even though my mother wants to learn English, but</u> she finds studying it difficult.

Correct:
<u>Even though my mother wants to learn English,</u> she finds studying it difficult.

Correct:
My mother wants to learn English, <u>but</u> she finds studying it difficult.

> **Note:** In the preceding corrected sentences, note that you have the option of using either a subordinating or a coordinating conjunction but not *both*.

Problem 2

A subordinating conjunction with the wrong meaning has been used in an adverbial clause.

Incorrect:
adv cl
Bob refuses to wear a tie <u>while the restaurant requires one.</u>

Correct:
Bob refuses to wear a tie <u>even though the restaurant requires one.</u> (In the incorrect sentence, subordinating conjunction of contrast has been used where a subordinating conjunction of concession is needed.)

> SELF-HELP STRATEGY: Make sure that the connector you have chosen gives the correct meaning to the sentence. Refer to Item 3 on page 135.

Problem 3

A prepositional phrase has been used instead of a subordinating conjunction in an adverbial clause.

Incorrect:
adv cl
Pierre could not travel to Mexico <u>because of his passport had expired.</u>

Correct:
Pierre could not travel to Mexico <u>because his passport had expired.</u>

> **Note:** *Because of* is a prepositional phrase. A prepositional phrase cannot be used in place of a conjunction to connect two clauses, but it can function as a transition to link one sentence to another. Prepositional phrases commonly used as transitional words are *in addition to, because of, in spite of, in contrast with, in contrast to,* and *in comparison with.*

Example:

Dimitri broke his leg while skiing. <u>Because of his accident,</u> he has to use crutches. (*Because of his accident* connects the information in the first sentence to the new information in the following sentence.)

Problem 4

An adverb has been used instead of a subordinating conjunction in an adverbial clause.

Incorrect:
adv cl
<u>Especially</u> my aunt likes hamburgers, we always buy one for her.

Correct:
<u>Because</u> my aunt likes hamburgers, we always buy one for her.

Note: *Especially* is an adverb. (*I am especially tired.*)

Problem 5

An adverbial clause is a fragment.

Incorrect: *adv cl*
<u>While the store was still open.</u> Harriet bought some soft drinks.

Correct: <u>While the store was still open</u>, Harriet bought some soft drinks.

(An adverbial clause is dependent and cannot stand alone as a sentence.)

Incorrect: *adv cl*
<u>While we were on vacation</u> my brother stayed in our house.

Correct: <u>While we were on vacation</u>, my brother stayed in our house.

Problem 6

The adverbial clause is not followed by a comma or a comma has been used where it is not needed.

Incorrect: *adv cl*
Marjorie likes Davis, <u>because it is a small university town</u>.

Correct: Marjorie likes Davis <u>because it is a small university town</u>.

Note: See Grammar Solutions, item 2 for exceptions, such as *although*.

Problem 7

The future tense has been used in an adverbial clause of time.

Incorrect: *adv cl*
<u>When we *will get* home,</u> we will call you.

Correct: <u>When we get home,</u> we will call you.

Incorrect: *adv cl*
<u>After we *will have finished* dinner,</u> we will go for a drive.

Correct: <u>After we have finished dinner</u>, we will go for a drive.

Note: The future tense is not used in adverbial clauses of time. It can only be used in the independent clause.

REVIEW GRAMMAR SOLUTIONS FOR ADVERBIAL CLAUSE ERRORS

Adverbial clauses are dependent clauses that begin with a subordinating conjunction and show a relationship to the independent (main) clause, such as reason *(because)*, concession *(although, even though)*, or time *(as, while, when)*. *If*-clauses are treated separately in Unit 4, "Conditional Sentences."

1. **An adverbial clause can be placed before or after the independent clause, usually without changing the meaning of the whole sentence.**

Examples:

<u>Because Kanya is interested in protecting the environment</u>, she recycles paper, plastic, glass, and aluminum.

Kanya recycles paper, plastic, glass, and aluminum <u>because she is interested in protecting the environment</u>.

<u>When the end of the semester is near</u>, students and teachers often begin to feel nervous about final exams.

Students and teachers often begin to feel nervous about final exams <u>when the end of the semester is near</u>.

2. **Put a comma after a subordinate clause that introduces a sentence.** Do not use a comma before a subordinate clause that follows the independent clause. (Exceptions: *While, whereas, although, even though,* and *though* are usually separated from the independent clause with a comma.)

Examples:

<u>While I was busy registering for my classes and buying my books</u>, my friend Kerry was enjoying her vacation in Canada.

The dog finally stopped barking <u>after his owner came home and fed him</u>.

Our town voted not to ban plastic bags, <u>whereas some towns in our area already have regulations against them</u>.

<u>When I was particularly tired one day</u>, I got angry at my boss.

3. **Subordinating conjunctions are used according to the meaning the writer wants to convey.**

concession	*although, even though, despite the fact that*	<u>Although</u> the building looks safe, it has not been checked by the building inspector.
condition	*if, even if, unless, when, whenever*	<u>If</u> you study hard enough, you should pass the test.
contrast	*while, whereas*	Some people like coffee, <u>while</u> others prefer tea.
place	*where, wherever*	<u>Wherever</u> I travel, I usually meet someone who can speak English.
purpose	*so that, in order to*	My brother booked his flight early <u>so that</u> he could get a good price.
reason	*because, since*	Jason got a parking ticket <u>because</u> the time on the meter had expired.
result	*so . . . that*	Hiroshi is <u>so</u> happy about his grade <u>that</u> he is telling everyone.
time or order	*after, as soon as, before, when, while, until, whenever, as, as long as*	<u>While</u> my sister was working outside, someone called her.
		The teacher will return our essays <u>as soon as</u> she finishes correcting them.

IMPROVE YOUR WRITING STYLE
CHANGING AND REDUCING ADVERBIAL CLAUSES

You can reduce adverbial clauses to add variety to your sentences.

1. *An adverbial clause beginning with* so that *or* because *can be changed to an infinitive phrase when it has the same subject as the independent clause.*

Example:

Maren took good notes <u>so that she could share them with her sick roommate.</u>

Maren took good notes <u>to share them with her sick roommate.</u>

2. *An adverbial clause can be reduced to a participial phrase when it has the same subject as the independent clause.*

Example:

<u>While she was studying</u>, Amy discovered she had not yet read an assigned chapter.

<u>While studying</u>, Amy discovered she had not yet read an assigned chapter.

3. *An adverbial clause can be reduced to a prepositional phrase or an absolute phrase. (An absolute phrase = a noun or pronoun + a present or past participle.)*

Example:

<u>After he finished his lecture</u>, the professor encouraged the students to ask questions.

<u>His lecture finished</u>, the professor encouraged the students to ask questions.

Note: *Do not reduce every adverbial clause but rather use some reduced and some full-length adverbial clauses to provide sentence variety.*

Part C: Noun Clauses

UNDERSTAND COMMON PROBLEMS

This section presents problems that writers commonly encounter with noun clauses. As you study Part C, first take the pre-test to see what you already know. When you finish, check your answers on page 351. Then, carefully study each problem and the examples that illustrate it. Pay particular attention to those problems that correspond to the pre-test questions you had difficulty with. Remember that becoming aware of the types of errors you most often make with noun clauses will increase your chances of avoiding these errors in your writing.

Note: Your instructor may mark this error *n cl*.

Pre-test   **What Do You Already Know?**

Test your ability to recognize and correct noun clause errors.

A Correct the marked noun-clause errors. These are examples of the seven common problems that are presented in Part C of this unit.

Problem 1 She got a job so quickly is amazing.

Problem 2 Barry needs to find out his supervisor wants him to proceed on the project.

Problem 3 Christy needs to face up to that she is not prepared for the exam.

Problem 4 Matthew promised that he go to the potluck.

Problem 5 Marcel is not sure what is the assignment for tomorrow.

Problem 6 Her professor prefers that Marta writes a thesis.

Problem 7 The students were surprised. That the exam was going to be on Monday.

B Underline and correct the one error in each of the following sentences. (The errors are not in any particular order.)

1. I cannot agree with you just said.

2. Jill wonders what will the next chapter cover.

3. What the question says. The students cannot understand.

4. The researcher said the experiment is a success.

5. He received a scholarship is good news.

6. The professor insists that Paul gets his essay finished by Monday.

7. We are very concerned about that the test yesterday was so difficult.

Seven Common Problems with Noun Clauses

Problem 1

A noun clause has not been used as a subject of a sentence or as an adjective complement where it is needed.

An **adjective complement** is a "that" clause which follows a phrase such as "it is necessary, it is unfair, it is common" or a "that" clause which follows an adjective, as in *The mother felt embarrassed that her child was screaming during the movie.*

Incorrect: Famous athletes and entertainers earn millions of dollars a year
                   n cl
                   seems unfair.

Correct: That famous athletes and entertainers earn millions of dollars a
                   year seems unfair. (Here the noun clause is used as a subject.)

Correct: It seems unfair that athletes and entertainers earn millions of
                   dollars a year. (Here the noun clause is used as an adjective complement and
                   the dummy subject "it" is used as the subject.)

Incorrect: Karen is afraid lose money in the stock market.
                                        n cl

Correct: Karen is afraid that she will lose money in the stock market.

                   (Also correct: Karen is afraid of losing money in the stock market.)

Problem 2

A noun clause has not been used as an object of a verb or a preposition.

Incorrect: I dreamed the midterm difficult.
                                  n cl

Correct: I dreamed (that) the midterm would be difficult.

Incorrect: I wonder this airport provides free Internet access.
                                                       n cl

Correct: I wonder whether this airport provides free Internet access.

Incorrect: Helen did not agree with they said.
                                                    n cl

Correct: Helen did not agree with what they said.

Problem 3

A noun phrase like "the possibility that," "the idea that," or "the fact that" has not been used where it is needed with a noun clause.

a. A noun phrase after a phrasal verb

A **phrasal verb** is a verb plus a preposition or an adverb.

Incorrect: We are concerned <u>about that there will be a food shortage</u>.

Correct: We are concerned <u>about *the possibility that* there will be a food shortage</u>.

Incorrect: We will just have to put up <u>with that this apartment is noisy</u>.

Correct: We will just have to put up <u>with *the reality that* this apartment is noisy</u>.

b. A noun phrase when a main verb or an adjective with a preposition requires it

Incorrect: Franklin D. Roosevelt <u>concealed that he could not walk without support</u>.

Correct: Franklin D. Roosevelt <u>concealed *the fact that* he could not walk without support</u>.

Incorrect: We can no longer <u>dispute that the earth is round</u>.

Correct: We can no longer <u>dispute *the theory that* the earth is round</u>.

Incorrect: Our teacher is unhappy <u>about that the textbook has not arrived</u>.

Correct: Our teacher is unhappy <u>about *the fact that* the textbook has not arrived</u>.

Problem 4

The verb tense in a noun clause in reported speech is incorrect.

Incorrect: <u>She said she is going</u> to Hawaii for spring break.

Correct: <u>She said (that) she was going</u> to Hawaii for spring break.

Correct: <u>She said (that) she would go</u> to Hawaii for spring break.

Incorrect: <u>The author stated she has worked</u> in Mexico City as a nurse ten years ago.

Correct: <u>The author stated (that) she had worked</u> in Mexico City as a nurse ten years ago.

Problem 5

A noun clause that is a reported question has been incorrectly formed because either the wrong connecting word or incorrect word order has been used.

a. Errors with the wrong connecting word

Incorrect: The researcher hopes to discover <u>that the function of this</u> ^{n cl}
              <u>chemical is</u>.

Correct: The researcher hopes to discover <u>what</u> the function of this
              chemical <u>is</u>.

b. Word order errors

Incorrect: The researcher hopes to discover <u>what is the function of this</u> ^{n cl}
              <u>chemical</u>.

Correct: The researcher hopes to discover <u>what</u> the function of this chemical <u>is</u>.
              Note: This error is also covered in Unit 8, "Word Order."

Problem 6

The subjunctive form of the verb (base form) has not been used in a noun clause that expresses a demand, recommendation, requirement, advice, or expectation.

Incorrect: His friends <u>recommended John to take</u> the course. ^{n cl}

Incorrect: His friends <u>recommended that John takes</u> the course. ^{n cl}

Correct: His friends recommended (that) John <u>take</u> the course.

Correct: His friend recommended (that) John <u>should take</u> the course.
              Note: The use of "should" in this situation is optional and is more
              common in British English than in American English.

Problem 7

The noun clause is a fragment.

Incorrect: Pat already told his boss. <u>That the report would be a little late</u>. ^{n cl}

Correct: Pat already told his boss <u>(that) the report would be a little late</u>.
              Note: Fragments are also covered in Unit 7, "Sentence Structure."

REVIEW GRAMMAR SOLUTIONS FOR NOUN CLAUSE ERRORS

1. **Like all clauses, noun clauses contain a subject and a verb. Noun clauses**, like single-word nouns or noun phrases, function as subjects of sentences or as objects of verbs or prepositions. They are introduced by the connecting word *that*, or if they are derived from information questions, are introduced by connecting words such as *what, why, where, whether,* or *how. Whatever, whether, how long,* and *how often* are examples of other connecting words.

Examples of noun clauses as subjects:

That calcium strengthens bones is a scientific fact.

That you have graduated makes the whole family proud.

How the experiment was done confuses me.

Examples of noun clauses as objects:

The students have been complaining (that) the room is too cold.

She asked me where I lived.

I am not sure how the experiment was done.

The professor cannot understand why the students failed the test.

The tutor looked at what I had written and made some suggestions.

2. A noun clause can follow an adjective. These structures are called **adjective complements**.

Examples of adjective complements:

It is obvious (that) John did not prepare for the meeting.

It was necessary (that) we attend the meeting.

(In the above two examples, the noun clause can also be used as a subject as in *That we attend the meeting was necessary.*)

I am sure (that) you were invited to the party.

3. The connecting word *that* can be omitted when the noun clause is in the object position. Note that omitting *that* may make your writing seem less formal.

Examples:

On New Year's Eve, the couple announced (that) they were getting married.

I doubt (that) the experiment has been properly designed.

4. Phrasal verbs as well as adjectives that take prepositions must be followed by a noun phrase + *that*, such as *the fact that, the idea that, the possibility that, the notion that.*

Examples:

The tourists complained about *the fact that* the tour bus was not air-conditioned.

The mayor is worried about *the fact that* so many homeless are in her city.

5. Certain verbs must also be followed by a noun phrase + *that*. Such verbs include *accept, conceal, discuss, dispute, disregard, overlook, hide,* and *support.*

Examples:

The employees resented *the fact that* their vacation time was cut.

The hikers disregarded *the possibility that* it might snow.

6. **Two main groups of verbs—verbs of indirect speech and verbs of mental activity—are frequently followed by noun clauses.**

Common verbs of indirect speech: *admit, announce, claim, complain, confess, declare, explain, hint, inform, mention, tell, remark, report, say, state, swear.*

Common verbs of mental activity: *assume, believe, conclude, decide, discover, doubt, dream, feel, find out, forget, guess, hope, hear, imagine, indicate, know, learn, notice, pretend, question, realize, recall, regret, remember, think, understand.*

a. Noun clauses used with verbs of indirect speech

Examples:

The witness reported <u>(that) he had seen two people</u>.

The professor explained <u>(that) he wanted the report done by May 1</u>.

Note: Some verbs of indirect speech must be followed by an indirect object before the noun clause as in the following examples:

Examples:

The president informed <u>his staff</u> (that) he would be out of town for a week.

She told <u>me</u> (that) she needed help moving into her new apartment.

b. Noun clauses used with verbs of mental activity

Examples:

I have always believed <u>(that) it is beneficial to think positively</u>.

Amir doubts <u>(that) he will be admitted to Harvard Medical School</u>.

7. **In noun clauses following verbs of indirect speech, the verb tense in the noun clause changes to past time when the tense of the main verb changes to past.**

Examples:

She <u>says</u> (that) she <u>will go</u> to the party.

She <u>said</u> (that) she <u>would go</u> to the party.

Mark <u>says</u> (that) the plane <u>took off</u> ten minutes ago.

Mark <u>said</u> (that) the plane <u>had taken off</u> ten minutes ago.

8. **Noun clauses in reported questions are common and may be introduced with question-word, connecting words, such as *who, where, whether,* or *how*.** Note that the word order in these noun clauses is: connecting word + subject + verb. See Unit 8, "Word Order," for a more detailed explanation.

Examples:

She asked me <u>where I lived</u>.

She asked me <u>whether I had Tom's e-mail address</u>.

I do not know <u>what the answer is</u>.

I wonder <u>what the next lecture will cover</u>.

9. **The base form of the verb is used in a noun clause after verbs expressing an idea, such as a *demand, recommendation, requirement, advice,* or *explanation*.** The base form is not affected by tense or number.

Common verbs followed by noun clauses: *ask, advise, beg, demand, forbid, insist, order, prefer, propose, require, recommend, request, suggest, urge.*

Examples:

The board recommended (that) he <u>resign</u>.

The board recommended (that) he <u>should resign</u>. (The use of *should* is more common in British than in American English.)

We suggest (that) Alex <u>be</u> the chairman.

We suggested (that) Alex <u>be</u> the chairman.

IMPROVE YOUR WRITING STYLE
USING *THAT* IN A NOUN CLAUSE

It helps your reader if you include the word that *in noun clauses even when technically it is not needed to make the sentence grammatically correct. Note that including the word* that *is especially helpful in situations in which the noun following the initial verb could also possibly be an object of the verb.*

Acceptable: We concluded the experimental design was flawed.
Better: We concluded <u>that</u> the experimental design was flawed.

Acceptable: They found out the problem with the computer was solved.
Better: They found out <u>that</u> the problem with the computer was solved.

Note: For details on omitting *that,* see item 3 on page 141.

Continued on page 144.

IMPROVE YOUR WRITING STYLE (*CONT.*)

VARIATIONS ON NOUN CLAUSES

Improve your writing style by using variations on noun clauses.

A noun clause used as a subject:

Example:

That he can walk again after his accident is a miracle.

Variation: His being able to walk again after his accident is a miracle.
Variation: For him to be able to walk again after his accident is a miracle.
Variation: His ability to walk again after his accident is a miracle.

A noun clause used as an adjective complement:

Example:

Charles is afraid that he will lose his money.

Variation: Charles is afraid of losing his money.

SO ... THAT, SO MANY ... THAT, AND *SO MUCH ... THAT* FOR EMPHASIS

To emphasize an adjective or adverb, use so *+ adjective* or *adverb.* Then add *that.*

Examples:

Our teacher was so exhausted (adjective) last night that she could not grade our tests.

My new yoga class lasts an hour and a half, but the time passed by so quickly (adverb) that the class was over before I knew it.

To emphasize quantity with a noun, use so many or so much + noun. Then, add that.

Examples:

Biochemistry 17 has so many difficult labs (emphasizes quantity and is used with plural nouns) that students are often reluctant to take the course.

My roommate has so much reading (emphasizes quantity and is used with uncountable nouns) to catch up on that he is going to cancel all social activities for a week.

Be aware of common errors like the following with this construction.

Incorrect: My chemistry book <u>is heavy that</u> I cannot carry it in my backpack.

Incorrect: My chemistry book <u>is heavy in that</u> I cannot carry it in my backpack.

Incorrect: My chemistry book <u>is heavy so that</u> I cannot carry it in my backpack.

Correct: My chemistry book <u>is so heavy that</u> I cannot carry it in my backpack.

PRACTICE WHAT YOU HAVE LEARNED

PART A: Relative Clauses

EXERCISE 1

Directions: Fill in each blank with the correct relative pronoun *who, whom, whose, which,* or *that.* In some cases, more than one answer is possible.

1. Mark thanked the tutor _____ had worked with him for the whole semester.

2. Dr. Ruiz is the professor _____ economics course I am planning to take next semester.

3. The person with _____ I share a locker is over there.

4. The backpack _____ is on the chair is mine.

5. New York is a city _____ residents tend to be always in a rush.

EXERCISE 2

Directions: Combine each pair of sentences into one sentence, using a
relative clause.

Example: The trail guide stayed behind with the hikers. Those hikers
were too tired to hike any farther.

The trail guide stayed behind with those hikers who were too tired to hike

any farther.

1. Phonetics is a branch of linguistics. It focuses on the sounds of
languages.

   _____

2. Mark knows the artist. The artist's painting received first prize in the
art show.

   _____

3. The people were late. We were waiting for them.

   _____

4. She borrowed a bicycle. Its tires were slightly flat.

   _____

5. Today, Michael plans to do the recording. He was unable to do the
recording last week.

   _____

6. The student was asked to give a speech at the graduation ceremony.
The student got the highest grades in the class.

   _____

7. Some bike riders do not stop at stop signs. These bikers may be given
either a warning or a ticket.

   _____

EXERCISE 3

Directions: Decide if the relative clauses in the following sentences are correct (C) or incorrect (I). If the relative clause is incorrect, correct the error.

__I__ 1. The person ^with^ whom I went to the movies fell asleep during the film.

_____ 2. A student who plagiarizes on a paper will get an F on the paper and possibly in the whole course which he wrote the paper.

_____ 3. The man whom I met last night and who immigrated to the United States a year ago speaks English well.

_____ 4. I wrote a thank-you note to the people whom I visited their home over the holidays.

_____ 5. The instructor teaches that course is very well organized.

PART B: Adverbial Clauses

EXERCISE 4

Directions: Fill in the blanks with subordinating conjunctions from the list to create correct adverbial clauses. You may need to use a specific conjunction more than once, and you will not use all of the conjunctions in the list.

| after | as soon as | even though | when | whereas |
| although | because | so that | whenever | while |

1. The day _____ I received my first midterm back in math, I decided that I had to improve my study habits _____ I would not fail the class.

2. One of the reasons I feel I did poorly, _____ I had studied, was that my roommates had a big, noisy party the night before the exam _____ I was in my room trying to prepare for it.

3. Unfortunately, I joined them. However, _____ the party was over, I tried to study but I really needed more time than I had.

4. The serious students did very well, _____ my friends and I, who had partied too much, placed way below the average on the exam.

5. _____ the final exam counts for 50 percent of the grade and I have only a C average so far, I think I will have to move into the library so that I can stay away from parties.

EXERCISE 5

Directions: Find the adverbial clause error in each of the following sentences and correct it. The first one has been done for you.

1. When my parents ~~will~~ buy me a car, I will not have to ask for rides from my friends.

2. Beverly did not ask her tutor for help. Although she needed it.

3. Even though I like to watch television, but I only watch the news during the week.

4. She cannot get good grades whereas she does not study.

5. Especially I have been attending college, I have become more independent.

6. My car often breaks down, when I really need it.

7. After Roger has cleaned his apartment he will go play tennis.

PART C: Noun Clauses

EXERCISE 6

Directions: Complete the following sentences with a noun clause or adjective complement.

1. The doctor suggested that _____.

2. The instructor observed that _____.

3. I did not understand what _____.

4. Peter's teacher recommended that _____.

5. It is obvious to everyone that _____.

6. _____ bothers me.

7. The department requires that _____.

8. The committee does not know whether _____.

9. The researcher explained that _____.

10. The news reporter stated that _____.

EXERCISE 7

Directions: Decide whether the following sentences are correct (C) or incorrect (I). If a sentence is incorrect, find the error and correct it.

_____ 1. That the potluck dinner was already over. We were disappointed.

_____ 2. The school requires that every student takes 15 credits each semester.

_____ 3. Elizabeth hopes that her grant will be approved soon.

_____ 4. What are you doing is not my business.

_____ 5. The magicians did so many tricks amazed the audience.

_____ 6. Mr. Smith's manager knows him one of the best workers.

_____ 7. The young mother worries her child get lost.

_____ 8. Many residents feel that the city has grown too quickly.

_____ 9. The students had no idea the answer.

_____ 10. The study group could not determine what was the answer.

PART D: Adjective, Noun, and Adverbial Clauses

EXERCISE 8

Directions: Examine the six clause errors that are marked with a star (*) in the following student paragraph. Rewrite each incorrect sentence correctly below the paragraph. The first one has been done for you.

*Some couples are childless have made a decision not to have children. It is clear that this type of family is rapidly growing in the United States. These couples choose to be childless for various reasons. *However, I personally have a hard time understanding people choose to live without children.

Many couples think that today's society is not "a good environment" for children to grow up in. *Other couples think they not have enough time and money to raise children. Still others want to focus on developing their careers rather than on raising children.

For me, having children is one of the most essential parts of life. *Because I have always wanted children. It would be hard for me to view a career as being more important than having a family. I am sure I would feel disappointed with my life when I got older if I did not have children or grandchildren. I understand that the world is overpopulated, but having children is one of our basic instincts. *Although I do not want many children, but I certainly hope to have one or two of my own. I believe that children are our future. Although I recognize that having children is not for everyone, *I recommend that everyone who wants to has children.

1. _Some couples who (or that) are childless have made a decision not to have children._

2. _____

3. _____

4. _____

5. _____

6. _____

EXERCISE 9

Directions: Combine each pair of sentences into one sentence using a relative, noun, or adverbial clause. Follow the example. Note that in some cases more than one correct answer is possible.

Example:

No notes will be allowed during the examination.
This announcement surprised the students.

The announcement that no notes will be allowed during the examination surprised the students.

OR

The students were surprised that no notes would be allowed during the examination.

OR

Although the announcement surprised the students, no notes will be allowed on the examination.

1. Mark is currently taking chemistry.

   Chemistry is not a requirement for his major.

   _____

   _____

2. Her grandfather is in a nursing care facility and often gets lonely.

   She tries to visit him at least once a week.

   _____

   _____

3. Her skis are bright yellow with a purple design.

She just bought them this season.

_____

_____

4. Jackson gets very stressed out at work.

He sometimes asks for a day off to calm down.

_____

_____

5. London is a very old city.

This fact attracts many visitors.

_____

_____

Post-test   **What Do You Know Now?**

A   Fill in each blank with the correct relative pronoun.

1. On our campus, the student recreation center is the place
   _____ students like to go to work out.

2. The reason _____ I was late to class was that I missed
   the bus.

3. The group _____ I worked with on our project met for six
   hours straight.

4. The student _____ I borrowed the practice test from got
   an A on the midterm, and I only got a B.

5. The author _____ novel we chose to read in our book
   club will be visiting our town next month.

6. Former President Bill Clinton, _____ served for two terms, became active in humanitarian issues.

7. There are certain majors _____ are more popular than others.

8. The professor has set new office hours for the times _____ we can go to get help with assignments.

B   Find and correct the mistake with the adverbial clause in each sentence.

1. When more Americans can speak Chinese.

2. Many high school students are studying foreign languages, because they can see the benefit of doing so.

3. Although many immigrants would like to learn English, but it is difficult for them to do so if they are working seven days a week.

4. When we will have more adult classes, more parents will start learning English.

5. Especially it is hard for older adults to learn a new language, they often prefer to speak their first language.

6. Because of he wants to get a better job, my neighbor, Mr. Chan, is going to adult school to learn English.

C   Underline and correct the one error with a noun clause in each sentence.

1. I wonder what will the instructor cover in the next lecture.

2. The store manager said that she will give me a refund for my defective ink cartridge.

3. The pharmacist advises that Steven takes the medicine with a glass of water.

4. The teacher could not find he was looking for.

5. We cannot forget about that we have to attend Sheila's going-away party.

D Fill in each blank with the correct connecting word for a noun clause.

1. When my roommate called, my mother could not understand _____ she was saying because she talked so fast.

2. _____ he lives in the mountains is a very beautiful, quiet place.

3. It is common knowledge _____ good students like to get good grades.

4. Even though he did so poorly on his presentation, the student did want to know _____ he could do to improve.

5. Carl never thinks about _____ he will pay his bills.

6. Some teachers are convinced _____ students never study.

7. His roommate is uncertain about _____ to go home or stay in town over the holidays.

8. It is necessary _____ we decide very soon when to work on our team project.

9. _____ Einstein was considered a genius has never been questioned.

10. My mechanic recommends _____ I change the oil in my car more often.

E Fill in each blank with a connector to create correct relative, adverbial, or noun clauses. Choose from the list below.

when	for example	that (3 times)	even though	because
as	which	before	what	

The most difficult class _____ I am enrolled in this semester
                          (1)
is Japanese 4, the intermediate level. _____ makes this class
                                        (2)
particularly hard is the fact that the professor, Dr. Fujimoto, gives so many
long homework assignments. _____, he assigns us 30 new
                            (3)
vocabulary words to memorize _____ each class session
                              (4)
meets. We also must do the exercises _____ he hands out. As if
                                      (5)

that were not enough, to finish the lab assignment, most students must

spend three to four hours in the language lab each week, _____
(6)

he has not put the lab assignments online. _____ the
(7)

homework is so time-consuming, many students find that they cannot

finish it _____ they have to study for tests in their other classes.
(8)

However, _____ this class is so difficult, most students realize
(9)

_____ it is an investment upon _____ advancement in
(10) (11)

their future careers may well depend.

APPLY WHAT YOU HAVE LEARNED TO WRITING

Select a writing topic and follow the steps in Appendix A on page 337.

Topic 1:

Many people believe in the connection between what we eat and our health, as indicated in the often-heard statement, "You are what you eat." Write about one or more foods that you believe are particularly healthful to eat. Then, comment on what you think is important, overall, in maintaining a diet that is good for one's health.

Topic 2:

Write about a current news event. First, summarize the news item. Then, explain why it is interesting or particularly important to you.

Topic 3:

Choose a problem currently facing society that you are interested in, such as homelessness, gangs, drugs, or school stress. Explain what the problem is and its possible causes. Then, suggest some possible solutions.

SENTENCE STRUCTURE

GOALS

- Learn why mastering sentence structure is important in writing

- Understand seven problems writers commonly encounter with sentence structure

- Learn and apply rules for correct sentence structure in exercises and writing assignments

What technological advances are of most interest to you and how are they beneficial? Do they have any drawbacks?

LEARN WHAT THE ERROR IS

Errors with Sentence Structure

A **sentence-structure** error is an error in which part of the grammatical structure of a sentence is incorrect. There are several types of sentence-structure errors, including missing sentence parts, unnecessary repetition of the subject of a sentence, two clauses joined that do not fit together in a sentence, or problems with parallel structure. **Fragments** (sentences that are less than complete) and **run-on** sentences (two or more sentences that are joined with no connecting word or punctuation) are sentence boundary problems, which are also addressed in this unit. As you work through this unit, remember that a complete sentence in English must have at least a subject and a verb. The editing symbol for sentence-structure errors is *ss*.

You need to be aware that sentences marked *ss* may also have other errors, but your instructor may choose not to mark them. For instance, in the sentence *By assisting to a person who does not needs help can be embarrassing,* there is an overall problem with sentence structure. The sentence does not have a subject. *(Note: By assisting to a person who does not needs help is not a sentence subject; it is an introductory phrase.)* However, the sentence also contains a verb-form *(a person who does not needs help)* and a preposition error *(by assisting to).* However, the most serious problem with the sentence is its incorrect sentence structure.

Sentence-structure errors are global (more serious) errors. As such, they not only cause readers great difficulty in understanding a piece of writing but also are highly noticeable to readers. In the sentence, *A person who does not exercise regularly is not because they don't care their health,* the reader has to go back and mentally change the sentence to *A person's failure to exercise regularly may not indicate a lack of concern about his or her health* to make it correct and to be able to comprehend it. Thus, the reader must edit the text while reading its content. Sentence-structure errors are also highly noticeable to readers in the academic and professional worlds because writers are expected to have good control of sentence structure. Thus, writers who are making sentence-structure errors will want to give high priority to reducing these errors in their writing.

Suggestions for Reducing Errors

- Try to determine if there is a pattern in the sentence-structure errors you are making. Examine your essays and ask yourself whether your sentence-structure errors are of one particular type or of several different types.

- Once you know what your sentence-structure problems are, study the specific rules in this unit. Then, if you know you have a tendency to omit the verb *to be* in your sentences, for example, you can begin to consciously monitor your writing for this error.

- If possible, try to figure out why you are making sentence-structure errors. For example, perhaps you are having difficulty with leaving out or repeating the subject of a sentence because such a structure is permitted in your native language or perhaps it is a structure you need to study further and practice.

- Read extensively in English. Although you may not notice its impact on your writing immediately, reading will help you become more familiar with English sentence structure and help you improve your ability to write correct sentences in English.

Check Your Understanding

Write answers to the following questions. Share your answers with another student.

1. What are two different kinds of sentence-structure problems?

2. Why do sentence-structure errors make a piece of writing particularly difficult for the reader to comprehend?

GRAMMAR JOURNAL ENTRY 7   SENTENCE STRUCTURE

Respond to the following in your grammar journal.

1. Write about your career plans and goals. If you are a student, discuss what ideas you have about your future career. If you are already working, discuss whether or not you are satisfied with your current position or whether you hope to do something different.

2. Underline or highlight five sentences in your response to question 1. Then, mark the subject and the verb in each sentence. If the sentence has other parts that you can identify (for example, a prepositional phrase or an object), mark those also.

UNDERSTAND COMMON PROBLEMS

This section presents seven problems that writers commonly encounter with sentence structure. First, take the pre-test to see what you already know about sentence structure. When you finish, check your answers on page 352. Then, carefully study each problem and the examples that illustrate it. Pay particular attention to those problems that correspond to the pre-test questions you had difficulty with. Remember that becoming aware of the types of errors you most often make with sentence structure will increase your chances of avoiding these errors in your writing.

Pre-test   **What Do You Already Know?**

Test your ability to recognize and correct errors with sentence structure.

A   Correct the marked sentence-structure errors. These are examples of the seven common problems that are presented in this unit.

Problem 1 In my opinion, <u>speaking in English easier</u>^{ss} than writing in English.

Problem 2 <u>Is a very interesting point</u>^{ss} you have raised.

Problem 3 <u>My summer internship, for example, it is</u>^{ss} one way for me to obtain valuable work experience.

Problem 4 My parents are first-generation immigrants to the United States, and they communicate <u>mostly native language</u>^{ss}.

Problem 5 <u>After celebrating a holiday and having time off</u>^{ss} makes it difficult to start studying again.

Problem 6 At present, I am finishing a project and <u>also I start</u>^{ss} a new one.

Problem 7 If you are working as an attorney, the problem is not the quantity of work <u>itself it is</u>^{ss} the responsibility you feel for your clients.

B   Correct the one error in each of the following sentences. (The errors are not in any particular order.)

1.   Malnutrition in children is a problem in many poor countries childhood obesity is a growing problem in the United States.

2.   Is a very hard adjustment to have a roommate if a student has always had a single room at home.

3. Unlike lots friends who like dining out in restaurants, I prefer to eat at home.

4. Most of the athletes at my university they have full scholarships.

5. Students in a recent survey reported that they liked the new library but wanting a new gym as well.

6. If they have not studied enough, most students think the test they are taking very hard.

7. In the beginning of a new school year is difficult for teachers and students.

Seven Common Problems

Problem 1

The verb *to be* is missing.

Incorrect: My cousin probably a very rich man in Vietnam since he owned many houses.

Correct: My cousin <u>was</u> probably a very rich man in Vietnam since he owned many houses.

Incorrect: There many majors to choose from on this campus.

Correct: There <u>are</u> many majors to choose from on this campus.

SELF-HELP STRATEGY: Be particularly careful to include the verb *to be* when it is needed in English, particularly if the verb *to be* does not exist or is used in a different way in your native language. Also be aware that *be* is often contracted and is hard to hear in spoken English.

Problem 2

The subject of a sentence or clause is missing.

Incorrect: <u>When we meet new people and start living in a totally new environment is scary.</u>

Correct: <u>Meeting</u> new people and <u>living</u> in a totally new environment is scary.

Note: In the incorrect sentence above, the adverb clause beginning with *when* cannot be the subject of the verb *is*. Thus, the sentence does not have a subject.

Incorrect: *ss*
When realized his son was frequently skipping class, Mr. Simon was angry.

Correct: When he realized his son was frequently skipping class, Mr. Simon was angry.

Incorrect: *ss*
Is an interesting class in which I am learning a great deal.

Correct: It is an interesting class in which I am learning a great deal.

> **SELF-HELP STRATEGY:** Make sure all verbs have subjects when you are making statements in English. The verb *to be* sometimes requires the "dummy subject" *it* as in the example above or in the structure [*it is* + adjective]. (*It is easy* to park on campus. *It is useful* to have a dictionary.)
>
> **Note:** Verbs in the imperative or command form have an implied subject *you*, as in the sentence *Feel free to leave early*. (The implied subject is *you*.)

Problem 3
The subject of a sentence has been unnecessarily repeated.

Incorrect: *ss*
The mechanic he said the car's brakes were worn.

Correct: The mechanic said the car's brakes were worn.

> **SELF-HELP STRATEGY:** Remember that, in conversation, English speakers sometimes repeat the subject of a sentence as in the incorrect example above. In formal writing, however, this kind of repetition is incorrect.

Problem 4
Words in a sentence are missing.

Incorrect: *ss*
They do not want their children to grow up in a broken family father's or mother's love.

Correct: They do not want their children to grow up in a broken family without a father's or mother's love.

Incorrect: He also knew that he didn't possess <u>enough power to against the</u> ^{ss} <u>current government</u>.

Correct: He also knew that he didn't possess enough power to <u>fight</u> against the current government.

Problem 5

Two clauses or a clause and a phrase have been used that do not fit together grammatically.

Incorrect: <u>As my brother said to my mother</u> ^{ss} <u>that he did not feel like having</u> <u>children</u>.

Correct: My brother said to my mother <u>that he did not feel</u> like having children.

Correct: <u>As</u> my brother said to my mother, <u>he does not feel</u> like having children.

Incorrect: <u>In the article, "Vitamin C Under Attack,"</u> ^{ss} <u>by Mario Nevares,</u> <u>explains some possible negative effects</u> of taking large doses of vitamin C.

Correct: <u>In the article, "Vitamin C Under Attack," Mario Nevares explains</u> some possible negative effects of taking large doses of vitamin C.
Note: This error is sometimes called *mixed sentence structure*.

Problem 6

A parallel structure has not been used when needed.

Incorrect: My advisor told me to find the article online <u>and that reading it</u> ^{ss (not //)} <u>as soon as possible was necessary</u>.

Correct: My advisor told me <u>to find</u> the article online and <u>to read</u> it as soon as possible.

Incorrect: Most successful students are skilled at taking notes, summarizing, ^{ss (not //)} <u>and are able to read critically</u>.

Correct: Most successful students are skilled at <u>taking</u> notes, <u>summarizing</u>, and <u>reading</u> critically.
Note: Your instructor may mark this kind of error *ss (not //)*.

Problem 7

A sentence boundary problem has occurred. Either the sentence is a fragment (less than a complete sentence), a run-on sentence (two complete sentences with no punctuation between them), or a comma splice (two complete sentences connected with a comma).

Incorrect: *ss (ro)*
On the river rafting trip, please bring clothes that will dry quickly and keep you warm polyester and wool are the best.

Correct: On the river rafting trip, please bring clothes that will dry quickly and keep you warm. Polyester and wool are the best.

Incorrect: *ss (frag)*
After having had the experience of traveling abroad. An individual has a broader perspective on the world.

Correct: After having had the experience of traveling abroad, an individual has a broader perspective on the world.

Incorrect: Lidia keeps her passport in a security pocket when she travels, *ss (cs)* she then knows where it is at all times.

Correct: Lidia keeps her passport in a security pocket when she travels; she then knows where it is at all times.

Note: Your instructor may mark these errors *ss (frag)* for a fragment, *ss (ro)* for a run-on sentence, or *ss (cs)* for a comma splice.

REVIEW GRAMMAR SOLUTIONS

Understanding English Sentences

If you learn the following important information about English sentence structure, you will be able to avoid many of the sentence-structure problems illustrated above. However, English sentence structure is complex and cannot be covered in full detail in these guidelines.

1. A sentence is a group of words that can stand by itself as a complete idea. It must have at least a subject and a main verb in order to be complete. For example, the sentence *Cats meow* is complete because *cats* is the subject and *meow* is the main verb. Some verbs require objects or complements to follow them in order to make the sentence complete. For example, *The wall is red* is a complete sentence because it has a subject *(the wall)* and a verb *(is)*. However, it also needs a complement to make it complete *(red)*. The sentence, *John gave a speech* is a complete sentence because it has a subject *(John)* and a verb *(gave)*. *John gave* is not a complete sentence because the verb needs a direct object *(a speech)* to make it complete.

2. **Sentences are sometimes defined as having a subject and a predicate.** The predicate is the verb or verb phrase and all of its complements (such as adverbs, direct and indirect objects, auxiliary verbs, and prepositional phrases).

Examples:

subject *predicate*
The wall / is red.

subject *predicate*
John / gave a speech.

Note: A verb in the imperative, or command form, does not have a stated subject in English because the subject *you* is implied, as in the sentence, *Please <u>give</u> me your e-mail address*, where the verb *give* is a command. The imperative is the only type of verb that does not need a stated subject in an English sentence.

3. **Standard word order for sentences in English is [subject-verb-object] or [subject-verb complement].** For more information on word order in sentences, see Unit 8, "Word Order."

4. **A sentence must have at least one independent clause.** A dependent clause is not a complete sentence even though it has a subject and a verb. However, when a dependent clause is connected to an independent clause, the entire structure is a complete sentence. When you write sentences of more than one clause, make sure that the two clauses you have chosen fit together correctly. If not, you will have a mixed construction or a sentence-structure error, as illustrated in Problem 5.

Examples:

New York is on the east coast of the United States. (independent clause = complete sentence)

While New York is on the east coast of the United States. (dependent clause = *not* a complete sentence)

While Los Angeles is on the west coast, New York is on the east coast of the United States. (one independent clause and one dependent clause = complete sentence)

5. **The subject of a sentence can be one of the following:**

- a noun *(the book; Maria; an engineer)*

- a pronoun *(I; you; he, she, it; we; they)*

- a noun clause *(what the engineer said; that you were late)*

- a gerund or infinitive *(reading; to read)*

See Unit 6, "Relative, Adverbial, and Noun Clauses," for more information on dependent clauses and how they work together with independent clauses.

For more information on verb phrases, see Unit 2, "Verb Forms."

Note: A prepositional phrase *(in the article by Leon Smith; at the movies)* <u>cannot</u> serve as a sentence subject.

6. The verb in a sentence can be one main verb or a main verb in a verb phrase.

Examples:

Norman <u>bicycles</u> to work every day. (main verb)

Norman <u>has been bicycling</u> to work every day for a year. (verb phrase: main verb with two auxiliary verbs preceding it)

Avoiding Sentence Boundary Problems

1. A complete sentence begins with a capital letter (upper case) and ends with a punctuation mark (a period, a question mark, or an exclamation point), as shown in the following examples:

Examples:

Employees generally have a four-day weekend for Thanksgiving.
Do employees have a four-day weekend for Thanksgiving?
I am so happy that this coming weekend is a four-day weekend!

2. A fragment is less than a sentence. The sentence that follows is not complete because it is a dependent clause and needs to be connected to an independent clause to make it a complete sentence.

Examples:

(Fragment)   Even though employees generally have a four-day weekend for Thanksgiving.

(Revision)   Even though employees generally have a four-day weekend for Thanksgiving, some will have to remain on call for emergencies.

Avoid fragments by making sure that your sentences have at least a subject and a main verb and one independent clause.

3. A run-on sentence is defined as two sentences that have not been separated by any punctuation. The sentence that follows is a run-on because it consists of two independent clauses without any punctuation. These clauses must be separated by a punctuation mark or be joined with a connecting word.

Examples:

(Run-on)   Living away from home for the first time has been a learning experience for me I have become a much more independent and self-sufficient person.

(Revision 1)   Living away from home for the first time has been a learning experience for me. I have become a much more independent and self-sufficient person.

(Revision 2)   Living away from home for the first time has been a learning experience for me, for I have become a much more independent and self-sufficient person.

4. A comma splice is a type of run-on sentence in which two independent clauses are incorrectly separated with a comma instead of a period or semicolon.

Examples:

(Comma splice)   One option is to listen to music, another option is to watch a video.

(Revision 1)   One option is to listen to music; another option is to watch a video.

(Revision 2)   One option is to listen to music. Another option is to watch a video.

(Revision 3)   One option is to listen to music, while another option is to watch a video.

(Revision 4)   One option is to listen to music, but another option is to watch a video.

(Revision 5)   One option is to listen to music; however, another option is to watch a video.

Avoid run-on sentences and comma splices by making sure that complete sentences (independent clauses) end with either a period, question mark, or exclamation mark. You can also join two independent clauses with a connecting word (for example: *and, but, for, after, before, while, because*) or with a semicolon or colon.

Using Parallel Structure

Whenever one or more items in a sentence are joined by the words *and, but, or, nor, yet,* these parts of the sentence should be parallel in structure. That is, they should have the same grammatical form (for example, all infinitives, all noun clauses, or all prepositional phrases).

Examples of Parallel Structure

Verbs (infinitives):

I like to swim, to surf, and to waterski.

Verbs (base forms):

I like to swim, surf, and waterski.

Verbs (gerunds):

I enjoy <u>swimming</u>, <u>surfing</u>, and <u>waterskiing</u>.

Verbs (present participles):

While he was <u>thinking about</u> the class lectures and <u>reviewing</u> some articles, he got an idea for his term paper.

Prepositional phrases:

Nowadays, social networking websites are used heavily <u>by many people</u> and <u>in many different ways</u>.

Nouns:

Next week Kazu has to work on a <u>term paper</u>, a <u>problem set</u>, and a <u>laboratory report</u>.

Noun clauses:

Professor Allen has promised <u>that the exam will be graded by 5:00 PM</u> and <u>that the scores will be posted online by 5:30 PM</u>.

Adjectives:

The teacher is <u>friendly</u> and <u>helpful</u> but somewhat <u>disorganized</u>.

IMPROVE YOUR WRITING STYLE

IMPROVING SENTENCE VARIETY

Although every complete sentence needs to have a subject and a verb, the subject does not always have to be the first word in a sentence in English. You can improve sentence variety in your writing by using other kinds of structures at the beginning of some of your sentences.

A time word or phrase:

<u>Yesterday</u> we decided to go on a hike in the mountains.

An infinitive phrase to show purpose:

<u>To avoid being indoors all day</u>, we decided to go on a hike in the mountains.

A dependent clause:

<u>Because the weather was so beautiful</u>, we decided to walk on the beach.

A prepositional phrase:

<u>In my hometown</u>, a beautiful lake attracts visitors and residents alike.

An adverb:

<u>Certainly</u>, I can see your point.

A transitional word or phrase:

<u>On the other hand</u>, I can see you have a point, even though I do not fully agree.

VARYING SENTENCE LENGTH

Vary the length of your sentences. Although in academic writing, long and complex sentences are common, including a short sentence in a text from time to time is very effective because it helps change the rhythm of the text. Shorter sentences are also effective ways to provide emphasis.

PRACTICE WHAT YOU HAVE LEARNED

EXERCISE 1

Directions: Some of the following sentences contain sentence-structure errors. First, decide whether a sentence is correct (C) or incorrect (I). Then, rewrite the incorrect sentences.

__*I*__ 1. Molecular genetics a field that is progressing very quickly.

   Molecular genetics is a field that is progressing very quickly.

_____ 2. To know their native language should be proud instead of embarrassed.

   _____

_____ 3. She wonders whether studying so hard worth it.

   _____

_____ 4. Engineering 101, it is the course that I spend the least time on.

   _____

_____ 5. Room 100 Smith Hall is one of the largest classrooms on my campus it can hold around 500 students.

   _____

_____ 6. As grow up, many children develop attitudes they will later have as adults.

_____

_____ 7. To improve her writing skills, Ana keeps a writing journal and reads as much as possible.

_____

_____ 8. Astronauts need to be prepared for every obstacle that could encounter in space.

_____

_____ 9. When she has time, Kim likes to take bike rides, read novels, and visiting her friends.

_____

_____10. The office is well equipped has a lot of antique furniture.

_____

_____11. By putting up beautiful art has made me feel more relaxed in my office.

_____

EXERCISE 2

Directions: Some of the following sentences have parallel-structure problems. First, decide whether the sentence is correct (C) or incorrect (I). Then, rewrite any incorrect sentences.

_I_ 1. That Jack arrived late and his not being prepared angered his supervisor.

That Jack arrived late and that he was not prepared angered his supervisor.

_____ 2. That is Dr. Wood, my thesis advisor and who chairs the Chemistry Department.

_____

_____ 3. In college, what classes you take and when you take them is generally your own decision.

_____

_____ 4. His job involves washing lab equipment, to set up experiments, and recording data.

_____

_____ 5. Sitting in a coffee shop and search the Internet is one of my favorite evening activities.

_____

_____ 6. I spent the day in San Francisco walk on the Golden Gate Bridge, visiting Chinatown, and do many other things.

_____

EXERCISE 3

Directions: Complete the following sentences in your own words. Make sure you use parallel structure.

1. Three things I enjoy doing in my free time are

_____.

2. We are looking for the following characteristics in a job applicant:

_____.

3. Several good places to go for a bicycle ride in my area are

_____.

4. Below are some ways to avoid feeling homesick in a new environment:

- *Stay active* _____

- _____

- _____

- _____

EXERCISE 4

Directions: Four of the following sentences have sentence-boundary problems, while one is correct. Circle the number of the correct sentence. Correct the incorrect sentences.

1. The most useful class I took was statistics, it was very challenging for me.

2. Thus far, school is more fun than work however I find the studies quite hard.

3. Statistics is a very useful class for me, as I am learning how to analyze my research data.

4. Chicago is such an interesting city I love going there.

5. Another reason why some people do not exercise regularly. Simply a lack of time.

EXERCISE 5

Directions: Copy at least five sentences from one of your textbooks, a journal, a news article, or a magazine. Examine each sentence carefully and look at its structure. Try to notice how the sentences are constructed, including how each sentence begins and how each is punctuated. Label the subject and main verb and note whether the sentence is made up of one or more clauses.

Post-test   **What Do You Know Now?**

A   Correct the marked sentence-structure errors.

1.   My teacher, who uses computers, she asks the students to tell her
     about new grammar resources they have discovered on the Internet.

2.   My teacher older but she has a lot of energy and experience.

3.   As for the class in advanced physics is going very well.

4.   By having the students come in for conferences is helping them
     learn individually and work on specific problems in their writing.

5.   The grammar that will be covered on the grammar exam is as follows:
     sentence structure, finding the correct verb tense, verb form,
     dependent clauses, modals, and reviewing conditional sentences.

6.   My grandparents they like to visit us often.

7.   How to solve that problem not clear to me.

8.   The best formula for success college is to study hard, find a study
     group, and exercise.

9.   When students first get to college is a difficult adjustment because
     high school is so different.

10. As many new students find out after their first tests that they must
     study harder than before.

B   Find the sentence-structure errors and rewrite the sentences.

1.   Depending on the weather and the time of year determines which
     route we take.

     _____

2.   Eating, watching the football game, and we talked a lot added up to
     a wonderful Thanksgiving Day.

     _____

3. My sister Susan, she works harder than any person I know.

_____

4. By memorizing the formulas will help me pass the chemistry exam.

_____

5. Getting good grades a must in today's competitive world.

_____

C   Identify sentence boundary problems in the following sentences. Label each sentence as *ro* (run-on), *cs* (comma splice), or *frag* (fragment). Then, correct the sentence.

_____ 1. Intercultural marriages are becoming more common however some people still think that they will not work.

_____ 2. Even though it is summer.

_____ 3. At the end of a semester, students usually feel very stressed, what is worrying them is all the work they have to complete before final exams.

_____ 4. It is going to snow tonight, drivers need to be very cautious on the highways.

_____ 5. Although we have talked about this problem many times before.

_____ 6. My mother would dedicate time to studying grammar and making vocabulary lists as a way to learn new vocabulary in English all this work did not help her that much because she really needed to go out and speak English in public.

D   Complete each sentence below with a parallel structure.

1.   The four courses I am taking this quarter are _____.

2.   I get really nervous when I think about what I have to study this week

     and _____.

3.   Next week, when I do not have any midterms, I am going to read a

     book, _____.

4.   The two universities which my sister is thinking of applying to are

     _____.

APPLY WHAT YOU HAVE LEARNED TO WRITING

Select a writing topic and follow the steps in Appendix A on page 337.

Topic 1:

What are some advantages and disadvantages of using e-readers or tablets such as the one shown in the photo? Will physical books disappear anytime soon with the popularity of e-readers?

Topic 2:

Write about something you have always thought about doing but have never done, perhaps because the opportunity never presented itself or because you were afraid or reluctant to carry out your plans. Explain what you have always wanted to do and why you would like to do it or would have liked to do it.

Topic 3:

Most individuals would agree that we learn not only in formal classroom situations but that much of our learning also goes on outside of school. Write about an important learning experience that you have had outside of the classroom. Explain the experience and what you learned from it.

WORD ORDER

GOALS

- Learn why mastering word order is important in writing

- Understand seven problems writers commonly encounter with word order

- Learn and correctly apply rules for word order in exercises and writing assignments

What is one of the most memorable famous places you have visited? What about it impressed you the most? What other famous places would you like to visit and why?

LEARN WHAT THE ERROR IS

Errors with Word Order

A **word-order** error is one in which the order of words in a sentence is incorrect or awkward. For example, in the sentence *The basketball team was exhausted* <u>*completely*</u> *after the game*, the word *completely* is in an incorrect position in the sentence; it should come before the adjective *exhausted*. In the sentence *Mary* <u>*yesterday*</u> *went to the library*, the word *yesterday* is in an awkward position in the sentence; it usually comes at the beginning or the end of the sentence. The editing symbol for a word-order error is *wo*.

Word-order errors are global (more serious) errors because in some cases they can affect the organization of a whole sentence. For example, in the sentence *Spanish language speak many people in Latin America*, the word order, which is not English word order, affects the whole sentence, making it difficult for the reader to understand. Some word-order errors, however, may not be as serious and may not affect the reader's understanding of the overall sentence. For example, in the sentence *Mary lent to John the book*, the word order is incorrect, but the reader can still easily understand the message. Nevertheless, incorrect or awkward word order, whether serious or less serious, will distract the reader and make a piece of writing difficult to read, particularly if the error is frequent.

Suggestions for Reducing Errors

• Keep in mind that not all writers have problems with English word order. Some writers, however, tend to experience problems with word order when using certain grammatical structures, such as indirect questions, adverbs, or adverbial phrases. These problems are covered in the next section, "Understand Common Problems."

• Think about the word order used in your native language in order to become aware of any patterns that you might be incorrectly transferring into English. In English, the basic word order is [subject + verb + object] as in *Gene* + *is reading* + *the newspaper* or [subject + verb + complement] as in *Gene* + *is* + *happy*. In some languages, such as Japanese and Korean, the basic word order is [subject + object + verb]. In other languages, such as Tagalog, the basic word order is [verb + subject + object]. Even if your native language has the same basic word order as English does, there still may be other differences. For example, although Spanish and English have the same basic word order [subject + verb + object], word-order differences still occur. In Spanish, adjectives usually come after the noun they modify, while, in English, they usually come before the noun they modify, as in *These* <u>*black*</u> *shoes belong to Jessica*.

- Keep in mind that in some cases—for example, with adverbs—you will have options with word order. Notice how the adverb *sometimes* can be placed in three different locations in the sentences <u>Sometimes</u> *I go to the movies, I go to the movies* <u>sometimes</u>, and *I* <u>sometimes</u> *go to the movies*. This means that, in these cases, you as the writer will choose which word order you want to use and it becomes a question of style.

- Remember that perhaps the best way to master English word order is by reading extensively. You can focus on the word order used in your textbooks as well as in the books, magazines, news articles, and online materials that you read.

Check Your Understanding

Write answers to the following questions. Share your answers with another student.

1. Why can word-order errors be either serious or less serious?

2. What is the basic word order of English? Is word order always fixed in English? Explain.

GRAMMAR JOURNAL ENTRY 8   WORD ORDER

Respond to the following in your grammar journal.

1. Describe a place that you frequently go to. It could be a café, restaurant, supermarket, store, park, or other location. Explain what the place looks like, what people do there, and why you like to go there.

2. Are there any differences in word order that you can identify between English and your native language? Write two simple sentences in your language and label the basic word-order patterns that you see. In each sentence, include at least a subject, a verb, and an object. You can include nouns and adjectives if you wish. Then, write the sentences in English and label them. Compare the word-order patterns.

UNDERSTAND COMMON PROBLEMS

This section presents seven problems that writers commonly encounter with word order. First, take the pre-test to see what you already know about word order. When you finish, check your answers on page 352. Then, carefully study each problem and the examples that illustrate it. Pay particular attention to those problems that correspond to the pre-test questions you had difficulty with. Remember that becoming aware of the types of errors you most often make with word order will increase your chances of avoiding these errors in your writing.

Pre-test

What Do You Already Know?

Test your ability to recognize errors with word order.

A   Correct the marked word-order errors. These are examples of the seven common problems that are presented in this unit.

Problem 1   I do not remember <u>when is the job application due</u>.

Problem 2   Our alarm system went off unexpectedly, and I had trouble figuring out how <u>to turn off it</u>.

Problem 3   O'Hare airport in Chicago is <u>busy extremely</u>.

Problem 4   The <u>roses red long-stemmed</u> are the loveliest.

Problem 5   My department <u>gave to me an award</u> for ten years of service.

Problem 6   The movies at the six-screen cinema <u>change always</u> on Fridays.

Problem 7   We left the laboratory because we did not have time to finish the experiment <u>at 7:00 PM</u>.

B   Underline and correct the one error in each of the following sentences. (The errors are not in any particular order.)

1.   She is tired always after playing tennis.

2.   The hikers walked this afternoon over ten miles.

3.   The student felt he answered adequately the question, but he still lost five points.

4.   On some products, the government determines what is the price.

5.   That is a very difficult question, and I'll need to think over it.

6.   The laptop light gray is the newest model.

7.   The instructor gave to me an A- on my essay.

Seven Common Problems

Problem 1
The word order is incorrect in an indirect question that makes up a noun clause.

Incorrect: When I came home, I wondered <u>where were my roommates</u>.

Correct: When I came home, I wondered <u>where my roommates were</u>.

Incorrect: I don't know <u>what did the instructor say</u> about the next lab

assignment.

Correct: I don't know <u>what the instructor said</u> about the next lab

assignment.

This error is also covered in Unit 6, "Relative, Adverbial, and Noun Clauses," in the section on noun clauses.

Incorrect: The article does not clearly explain <u>how was the experiment</u>

<u>performed</u>.

Correct: The article does not clearly explain <u>how the experiment was</u>

<u>performed</u>.

Problem 2

The pronoun that accompanies a two-word verb (such as *hand in*, *pick up*, *throw out*) has been incorrectly placed.

Incorrect: I don't like these posters anymore. I have decided to <u>throw out them</u>.

Correct: I don't like these posters anymore. I have decided to <u>throw them out</u>.

Incorrect: Any student who misses a quiz cannot <u>make up it</u>.

Correct: Any student who misses a quiz cannot <u>make it up</u>.

Note: These verbs are often called *phrasal verbs*, and the prepositions that go with these verbs are called *particles*.

SELF-HELP STRATEGY: Review the word-order guidelines in this section for information on when two-word verbs can or cannot be separated. Keep in mind that you will need to memorize, on a case-by-case basis, whether each two-word verb is always separable, optionally separable, or never separable. A learner's dictionary will indicate whether or not a phrasal verb is separable.

Problem 3

An adverb that modifies an adjective has been incorrectly placed.

Incorrect: The mayor had become <u>aware more</u> of his reputation in the town.

Correct: The mayor had become <u>more aware</u> of his reputation in the town.

Incorrect: I felt <u>exhausted completely</u> after the all-day hike.

Correct: I felt <u>completely exhausted</u> after the all-day hike.

Problem 4

An adjective that modifies a noun has been incorrectly placed.

Incorrect: The notebook blue is Jerry's.

Correct: The blue notebook is Jerry's.

Incorrect: The blue large notebook is Jerry's.

Correct: The large blue notebook is Jerry's.

> **SELF-HELP STRATEGY:** Remember that in English adjectives come *before* the nouns they modify. See the word-order guidelines later in Review Grammar Solutions for cases in which more than one adjective modifies a noun.

Problem 5

The word order is incorrect after a verb that has both a direct object and an indirect object.

Incorrect: The president of the company gave to Jenna a special assignment.

Correct: The president of the company gave a special assignment to Jenna.

Correct: The president of the company gave Jenna a special assignment.

Incorrect: Matt bought for me a present.

Correct: Matt bought a present for me.

Correct: Matt bought me a present.

Problem 6

An adverb has been incorrectly placed.

Incorrect: I went yesterday to the movies with Johan.

Correct: I went to the movies with Johan yesterday.

Correct: Yesterday, I went to the movies with Johan.

Correct: I went to the movies yesterday with Johan.

Incorrect: Very poorly, Bill did that cleaning job.

Correct: Bill did that cleaning job very poorly.

Incorrect: My cousin has taken always his schoolwork very seriously.

Correct: My cousin has always taken his schoolwork very seriously.

Incorrect: In a rush to get things done, small details will be <u>sometimes</u>
overlooked.

Correct: In a rush to get things done, small details will <u>sometimes</u> be
overlooked.

> **Note:** In the last two correct examples, the adverb has been placed after the first auxiliary verb to achieve a formal style.

Problem 7
Adverbial phrases or clauses at the end of a sentence are not in the correct order.

Incorrect: Mark lifts weights <u>to keep in shape every morning</u>.

Correct: Mark lifts weights <u>every morning to keep in shape</u>.

Correct: <u>Every morning</u>, Mark lifts weights <u>to keep in shape</u>.

Correct: <u>To keep in shape</u>, Mark lifts weights <u>every morning</u>.

Incorrect: We left the movie <u>because it was boring before it was over</u>.

Correct: We left the movie <u>before it was over because it was boring</u>.

Correct: <u>Because it was boring</u>, we left the movie <u>before it was over</u>.

Incorrect: I walked <u>this morning to the cafeteria</u>.

Correct: I walked <u>to the cafeteria this morning</u>.

Correct: <u>This morning</u>, I walked <u>to the cafeteria</u>.

> **Note:** In English more than one adverbial phrase or clause can occur at the end of a sentence. Some of these adverbial phrases or clauses can also occur at the beginning of the sentence. However, usually only one adverbial clause or phrase can occur at the beginning of a sentence.

REVIEW GRAMMAR SOLUTIONS

Basic Word Order in English

The basic word order in English follows two patterns. One is subject + verb + object: *Gene* + *is reading* + *the newspaper.* The other is subject + verb + complement: *Gene* + *is* + *happy.*

Word Order in Indirect Questions

Always use statement word order (not direct-question word order) for noun-clause indirect questions. In other words, do not invert the subject and the verb as you would when asking a direct question.

1. **Direct-question word order:** Invert the subject and first auxiliary verb.

Examples:

Where <u>have you</u> been living?

<u>Did Paul</u> pass the midterm?

2. **Indirect-question word order:** Do not invert the subject and verb.

Examples:

I don't know where <u>you live</u>.

I wonder whether <u>Paul passed</u> the exam.

Some common phrases followed by noun-clause indirect questions include those in italics in the sentences below.

I wonder where the post office is.

I don't know whether (or not) Tom will be coming to the potluck.

I cannot remember why my supervisor wants to meet with me.

I do not understand what the lecture was about.

I am not sure if the meeting is tomorrow or the next day.

Could you please tell me what your date of birth is?

I asked where the nearest gas station was.

Note: In spoken English, you will sometimes hear inverted word order such as "Could you please tell me what is your date of birth?" or "I asked where was the nearest gas station." However, in academic writing, indirect-question word order should be followed.

Word Order for Two-Word (Phrasal) Verbs

Using two-word verbs can be challenging because some two-word verbs cannot be separated, meaning the object must always come after the verb and its particle. Some two-word verbs can be separated or not, meaning the object can either come after the verb and particle or between them. Other two-word verbs must always be separated, meaning the object must come between the verb and particle. You can review the word-order guidelines in this section for more detailed information on two-word verbs, but keep in mind that you will need to memorize on a case-by-case basis whether each two-word verb is always separable, optionally separable, or never separable. Also remember that a learner's dictionary will indicate whether or not a phrasal verb is separable.

Examples:

Half of the voters <u>sided with</u> the governor on the tax issue. (cannot be separated)

Marsha <u>filled up</u> the water bottle. *or* Marsha filled the water bottle <u>up</u>. (can be separated or not separated)

John finally decided to <u>ask</u> Christy <u>out</u>. (must be separated)

If a phrasal verb can be separated and it has an object pronoun, this pronoun will always be between the verb and the particle. If the phrasal verb is not separable, the pronoun will come after the verb.

1. **Always separated: The object or object pronoun comes between the verb and its particle.**

Examples:

Martha <u>talked</u> her father <u>into</u> letting her use the car.

Martha <u>talked</u> him <u>into</u> letting her use the car.

2. **Can be separated: The object comes either after the verb and particle or between the verb and particle. An object pronoun always comes between the verb and its particle.**

Examples:

Jake said he wanted <u>to think over</u> the situation.

Jake said he wanted <u>to think</u> the situation <u>over</u>.

Jake said he wanted <u>to think</u> it <u>over</u>.

3. **Never separated: The object or object pronoun comes after the verb and its particle.**

Examples:

Katya <u>takes after</u> her mother.

Katya <u>takes after</u> her.

Word Order for Adjectives That Modify Nouns

In English, adjectives come **before** the nouns they modify.

Examples:

the <u>red</u> roses

a <u>cloning</u> technique

a <u>football</u> field

an <u>excellent</u> proposal

When more than one adjective modifies a noun, use the following guide to decide on the order of adjectives.

1	2	3	4	5	6

(number) + (general comment) + (size) + (shape) + (color) + (material) + NOUN

Examples:

> several high-strength black steel beams
>
> (a) long rectangular grey metal sheet
>
> numerous flashing multicolored lights
>
> several small black and white dogs

Word Order for Adverbs That Modify Adjectives

An adverb that modifies an adjective comes **before** the adjective.

Examples:

> San Francisco is <u>extremely</u> beautiful.
>
> This classroom is <u>unusually</u> small.
>
> They have a <u>completely</u> remodeled kitchen.

Word Order for Direct and Indirect Objects of Verbs

Not many verbs in English take both a direct and an indirect object. However, the following two rules will help you master word order in sentences containing both objects.

1. **When a verb (V) has both a direct object (DO) and an indirect object (IO), the direct object must come first if the indirect object is preceded by** *to* **or** *for.* If, however, *to* or *for* is omitted, then the indirect object must come first.

Examples:

>   *V   DO   IO*
> The clerk <u>sold</u> a <u>book</u> **to** <u>me</u>.
>
>   *V   IO   DO*
> The clerk <u>sold</u> <u>me</u> a <u>book</u>.
>
>   *V   DO   IO*
> Matt <u>bought</u> a <u>present</u> **for** <u>me</u>.
>
>   *V   IO   DO*
> Matt <u>bought</u> <u>me</u> a <u>present</u>.

Some common verbs that take an indirect object with *to* are *give, write, show, teach, sell, send, lend, bring,* and *hand.*

Some common verbs that take an indirect object with *for* are *buy, get, make,* and *bake.*

2. **A small number of verbs require that the indirect object follow the direct object, and this indirect object must be preceded by *to* or *for*.** Verbs that take indirect objects with *for* include *answer, open,* and *close.* Verbs that take indirect objects with *to* include *announce, introduce, suggest, mention,* and *describe.*

wo

Incorrect: Richard <u>explained Mary the math problem</u>.

Correct: Richard explained <u>the math problem to Mary</u>.

wo

Incorrect: Richard <u>answered Mary the question</u>.

Correct: Richard answered <u>the question for Mary</u>.

Word Order Guidelines for Placement of Adverbs

Generally, adverbs can be placed in several different positions in a sentence.

1. **Initial position** (at the beginning of the sentence)

Example:

> <u>Yesterday</u>, I sailed for four hours.

2. **Midposition** (before the verb or in the middle of the verb phrase)

Example:

> I <u>especially</u> like Boston.
>
> I do not <u>really</u> like peanut butter ice cream.

3. **End position** (at the end of the sentence)

Example:

> I expect my friend to arrive <u>tomorrow</u>.

However, not all adverbs can be placed in all three positions. What follows are some general guidelines for adverb placement according to the function of the adverb.

1. **Adverbs of place** usually take the end position.

wo

Incorrect: <u>Outside</u> John is sitting.

Correct: John is sitting <u>outside</u>.

Other common adverbs of place include *inside, here,* and *there.*

> **2. Adverbs of definite time** usually take the beginning or end position.

Incorrect:	I went <u>yesterday</u> to my aerobics class.
Correct:	I went to my aerobics class <u>yesterday</u>.
Correct:	<u>Yesterday</u>, I went to my aerobics class.

Other common adverbs of definite time include *today, tomorrow,* and *now.*

> **3. Adverbs of indefinite time** can take the initial, middle, or end position.

Correct:	<u>Recently</u>, I have become interested in karate.
Correct:	I have <u>recently</u> become interested in karate.
Correct:	I have become interested in karate <u>recently</u>.

Another adverb of indefinite time is *lately,* although it is not usually used in midposition.

> **4. Adverbs used to evaluate** usually take the end position.

Incorrect:	Bill did <u>well</u> that cleaning job.
Correct:	Bill did that cleaning job <u>well</u>.

Other common adverbs used to evaluate include *badly* and *poorly.*

> **5. Adverbs of manner** usually take the middle or end position but can take the initial position.

Correct:	Luis <u>quietly</u> opened the door to the baby's room.
Correct:	Luis opened the door to the baby's room <u>quietly</u>.
Correct:	<u>Quietly</u>, Luis opened the door to the baby's room.

Other common adverbs of manner include *quickly, carelessly,* and *softly.*

6. Adverbs of frequency follow very specific rules regarding their position in the sentence.

(Common adverbs of frequency include *always, frequently, occasionally, seldom, continually, hardly ever, often, sometimes, never, ever, rarely,* and *usually.*)

a. With the verb *to be*—**usually after the verb**

Correct: John is <u>never</u> at home when I call him.

Correct: Vincent is <u>continually</u> busy.

b. With the verb *to be + not*—**after** *not*

Correct: Brian is not <u>always</u> nice to his little sister.

Correct: It is not <u>usually</u> so hot here during the summer.

> **Note:** The adverbs *usually* and *often* can also be placed before *not* as in *It is usually <u>not</u> so hot here during the summer.*

c. With other verbs—before the verb

Correct: Lois <u>always</u> skates on the boardwalk.

Correct: I <u>never</u> ride my bicycle to class.

d. In a verb phrase—after the first auxiliary verb

Correct: Tim is <u>always</u> running out of money when we go out to eat.

Correct: I have <u>never</u> seen a comet.

e. In a verb phrase with *not*—**after** *not*

Correct: Maria does not <u>always</u> type her papers.

Correct: Mark does not <u>usually</u> have time to read the newspaper.

> **Note:** The adverbs *usually* and *often* can also be placed before the first auxiliary verb as in *Maria <u>usually</u> does not type her papers* or *Maria <u>often</u> does not type her papers.*

Word Order Guidelines for Adverbials

When several **adverbials** (phrases and/or clauses that function like adverbs) occur at the end of a sentence in English, word-order problems often occur. Although the order of these adverbials in relation to each other sometimes varies, you will find the following guidelines helpful. These guidelines are based on the different types of adverbials listed below.

Adverbials of time:	at six o'clock; this morning; in the evening
Adverbials of frequency:	every morning; every Tuesday
Adverbials of position:	in the cafeteria; at home; in the classroom
Adverbials of direction:	to the cafeteria; from the lab
Adverbials of purpose:	(in order) to lose weight; so that I could stay in shape
Adverbials of reason:	because it is hot; because it was interesting

1. Adverbials of time and frequency generally come after adverbials of position and direction.

Examples:

She walks <u>to campus every day at noon</u>.

She studies <u>at home every evening</u>.

2. Adverbials of time and frequency are generally interchangeable with each other in their position in a sentence.

Examples:

She walks to campus <u>every day at noon</u>.

She walks to campus <u>at noon every day</u>.

3. Adverbials of purpose and reason generally come after all other adverbials.

Examples:

Mark works out in the gym every night <u>to keep in shape</u>.

We left the party before 9:00 PM <u>because we had another commitment</u>.

IMPROVE YOUR WRITING STYLE

PLACEMENT OF ADVERBS IN FORMAL (OR ACADEMIC) WRITING

As explained in the word-order guidelines, adverbs in English can often be placed in a number of different positions within a sentence. These positions include initial position, final position, or midposition. To achieve a more formal writing style, place your adverbs midposition—that is, within the verb phrase either before the main verb (if there is only a main verb) or after the first auxiliary verb (if there is a verb phrase). See the examples below.

Examples:

<u>Then</u>, a solution can be found.

A solution can <u>then</u> be found. (more formal word order)

Since I have been here, my English skills have improved <u>gradually</u>.

Since I have been here, my English skills have <u>gradually</u> improved. (more formal word order)

<u>Slowly</u>, the mixture is heated to the boiling point.

The mixture is <u>slowly</u> heated to the boiling point. (more formal word order)

<u>Sometimes</u> I work on weekends.

I work on weekends <u>sometimes</u>.

I <u>sometimes</u> work on weekends. (more formal word order)

PRACTICE WHAT YOU HAVE LEARNED

EXERCISE 1

Directions: Some of the following sentences have incorrect or awkward word order. If a sentence is incorrect, rewrite the sentence correctly. If a sentence is correct, write *correct* on the line.

1. I do not really know what is this issue all about.

_____

2. I have been already accepted to the university I wanted to attend.

_____

3. The only concern I have is how much will it cost the students to pay the rent.

_____

4. I ran to the grocery store this morning because I needed some milk for my cereal.

_____

5. A potential candidate must consider what his chances for winning the election are.

_____

6. Tomás is planning to have for Luis a surprise birthday party.

_____

7. I have not gotten my term paper back even though I handed in it a week ago.

_____

8. I am going to buy my father a silk beautiful green tie for his birthday.

_____

9. Bill often goes swimming to get regular exercise in the evening.

_____

10. The professor comes every day to class on time.

_____

EXERCISE 2

Directions: Complete the following sentences using an indirect question.

Example: I wonder where _the chemistry building is_ _____.

1. The professor said he doesn't know when _____.

2. Your term paper does not cover how _____.

3. I am sorry but I did not understand what _____.

4. Could you please tell me where _____.

5. It is not clear whether _____.

EXERCISE 3

Directions: Underline the 13 word-order problems. Then, write the correct word order above each part you have underlined. The first error has been corrected for you.

You can learn vocabulary in your English classes and from your textbooks. However, you may not be taking advantage of some handy reference tools that you can use to build up your vocabulary. Have you ever thought, for instance, what a great teacher the supermarket can be? If you think about it, everything is labeled with pictures or signs, making it easy for you to connect _the words with the product_ with the product the words. The window on the chocolate chips package lets you see the chips, and there is a picture of tomatoes diced on a can. Besides, if you are still not sure about what is a product, you can ask in the store another customer to help you, and you will be practicing your communication skills. Have you ever thought, too, about how helpful the newspaper, magazine, or Internet ads can be? Just consider, for example, what about pizzas you can learn. You can find ads for different styles of pizzas and also learn just how many different kinds of crusts are there. Many pizza places have in their ads helpful pictures, and you can also learn some interesting slogans, too, such as "Fastest wheels west of the Rockies!" or "Only Chicago-style pizza in Montana!" Instead of throwing away those catalogs that to your mailbox come or ignoring them online, have you thought about ever what a useful resource they can be for words? Catalogs have excellent pictures with detailed descriptions of their products. For example, you could learn what is a frost-free refrigerator or what are the names of different golf clubs. As for clothes, you could learn names exotic for colors and see the color itself illustrated. So, the next time you complain about not knowing enough vocabulary, get out of the house and go to the supermarket, or if on staying home you insist, pick up the latest catalog that came in the mail or click on your Internet browser and get busy!

Post-test   What Do You Know Now?

A Put the word(s) in parentheses where they belong in the underlined part of the sentence.

1. Learning to manage time <u>is a challenge for first-year students</u>. (often)

2. <u>It is a difficult decision for students</u> to decide whether or not to take a job. (always)

3. <u>Some stores have been generous than others this year</u> in giving discounts to students. (more)

4. Last year the professor <u>gave out a special assignment for extra credit</u>. (to the class)

5. <u>That red sports car</u> belongs to one of the richest families in town. (new)

6. Although most people would like peace, <u>war exists in this world</u>. (still)

7. When I get behind in my reading assignments, <u>I get very nervous</u>. (sometimes)

B Decide if the word order in these indirect questions is correct (C) or incorrect (I). If it is incorrect, make the correction.

_____ 1. The judge explained how were the winners of the prize selected.

_____ 2. The new student wondered where the room for his first class was located.

_____ 3. In the middle of the lecture, some students could not figure out what was the professor trying to explain.

_____ 4. The teaching assistant announced when was the deadline for the paper.

_____ 5. We still do not know when will be the test.

C Decide whether the word order for these adverbial phrases or clauses is correct (C) or incorrect (I). If it is incorrect, make the correction.

_____ 1. We decided yesterday morning to go to the movies tonight.

_____ 2. Because we could not find a seat at the play, we decided to go back home.

_____ 3. Yesterday in the yard we found an abandoned bicycle, which we reported to the police.

_____ 4. We are planning tomorrow to go home for the weekend.

_____ 5. Next week, we will be going on a field trip for my biology class in the afternoon.

D In the following sentences, circle the number of the sentence that uses formal word order for adverbs.

1a. Before the test started, the instructor had checked in the students carefully.

1b. Before the test started, the instructor had carefully checked in the students.

2a. Even though I am a hard worker, I have sometimes struggled to get my assignments completed.

2b. Even though I am a hard worker, sometimes I have struggled to get my assignments completed.

3a. We have always had a review class before an exam, but the professor decided not to offer one this time.

3b. Always, we have had a review class before an exam, but the professor decided not to offer one this time.

4a. When we do not attend class, the professor feels we are not learning the material thoroughly.

4b. When we do not attend class, the professor feels we are not thoroughly learning the material.

5a. Most students prefer to write with a ball-point pen on exams; I have never felt comfortable with that and write with a pencil.

5b. Most students prefer to write with a ball-point pen on exams; I never have felt comfortable with that and write with a pencil.

E   In this student's e-mail to her instructor, there are eight word-order errors. Find and correct them.

Dear Ms. Carpenter,

I hope you are enjoying this weekend the nice weather. I am writing you about the volunteer position I spoke to you about this week earlier.

Yesterday, I received from the volunteer coordinator a phone call. She said that she would be soon sending you a form reference to fill out for the volunteer position that I spoke to you about earlier in the student crisis center. I would appreciate your as soon as possible filling it out because I cannot be accepted into the program until all my references have sent in their forms.

Thank you for all your help. I look forward to soon my volunteer work starting.

Sincerely,

Maria Cecilia Santos

APPLY WHAT YOU HAVE LEARNED TO WRITING

Select a writing topic and follow the steps in Appendix A on page 337.

Topic 1:

Why are monuments, such as the Lincoln Memorial, and famous places, such as the Eiffel Tower in France, the Great Wall of China, or the Pyramids of Egypt, important in our lives? Choose one monument or famous place anywhere in the world. Describe what it looks like and what it represents. Then, explain why it is of interest or importance to you or to others.

Topic 2:

Write about a problem that you are facing personally or that you have recently faced. Explain what the problem is, including its possible causes and/or effects. Then, suggest possible solutions to the problem. If you have already solved it, explain how you did so.

Topic 3:

Think about the friendships that you have or have had. What qualities are important to you in a close friend and why?

CONNECTING WORDS

GOALS

- Learn why mastering connecting words is important in writing

- Understand four problems writers commonly encounter with connecting words

- Form and use connecting words correctly in exercises and writing assignments

Do you usually ask questions in class or do you go to your instructor's office to ask questions? What are the pros and cons of each?

LEARN WHAT THE ERROR IS

Errors with Connecting Words

An error with a connecting word is a global (more serious) error in which the connection between words, clauses, sentences, or paragraphs is either unclear or illogical because of a missing, incorrect, or misplaced connecting word or phrase. The sentence *I studied the material for five hours, then I took a break* has a connector error: a comma cannot connect two independent clauses. (This error is also called a **comma splice**.) The sentence should read: *I studied the material for five hours; then I took a break* or *I studied the material for five hours, and then I took a break* or *After I studied the material for five hours, I took a break*. The editing symbol for a connecting word error is *conn*.

A **connector** is a word, or sometimes a phrase, used to link paragraphs, sentences, clauses, or words. To understand connecting words and phrases, you need to understand the types of connectors and their functions.

Types of Connectors and Their Functions

Coordinating conjunctions connect words or phrases.

Examples:

> The students bought juice, soft drinks, <u>and</u> cookies for the party.
>
> The dog ran out of the house <u>and</u> started chasing the car.
>
> Tonight we can go to a movie <u>or</u> to a concert.

Coordinating conjunctions connect independent clauses.

Example:

> Pedro wanted to study engineering, <u>but</u> his father convinced him to study medicine. (Note that the two clauses have equal emphasis. Each independent clause can stand alone as a sentence because its meaning is complete.)

Correlative conjunctions connect similar grammatical structures.

Examples:

> You will have to <u>either</u> get a job <u>or</u> cut down on your expenses to stay in school.
>
> Thuy <u>not only</u> has two classes today <u>but</u> she <u>also</u> has a term paper due.

Transitional words and phrases link sentences and link paragraphs.

> **Example:**
>
> I dislike working at night; <u>however</u>, I cannot find a day job. (Some texts refer to these connecting words as *conjunctive adverbs*.)

Subordinating conjunctions connect a dependent (or subordinate) clause with an independent clause.

> **Example:**
>
> <u>When</u> we have finished the chapter, we will have a test. (Note that the two clauses have unequal emphasis. The dependent clause is subordinate and thus has less emphasis.)

Subordinating conjunctions are treated separately in Unit 6, "Relative, Adverbial, and Noun Clauses," Part B, "Adverbial Clauses" on page 131.

Errors with connecting words are global (more serious) errors and, as such, affect the meaning of whole sentences. Connecting words are especially important because writers use them to link items together, such as two sentences, or to lead the reader to a new point *(for example)* or to show order of importance *(most importantly)*.

By providing smooth links between ideas, connecting words help make writing clear and easy for the reader to follow, but they are only one tool writers use to connect their ideas coherently. See Section 3, page 333, "Improve Flow of Ideas," for additional information on coherence.

Suggestions for Reducing Errors

- Be certain of the meaning of the connector you want to use. (Consult the chart in this unit to ensure that you are using the appropriate connector.)

- Become aware of how connectors are used and what their meaning is in the material that you read so that you can improve your ability to use connectors correctly.

- Remember that when using connecting words, you may have choices. For example, when connecting two independent clauses, you may wish to use the coordinating conjunction *but* or the transitional word *however* to show a contrast.

Check Your Understanding

Write answers to the following questions. Share your answers with another student.

1. What is the difference between a coordinating conjunction and a correlative conjunction?

2. What are some of the functions that connecting words perform in a piece of writing; that is, how do they help guide the reader through the text?

GRAMMAR JOURNAL ENTRY 9   CONNECTORS

Respond to the following in your grammar journal.

1. What was the best dream or worst nightmare that you have ever had?

2. What are five connecting words you frequently use? Use each one in a sentence.

UNDERSTAND COMMON PROBLEMS

This section presents four problems that writers commonly encounter with connecting words. First, take the pre-test to see what you already know about connecting words. When you finish, check your answers on page 353. Then, carefully study each problem and the examples that illustrate it. Pay particular attention to those problems that correspond to the pre-test questions you had difficulty with. Remember that becoming aware of the types of errors you most often make with connecting words will increase your chances of avoiding these errors in your writing.

Pre-test   **What Do You Already Know?**

Test your ability to recognize errors with connecting words.

A   Correct the marked connecting-word errors. These are examples of the four common problems that are presented in this unit.

Problem 1 Natasha hoped to find an acting job in Hollywood_, she had little talent.
conn

Problem 2 Global warming poses a continuing threat to our environment;
conn
for example, we are trying to solve the problem.

conn

Problem 3 Even though we should be saving money, <u>but</u> we are always going shopping.

conn

Problem 4 There are three obstacles to losing weight, however, they can be overcome with a strong commitment to having a healthier, better-looking body.

B   Underline and correct the one error in each of the following sentences. (The errors are not in any particular order.)

1.   Although most students would like to have brand-new textbooks, but those on a budget often buy used ones.

2.   Before we bought a car, we did research on car safety, in addition, we test drove different models.

3.   Our teacher wanted to schedule an extra class, we did not like that idea.

4.   A new bookstore has just opened downtown; moreover, I don't have any money to spend on new books right now.

Four Common Problems

Problem 1

A connecting word is missing where it is needed.

conn

Incorrect: I did not study; I got an A on the test.

(These two clauses are grammatically correct, but without a connector, the reader cannot see how the ideas are connected.)

conn

Incorrect: I did not study, I got an A on the test.

(Two independent clauses cannot be connected with a comma.)

Correct: I did not study, <u>but</u> I got an A on the test.

Correct: I did not study<u>; however</u>, I got an A on the test.

Correct: <u>Although</u> I did not study, I got an A on the test.

Note: An adverbial clause like the one above may also be used. To study these clauses, see Unit 6, "Relative, Adverbial, and Noun Clauses."

conn

Incorrect: I frequently read magazines, watch movies in my spare time.

Correct: I frequently read magazines <u>and</u> watch movies in my spare time.

Problem 2

A connecting word with the wrong meaning has been used to join two independent clauses.

Incorrect: I was very nervous about writing an essay in just one hour;
     conn
moreover, I conquered my fears and finished the essay.

Correct: I was very nervous about writing an essay in just one hour;

however, I conquered my fears and finished the essay.

(Moreover adds information, as in the sentence I am very tired right now; moreover, I am also hungry. However sets up a contrast.)

> SELF-HELP STRATEGY: Make sure the connecting word you have chosen gives the correct meaning to the sentence. Refer to Commonly Used Connecting Words and Their Meanings on page 205.

Problem 3

An adverbial clause is connected to an independent clause with a subordinating conjunction *and* a coordinating conjunction.

Incorrect: *conn*
Even though my uncle bought a bicycle, but he never rides it.

Correct: Even though my uncle bought a bicycle, he never rides it.

Correct: My uncle bought himself a bicycle, but he never rides it.

Note: You will also see this problem in Unit 6, "Relative, Adverbial, and Noun Clauses," Part B, "Adverbial Clauses," Problem 1 on page 133.

> SELF-HELP STRATEGY: Remember that a subordinating connector connects a dependent clause to an independent clause, and a coordinating connector connects two independent clauses. In the preceding corrected sentences, note that you have the option of using either a subordinating or a coordinating connector, but not both.

Problem 4

The wrong punctuation has been used with a connecting word.

Incorrect: *conn*
Arielle wanted to go home for vacation, however, she did not have the money.

Correct: Arielle wanted to go home for vacation; however, she did not have the money.

Incorrect: *conn*
Vladimir craves sweets. For example he loves cake, cookies, and candy.

Correct: Vladimir craves sweets. For example, he loves cake, cookies, and candy.

SELF-HELP STRATEGY: Make sure you know how to punctuate connecting words correctly. For help, refer to Punctuating Connecting Words on page 209.

REVIEW GRAMMAR SOLUTIONS

To use connecting words correctly, you need to know not only their grammatical function but also their meaning. You also need to know how to punctuate connecting words correctly. In the following sections, you will learn the meaning of the most commonly used connecting words and the rules for punctuating sentences with connecting words.

Commonly Used Connecting Words and Their Meanings

1. To add information

COORDINATING CONJUNCTIONS	CORRELATIVE CONJUNCTIONS	TRANSITIONAL WORDS AND PHRASES
and	not only … but also both … and	additionally also besides furthermore in addition moreover

Examples:

We have seen that new movie twice, <u>and</u> we plan to see it again.

<u>Both</u> my brother <u>and</u> I know how to play tennis.

Ahmed speaks Arabic and English; <u>in addition</u>, he can read German.

2. To give an example or illustrate a point

COORDINATING CONJUNCTIONS	CORRELATIVE CONJUNCTIONS	TRANSITIONAL WORDS AND PHRASES
		for example for instance in particular specifically to illustrate

Examples:

I like to travel; <u>specifically</u>, I visit countries where I can practice my Spanish.

<u>For example</u>, last summer I spent two weeks in Mexico.

3. To show a contrast

COORDINATING CONJUNCTIONS	CORRELATIVE CONJUNCTIONS	TRANSITIONAL WORDS AND PHRASES
but		conversely however in contrast instead on the contrary on the other hand otherwise still

Examples:

Bill received an A in his German class, <u>but</u> Antoinette got a B.

We were supposed to meet at 8:00 AM; <u>however</u>, Barry arrived at 8:30.

4. To show a concession

COORDINATING CONJUNCTIONS	CORRELATIVE CONJUNCTIONS	TRANSITIONAL WORDS AND PHRASES
yet		admittedly even so nevertheless

Examples:

Albert knows that he should take vitamins, <u>yet</u> he refuses to buy them.

I need to wear reading glasses; <u>nevertheless</u>, I try to read without them.

5. To show a similarity

COORDINATING CONJUNCTIONS	CORRELATIVE CONJUNCTIONS	TRANSITIONAL WORDS AND PHRASES
		in the same way likewise similarly

Example:

Algebra was hard for me in high school; <u>likewise</u>, I find calculus difficult in college.

6. To show a result

COORDINATING CONJUNCTIONS	CORRELATIVE CONJUNCTIONS	TRANSITIONAL WORDS AND PHRASES
so		accordingly as a consequence as a result consequently therefore thus

Examples:

Tran finally got all his verb tenses right in an essay, <u>so</u> he is very happy.

Tran finally got all his verb tenses right in an essay; <u>as a result</u>, he is very happy.

7. To give a reason or cause

COORDINATING CONJUNCTIONS	CORRELATIVE CONJUNCTIONS	TRANSITIONAL WORDS AND PHRASES
for		

Examples:

Mr. Cross received an award, <u>for</u> he was elected teacher of the year.

8. To show a time relationship or order

COORDINATING CONJUNCTIONS	CORRELATIVE CONJUNCTIONS	TRANSITIONAL WORDS AND PHRASES
		afterward finally first in conclusion meanwhile next previously second subsequently

Examples:

Martin is now a student; <u>previously</u>, he was a store manager.

9. To show a condition

COORDINATING CONJUNCTIONS	CORRELATIVE CONJUNCTIONS	TRANSITIONAL WORDS AND PHRASES
or	whether … or	

Examples:

I have to get dressed quickly, <u>or</u> I will be late for the movies.
(<u>Or else</u> can also be used.)

<u>Whether</u> she plans to accompany me <u>or</u> not, I still am going to the concert.

10. To explain or emphasize

COORDINATING CONJUNCTIONS	CORRELATIVE CONJUNCTIONS	TRANSITIONAL WORDS AND PHRASES
		actually in fact in other words namely that is

Examples:

The bookstore sells greeting cards; <u>in fact</u>, they have the best selection in town.

I have to study all weekend; <u>in other words</u>, I am behind in my homework.

11. To give a choice or alternative; to eliminate choices

COORDINATING CONJUNCTIONS	CORRELATIVE CONJUNCTIONS	TRANSITIONAL WORDS AND PHRASES
or	either . . . or neither . . . nor	

Examples:

We can go to the beach, <u>or</u> we can go to the mountains.

You can <u>either</u> ride the bus <u>or</u> take the subway to get downtown.

I was so surprised that I could <u>neither</u> speak <u>nor</u> cry out.

Punctuating Connecting Words

1. **Coordinating conjunctions.** Put a comma before a coordinating conjunction unless the two sentences it connects are very short.

Examples:

A new café has opened five blocks from my apartment, <u>and</u> I have noticed that it is offering many specials.

The movie has started, <u>but</u> Jane has not arrived. (Note that the comma could be omitted.)

2. **Correlative conjunctions.** Put a comma before the second correlative conjunction if it connects two clauses but not if it connects words or phrases.

Examples:

> Eric is <u>not only</u> an outstanding teacher, <u>but</u> he is <u>also</u> a gourmet cook.
>
> The French bakery downtown sells <u>not only</u> crusty bread <u>but also</u> flaky pastries.

3. **Transitional words and phrases.** Put a semicolon before and a comma after a transitional word or phrase if you want to use it to connect two independent clauses. Put a comma after a transitional word or phrase if you want to use it to introduce an independent or dependent clause. Put commas before and after a transitional word or phrase within a clause.

Examples:

> The weather forecast for today was for cooler temperatures with a possibility of rain; <u>however</u>, the sun is shining brightly. <u>Nevertheless</u>, I am going to take my umbrella to work. As an extra precaution, <u>moreover</u>, I am going to wear my raincoat.

IMPROVE YOUR WRITING STYLE
LINKING IDEAS

Writing without transitional words and phrases can make your writing choppy and make it hard for the reader to follow the flow of your ideas. With transitional words and phrases, you can move the reader smoothly from one idea to another. You can introduce an example, indicate the order of ideas, or tell the reader that you are about to show a contrast. For additional techniques you can use to link ideas, see Section 3, page 333.

In the student paragraph below, notice how the writer uses transitional words and phrases to keep the flow of ideas smooth.

<u>First of all</u>, in terms of communication, Asian families need to strike a balance between assimilation and cultural segregation. This balance can affect our lives socially and economically. As Asian Americans, we need to master a second language. <u>Yet</u>, we should still maintain fluency in our own language and never negate our cultural identity. <u>For instance</u>, my father had a difficult time finding a job because he was unable to communicate in the workplace. <u>Finally</u>, after going to adult school for two years to study English, he found a job. <u>However</u>, my father maintains his first language (Korean) because he says that it forms a bond between our ancestors and us. My father is absolutely right. It is important for us Asian Americans to learn how to fit in; <u>nevertheless</u>, we still need to remember who we are.

PRACTICE WHAT YOU HAVE LEARNED

EXERCISE 1

Directions: Some of the following sentences have errors with connecting words. If a sentence is correct, write (C). If it is incorrect, write (I). Then, underline the error and write the correction above it.

Examples: __*I*__ It's raining; *even so* <u>likewise</u>, I will go running.

         __*C*__ Sarah was angry at her brother; as a result, she could not think clearly.

_____ 1. My sister is an accountant, she is very busy during tax time.

_____ 2. The supermarket closes at 10:00 PM; however, it reopens at 6:00 AM if you need milk for breakfast.

_____ 3. He did not want to go to chemistry laboratory. He went anyway.

_____ 4. Although a car is expensive to maintain, but I need one to commute to work.

_____ 5. Not only did Ann dislike the color of my dress, she did not like its style.

_____ 6. They could buy neither coffee nor milk because the store was closed.

_____ 7. Even though I dislike fish, I ate it at my friend's house to be polite.

_____ 8. I went to the bank, I did not have any money.

EXERCISE 2

Directions: Write four different sentences, using a connecting word with a different meaning in each sentence. Refer to the charts on pages 205–209 of this unit. Be sure that you also understand the grammatical function of the connector.

Example: Canada's Northern Lights are fascinating; therefore, tourists come from all over the world to view them.

1. _____

_____

2. _____

_____

3. _____

_____

4. _____

_____

EXERCISE 3

Directions: Read the whole paragraph. Then, identify and discuss the type and meaning of the underlined connectors with your classmates.

coordinating conjunction/gives a reason

Today's modern airport resembles a city in itself, <u>for</u> it offers many services to travelers. <u>First</u>, like all cities, it offers food. If you want to purchase something to eat quickly, coffee shops <u>and</u> snack bars are everywhere along with numerous fast-food restaurants usually found around a food court. For just a quick energy booster, you can grab, <u>for example</u>, your favorite candy bar, a bag of chips, <u>or</u> a package of nuts from one of the many small shops, which offer magazines, newspapers, books, gifts, <u>and</u> toiletries as well. <u>In addition</u>, there is even a growing trend towards having gourmet restaurants in airports. <u>Second</u>, like any city, the modern airport offers entertainment. Most airports have wireless Internet access, so you can browse the Internet from your laptop. Television areas still exist <u>and</u> people also can spend their time reading in seating areas. <u>Moreover</u>, some airports now have art exhibits. Of course, you can always entertain yourself the old-fashioned way just by watching people. <u>Third</u>, many airports offer shopping. Some airports have outlets for major-brand stores <u>or</u> shops dedicated to selling an array of local products, such as smoked fish, maple syrup, or special cheeses. If you run out of things to do, you can get a manicure, have a massage, charge your telephone, <u>or</u> rent a DVD. Keeping all these activities in mind, we can safely say, <u>therefore</u>, that in modern airports, waiting for a flight no longer needs to be boring because an airport is often "a city" within a city.

EXERCISE 4

Directions: Fill in the blanks with the appropriate connector from the list.

as an example	first of all	however	second
but	for instance	moreover	therefore

Now that I am in college, I am becoming more proficient at and more comfortable with using my computer skills to do academic work. Having high-speed wireless access 24 hours a day is a real advantage, _____ that is not the whole story. _____, the class website serves as an adjunct (2) to my classes, expanding my understanding of class materials. _____, (3) my Chemistry 2A professor posts homework solutions, sample tests, and pre- and post-lecture notes online. After each lecture, I visit the site to compare my class notes with his to make sure my notes are accurate. In another science class, biology, we are required to complete a pre-lab worksheet online before we go to the laboratory session. That way, my classmates and I are all prepared and ready to get to work with our partners when we arrive. _____, (4) teaching sites are not just confined to class sites. I have recently heard about an excellent interactive website for Chinese language learners, where it is possible to walk on the Great Wall, all while listening to its history in Mandarin. The _____ reason why my computer skills are rapidly improving is (5) that I am also putting my social networking skills to work. I use these networks to contact other students when we are working on team projects or to get help from my professors. _____, last semester my macroeconomics (6) professor held open office hours from 7:00 to 9:00 PM, and she also managed several blogs and a wiki site where we could share information and give our opinions. _____, learning and using these new skills is very beneficial. (7) _____, I still need to develop better skills at balancing my time (8) between working and playing on the computer.

EXERCISE 5

Directions: Choose a short news article to read. Underline the connecting words in two paragraphs and write down the function and meaning of each connecting word. Check your work with a classmate.

Post-test   **What Do You Know Now?**

A   Decide whether each sentence is correct (C) or incorrect (I). If the sentence is incorrect, make the correction.

_____ 1. The shoes I ordered by mail did not fit; I sent them back.

_____ 2. Although the days are still warm in September, the nights are chilly.

_____ 3. My mother takes language classes on Fridays, exercise classes on Mondays.

_____ 4. My friends intended to vote yesterday, however, they forgot.

_____ 5. While she likes animals, my sister wants to have a pet.

_____ 6. Thanksgiving is a holiday for visiting relatives. Also, it is a time for eating traditional food for example turkey and mashed potatoes and gravy.

_____ 7. Although most children are fascinated by insects, many are scared of spiders.

_____ 8. Mira likes her cousin Jennifer very much; however, she visits her as often as she can.

_____ 9. Many students like to take trips during vacations however that takes time and money.

_____10. The price of gas is high, I will not drive my car much this month.

B   Fill in the blanks with the appropriate connecting word(s) from the list.

| but also | for example | in addition | or |
| even though | however | in fact | in the future |

_____ my social life in college is going well, I have a constant
(1)
source of stress from school: taking tests. The primary reason for this

stress is the very competitive grading system. In high school, grading was much easier because most course grades were based on a series of

quizzes; _____ (2), the teachers usually dropped the lowest grade.

_____ (3), here in college, _____ (4), two tests, a term

paper, and the final exam can constitute a course grade with no make-ups

_____ (5) extra credit. To make matters worse, one bad test can

lower one's grade. Last semester, I had one painful experience—the grade

on my second chemistry exam, which was so low that my grade went from

an A to a C. Another reason midterms are stressful is that the competition

is intense. Not only do I panic about the test itself _____ (6) about

the competition from my classmates, most of whom finished high school

with impressive grades. _____ (7), I must already have met at least

25 students who graduated at the top of their class. Even though I took

numerous tests in high school, it is still hard to deal with the stress of tests

in college. _____ (8), I do not think I will overcome the stress at all

since grades are so important to me. In the future, I hope to gain enough

confidence in my test-taking ability so that I can perform well on tests even

if I am still very nervous.

APPLY WHAT YOU HAVE LEARNED TO WRITING

Select a writing topic and follow the steps in Appendix A on page 337.

Topic 1:

Think about your favorite teachers. First, describe the qualities a teacher should have to be effective. Then, write about one of your very favorite teachers. As an alternative, you may wish to discuss the qualities of an effective supervisor or manager at work.

Topic 2:

Although most people see a college education as a good investment in the future, not everyone sees a college education as useful. What are some of the major benefits of a college education? When would a college education not be necessary or even desirable?

Topic 3:

Think about a custom from your culture of origin or from the United States that you either like or dislike. First, describe the custom. Then, explain why you either like or dislike it.

SECTION 2

LOCAL ERRORS

This section contains six units, each one addressing a local error that writers commonly have difficulty with. Each unit has an introduction to the error, examples of the kinds of problems writers frequently have with the error, grammar review with self-help strategies, exercises for practice, and writing assignments.

Local errors are less serious errors because they usually do not significantly affect the reader's ability to comprehend what you have written. However, when local errors are frequent, they are distracting to the reader, often making it difficult to concentrate on content. In addition, many local errors may lead the reader to question the writer's competence. Because of the high demands for accuracy in academic and professional writing, if you are making these errors in your writing, you should work on them along with your global errors.

SUBJECT-VERB AGREEMENT

GOALS

- Learn why mastering subject-verb agreement is important in writing

- Understand six problems writers commonly encounter with subject-verb agreement

- Learn and apply rules for correct subject-verb agreement in exercises and writing assignments

What are some of the advantages and disadvantages of having pets?

LEARN WHAT THE ERROR IS

Errors with Subject-Verb Agreement

A subject-verb agreement error is one in which a verb does not show agreement in number (singular or plural) with its subject. For example, *he see* and *she have* illustrate errors in subject-verb agreement. *He see* should be *he sees* (third person singular) while *she have* should be *she has* (third person singular). The editing symbol for a subject-verb agreement error is *sv*.

Subject-verb agreement errors are local (less serious) errors. Although a reader can still understand the meaning of a text even if it contains errors in subject-verb agreement, these errors will be highly noticeable and distracting and will make your writing appear less professional. Readers in the academic and professional worlds expect writers to use correct subject-verb agreement.

Suggestions for Reducing Errors

• Be aware that the rules for subject-verb agreement are relatively easy to master. If you tend to make this kind of error, study the rules covered in this unit.

• Make it a habit to check your writing for agreement errors by looking carefully at each subject and verb to see if they agree. In particular, check the following:

   1. Check for correct agreement when using the simple present tense (e.g., *she reads, they read*).

   2. Check for correct agreement when several words appear between the subject and verb (e.g., *The cabins near the lake are the most expensive and the most popular*).

   3. Check for correct agreement with forms of the verb *to have (has/have)*, *to be (am/is/are; was/were)*, and *to do (does, do)* (e.g., *My brother has sent me a gift*).

   4. Check for correct agreement when two verbs with the same subject appear in the sentence (e.g., *Johnny reads the newspaper and listens to music when he is riding the bus to work*).

   5. Be aware that grammar-checking computer software will not pick up all subject-verb agreement errors.

Check Your Understanding

Write answers to the following questions. Share your answers with another student.

1. What causes an error in subject-verb agreement?

2. What verb tense should you check carefully for correct subject-verb agreement?

GRAMMAR JOURNAL ENTRY 10   SUBJECT-VERB AGREEMENT

Respond to the following in your grammar journal.

1. Ask a classmate or friend what he or she likes to do when he or she has free time. In your journal, write about whether or not you and this person share the same free-time interests.

2. Write two sample sentences in the present tense. One should use the third person singular form (*he/she/it* or a singular noun as the subject), while the other should use the third person plural form (*they* or a plural noun as the subject). After checking them for subject-verb agreement, use these sentences as models when you are writing.

UNDERSTAND COMMON PROBLEMS

This section presents six problems that writers commonly encounter with subject-verb agreement. First, take the pre-test to see what you already know about subject-verb agreement. When you finish, check your answers on page 353. Then, carefully study each problem and the examples that illustrate it. Pay particular attention to those problems that correspond to the pre-test questions you had difficulty with. Remember that becoming aware of the types of errors you most often make with subject-verb agreement will increase your chances of avoiding these errors in your writing.

Pre-test   **What Do You Already Know?**

Test your ability to recognize and correct errors with subject-verb agreement.

A Correct the marked subject-verb agreement errors. These are examples of the six common problems that are presented in this unit.

Problem 1 A good scientist observes closely and <u>record</u>^{sv} data accurately.

Problem 2 An attorney from one of the most distinguished law firms <u>have</u>^{sv} <u>agreed</u> to represent the suspect.

Problem 3 A supervisor who <u>listen</u>^{sv} to others and whose style is collaborative is often the most effective leader.

Problem 4 Taking regular breaks often <u>help</u>^{sv} a person work more efficiently.

Problem 5 <u>There is</u>^{sv} six articles that I need to review this week in preparation for my presentation.

Problem 6 One of the two cars <u>consume</u>^{sv} significantly more gas than the other.

B Underline and correct the one error in each of the following sentences. (The errors are not in any particular order.)

1. There is indications that global warming is more complex than scientists originally thought.

2. One of the questions on the exam have a typing error in it and is hard to understand.

3. Most people feel comfortable around a person who listen to them.

4. Before buying a car, the smart consumer compares prices and check the car's safety rating.

5. Mica, like most of my friends, like to go out to a restaurant at least once a week.

6. Going shopping for clothes are something that always interests my sister.

Problem 1

The final -s or -es has been left off a verb in the third person singular form in the present tense.

Six Common Problems

Incorrect: Each spring my mother <u>tell</u>^{sv} my father to take a vacation.

Correct: Each spring my mother <u>tells</u> my father to take a vacation.

Problem 2

The subject and verb are not in agreement when words come between them.

Incorrect: Two members of the fire department <u>has</u> been commended for their bravery.

Correct: Two members of the fire department <u>have</u> been commended for their bravery.

Incorrect: My manager, like many other managers, <u>want</u> to offer better health benefits.

Correct: My manager, like many other managers, <u>wants</u> to offer better health benefits.

> **Note:** In the example sentences above, the subjects are *members* and *manager* (not *fire department* or *other managers*). The verb in each case must agree with these true subjects.

SELF-HELP STRATEGY: Remember that words that appear between the subject and the verb do not affect agreement.

Problem 3

The verb in a relative clause (sometimes called an adjective clause) does not agree with the noun that the relative clause is modifying.

Incorrect: Every person should choose a place to live that <u>suit</u> his or her needs.

Correct: Every person should choose a place to live that <u>suits</u> his or her needs.

Incorrect: The president, who <u>serve</u> a four-year term, lives in the White House.

Correct: The president, who <u>serves</u> a four-year term, lives in the White House.

> **Note:** In the first example sentence, the verb in the relative clause must agree with the noun *place*. In the second sentence, it must agree with the noun *president*.

SELF-HELP STRATEGY: Remember that the verb in a relative clause always agrees with the word that the relative pronoun (*that, which, who, whose, whom*) refers to.

Problem 4

The subject and verb do not agree when a gerund, infinitive, or noun clause is the subject of the verb.

Incorrect: *gerund*   *sv*
Being a workaholic have many disadvantages.

Correct: Being a workaholic has many disadvantages.

Incorrect: *infinitive*   *sv*
To copy someone else's answers on tests are wrong.

Correct: To copy someone else's answers on tests is wrong.

Incorrect: *noun clause*   *sv*
What we requested are more supplies for the workroom.

Correct: What we requested is more supplies for the workroom.

SELF-HELP STRATEGY: Remember that when a gerund, an infinitive, or a noun clause serves as the subject of a sentence, the verb connected with this subject will be in the singular form.

Problem 5

The subject and verb do not agree when the clause or sentence begins with *there is/there are, there was/there were,* or *there has been/ there have been.*

Incorrect: *sv*
There are a new 20-screen movie theater being built downtown.

Correct: There is a new 20-screen movie theater being built downtown. (The subject is *theater.*)

Incorrect: *sv*
There is ten students in my discussion class.

Correct: There are ten students in my discussion class.

(The subject is *ten students.*)

Note: Be aware that such mistakes are often made in spoken English.

Problem 6

The subject and verb do not agree following the words *one of the.*

Incorrect: *sv*
One of the students play the flute.

Correct: One of the students plays the flute.

SELF-HELP STRATEGY: Remember that the verb must agree with *one* (the true subject of the sentence) even though the phrase *one of the* is always followed by a plural noun.

REVIEW GRAMMAR SOLUTIONS

1. **In the present tense, a third person singular subject takes a verb that ends in *-s* or *-es*.** The third person singular subjects include the pronouns *he*, *she*, and *it*, as well as all other singular subjects, such as *the doctor*, *a dog*, and *an athlete*.

   Incorrect: Marta <u>work</u>^{sv} as a clerk at the grocery store. She <u>like</u>^{sv} her job.

   Correct: Marta <u>works</u> as a clerk at the grocery store. She <u>likes</u> her job.

   Incorrect: My back sometimes <u>hurt</u>^{sv} after I have done heavy lifting.

   Correct: My back sometimes <u>hurts</u> after I have done heavy lifting.

2. **All other pronouns** *(I, you, we, they)* **and plural subjects, such as** *books* **or** *classes*, **do not take a verb ending in** *-s* **or** *-es*.

   Incorrect: Many students <u>chooses</u>^{sv} sports to stay in shape. As a result, they also <u>has</u>^{sv} more energy to study hard.

   Correct: Many students <u>choose</u> sports to stay in shape. As a result, they also <u>have</u> more energy to study hard.

   Incorrect: Her children <u>has</u>^{sv} many different kinds of toys.

   Correct: Her children <u>have</u> many different kinds of toys.

3. **Compound subjects (two or more nouns or noun phrases joined by** *and*) **usually take a plural verb rather than a verb ending in** *-s* **or** *-es*.

   Incorrect: Hamburgers and pizza <u>is</u>^{sv} favorite American foods.

   Correct: Hamburgers and pizza <u>are</u> favorite American foods.

4. **Uncountable nouns take a singular verb.**

   Incorrect: The money <u>are</u>^{sv} in the wallet.

   Correct: The money <u>is</u> in the wallet.

5. **A few nouns that end in -s are actually singular.** Some of these include *sports*, *news*, and some fields of study (*physics*, *mathematics*, *economics*, *statistics*, for example).

Incorrect: Economics $\underset{sv}{\underline{are}}$ a very interesting field of study.

Correct: Economics <u>is</u> a very interesting field of study.

Incorrect: The news $\underset{sv}{\underline{begin}}$ at 6:00 PM.

Correct: The news <u>begins</u> at 6:00 PM.

6. **The commonly used noun *people* takes a plural verb.**

Incorrect: The people going on the trip $\underset{sv}{\underline{is}}$ already here.

Correct: The people going on the trip <u>are</u> already here.

7. **Collective nouns (nouns that define groups of people or animals) can take either a singular or plural verb.** When the singular verb is used, the focus is on the group as a whole. When the plural verb is used, the focus is on the individual members of the group.

Correct: The faculty <u>prefers</u> the semester system. (The focus is on the faculty as a whole group.)

Correct: The faculty <u>prefer</u> the semester system. (The focus is on the individual members that make up the faculty.)

Correct: The audience clearly <u>loves</u> the show. (The focus is on the audience as a whole group.)

Correct: The audience clearly <u>love</u> the show. (The focus is on the individual members of the audience.)

8. **When a sentence or clause begins with *there*, the verb agrees with the true subject, which follows the verb.**

   a. *There is* is used before a singular or uncountable subject.

   Examples:

   There <u>is</u> a new book on the bestseller list.

   There <u>is</u> enough air in the tires.

b. *There are* is used before a plural subject.

Example:

There <u>are</u> two new books on the bestseller list.

c. When *there* is followed by a compound subject (two noun phrases joined by *and*), the verb agrees with the noun immediately following it.

Example:

There <u>is</u> a new photo of her family and a new wall hanging in her room.

There <u>are</u> new twin beds and a desk in her room.

9. **Although many errors in subject-verb agreement involve verbs in the present tense, the verb *to be* in the past tense and the verb *to have* in the present perfect must always agree in number with the subject of the verb.**

Incorrect: Max <u>were</u> a student for four years.

Correct: Max <u>was</u> a student for four years.

Incorrect: Tomás and Blanca <u>was</u> students for four years.

Correct: Tomás and Blanca <u>were</u> students for four years.

Incorrect: The new laboratory samples <u>has</u> arrived.

Correct: The new laboratory samples <u>have</u> arrived.

10. **Rules for subject-verb agreement with quantifying words and phrases vary depending on the quantifying word or phrase.**

Examples:

• *all of the*

All of the students <u>are</u> working on the project. (Use a plural verb when the noun following *all of the* is plural.)

All of the money <u>has</u> been carefully invested. (Use a singular verb when the noun following *all of the* is uncountable.)

• *some*

Some samples <u>have</u> arrived. (Use a plural verb with *some*.)

• *none*

None of the samples <u>have</u> arrived. (Use a plural verb when the noun following *none of the* is plural.)

None of the furniture <u>has</u> arrived. (Use a singular verb when the noun following *none of the* is uncountable.)

- *everyone*

  Everyone <u>wants</u> to go away during spring break. (Use a singular verb with *everyone*.)

- *the number of*

  The number of voters <u>has</u> increased. (Use a singular verb with *the number of*.)

- *a number of*

  A number of voters <u>have</u> sent in absentee ballots. (Use a plural verb with *a number of*. It is similar in meaning to *a lot of*.)

IMPROVE YOUR WRITING STYLE

SUBJECT-VERB AGREEMENT WITH CORRELATIVE CONJUNCTIONS

1. *both … and (Use a plural verb when two subjects are connected in this way.)*

    Both Engineering 3 and Engineering 4 <u>fulfill</u> the elective requirement.

2. *either … or (The verb should agree with the noun after or.)*

    Either the textbook or the assigned journal articles <u>cover</u> this topic.

    Either the assigned journal articles or the textbook <u>covers</u> this topic.

    Note: *The following is also acceptable but considered less formal:*

    Either the assigned journal articles or the textbook <u>cover</u> this topic.

3. *neither … nor (The verb should agree with the noun after nor.)*

    Neither Amy nor her parents <u>have</u> a car.

    Neither the students nor the teaching assistant <u>understands</u> the situation fully.

    Note: *The following is also acceptable but considered less formal:*

    Neither the students nor the teaching assistant <u>understand</u> the situation fully.

SUBJECT-VERB AGREEMENT IN REPORTING NUMBERS AND DATA

The word data *is a plural noun. (The singular* datum *is rarely used.)*

The data <u>show</u> that college students are often sleep deprived.

When reporting percentages and proportions, if the noun after the of-*phrase is singular (or uncountable), use the singular verb; if it is plural, use the plural verb.*

Over 25 percent of the students <u>were</u> able to score above 90 percent on the final exam.

One quarter of the marathoners <u>were</u> not able to finish the race.

A large amount of water <u>was</u> wasted when the fire hydrant broke.

PRACTICE WHAT YOU HAVE LEARNED

EXERCISE 1

Directions: Decide whether the subject-verb agreement in each sentence is correct (C) or incorrect (I). Then, cross out and correct the incorrect verbs.

Example: _*I*_ A student in the Netherlands usually ~~learn~~ *learns* to speak English, French, and German in school.

_____ 1. A good presenter is aware of his or her audience and use eye contact.

_____ 2. Physics is a popular major at my university.

_____ 3. Matthew, who is in second grade, already know how to read and write.

_____ 4. One of the students in the class was selected to participate in the essay contest.

_____ 5. Having good computer skills are required for many jobs today.

_____ 6. The number of hybrid cars we see on freeways have increased.

_____ 7. Brainstorming help a writer to gather ideas and avoid writer's block.

_____ 8. There is several stages in the writing process, including prewriting, writing a draft, and revising.

_____ 9. Because of the drought, there are not enough water for all the farmers who need it.

_____10. All of the conference attendees receive complimentary parking passes.

EXERCISE 2

Directions: Fill in each blank with the correct form of the verb in parentheses. The paragraph comes from a student essay on the effects of technology and is written in the present.

Another way that people ____*are*____ (be) affected by our high-
(1)
tech society is that human contact _____ (be) missing from our
(2)
electronic wonderland. People who _____ (enjoy) high-tech
(3)
equipment _____ (run into) this trap without knowing it. Computers,
(4)
wireless networks, and cell phones _____ (tend) to isolate us from
(5)
one another. We _____ (send) messages through the Internet or
(6)
our cell phones rather than _____ (meet) each other over coffee.
(7)
When we _____ (be) watching TV or using the Internet, we often
(8)

_____ (ask) people around us to be quiet until the program we
(9)

_____ (be) enjoying is over or we are finished with what we were
(10)

doing on the Internet, even if someone _____ (have) something
(11)

important to say. Also, an individual who _____ (play) video-
(12)

computer games would probably prefer to continue playing rather than

go out with friends. He or she might end up spending less and less time

communicating with others because the games _____ (be) just
(13)

too attractive to stop playing. These high-tech electronics _____
(14)

(make) us feel less interested in the people around us. Thus, important aspects

of human interaction _____ (be) de-emphasized because of our
(15)

involvement with modern technology.

EXERCISE 3

Directions: The following paragraph contains 11 errors in subject-verb
agreement. Cross out each incorrect verb and write the
correct form above it. The first one has been done for you.

April 15 is a well-known date in the United States. By this date every year,

                    works
everyone who ~~work~~ must file his or her income tax forms with both the federal

and state governments. Completing these forms are no easy task. First, a

person needs to decide which forms to file. For federal income taxes, there is a

long form for people who wishes to itemize their deductions. This form have at

least five supplementary parts, called "schedules," and a person must decide

which of these, if any, to complete as well. Then, there is a short form for people

who plans to take the "standard" deduction, one that have been precalculated

and is the same for everyone. The state income tax forms are separate forms,

and these must also be filed. In California, there is at least four supplementary

schedules that a person may need to fill out. Once a person know which ones

to file, completing all of these forms are not easy either, and many people hires

an accountant to help them. Regardless of whether a taxpayer choose to

complete the forms on his or her own or to seek assistance, the forms must be

postmarked or filed electronically before midnight on April 15.

EXERCISE 4

Directions: Choose a newspaper or magazine and write down five headlines that are in the present tense. Underline the verbs and notice whether or not they are singular or plural. (Note that some words, such as articles and some forms of the verb "to be," are often omitted in headlines.)

Example: It <u>Takes</u> Good Genes to Live to be 100, Researchers <u>Confirm</u>

The verbs are underlined. Takes *is singular because it agrees with the pronoun* it. Confirm *is plural because it agrees with the plural noun* researchers.

(**Post-test**)   ## What Do You Know Now?

A Fill in each blank with the correct form of the verb. For items 7–10, add the correct auxiliary verb.

1. Marcos _____ a sports car.   have (simple present)

2. My brother _____ a bad   have (simple past)
   cold last week.

3. Statistics _____ a hard course.   be (simple present)

4. The mathematics quiz _____   be (simple past)
   hard.

5. That vision _____ only   exist (simple present)
    in your imagination.

6. My older sister _____ at a   teach (simple present)
   community college.

7. All the students _____ attending   (present progressive
   class regularly.   tense)

8. The university _____   (past progressive
   celebrating the team's win.   tense)

9. Someone _____ broken into   (present perfect)
   my car.

10. The bus _____ been coming   (present perfect
    late recently.   progressive)

B Fill in each blank with the correct form of the verb. All verbs are in the
simple present tense unless otherwise indicated.

1. My English textbook _____ (have) three hundred pages.

2. Their grandmother _____ (cook) from morning until
   night.

3. His cousins _____ (live) in California.

4. Nobody _____ (want) to have dessert after a big dinner.

5. The United States _____ (attract) people from many other
   countries.

6. Judy and Mike's cousin, Helen, _____ (study, present
   progressive) at Harvard.

7. The articles in today's newspaper _____ (be) interesting.

8. The story written by the children _____ (be, simple past)
   interesting.

9. One of the students _____ not _____ (come,
   present progressive) to class today.

10. All of the students _____ just _____ (go, present
    perfect) on vacation. They left two days ago.

C Decide whether the subject-verb agreement is correct (C) or incorrect
(I). If there is a subject-verb agreement error, make the correction.

_____ 1. Yesterday we went to a party at Elena's house. We left early,
       though, because there was too many people in the room.

_____ 2. When I taught at a rural secondary school, the classroom was very
       small and bare. The students did not have many supplies, but,
       thanks to our principal, there were textbooks for every student.

_____ 3. My brother liked living on a farm in the country, but there was
       never anything to do in the evening.

_____ 4. When we take the bus, we often find that there is hundreds of people going the same way.

_____ 5. Everyone secretly wants to be famous.

_____ 6. Thailand is a beautiful country. There is a lot of great places to visit there.

D   Correct the marked subject-verb agreement errors in the following paragraph.

Careers in Information Technology

The number of people choosing a career in information technology <u>are</u> increasing year by year. This decision is a smart one, for most companies now <u>needs</u> someone with advanced computer knowledge. Web design, computer graphics, and software development <u>is</u> just some of the areas that are in demand. Anyone with advanced computer skills and creativity has the opportunity to find an excellent position. For those who <u>is</u> not happy working for a company, other opportunities exist. Consulting for big corporations <u>are</u> an excellent way to make a good living but not be tied down to one job. People who <u>likes</u> to make their own hours, choose their contracts, and decide how hard they are willing to work thrive on consulting work. Overall, a career in information technology, one of the most promising job markets in today's world, is a smart choice.

E   Find and correct the six subject-verb agreement errors in the following paragraph.

One of the hardest jobs of being a parent involve motivating children to succeed without pressuring them. However, some parents would say that setting limits are even more difficult. Every parent face this dilemma. For example, if a parent have never allowed the child to go out to parties in high school, when the child goes away to college where more freedom exists, he or she may want to go out rather than concentrate on schoolwork. Most likely this child's grades will drop and his or her parents will be disappointed. If the parents is too controlling, children will sometimes get out of control rather than growing up to be responsible adults. Therefore, the job of being a parent and making such decisions about control are difficult indeed.

APPLY WHAT YOU HAVE LEARNED TO WRITING

Select a writing topic and follow the steps in Appendix A on page 337.

Topic 1:

Think about the relationship people have with pets either in the United States or in your country of origin. What can pets contribute to people's lives? Are there any drawbacks to having pets?

Topic 2:

Think of a person that you admire or greatly respect. This could be a relative, a friend, or a well-known person. Explain what this individual's qualities are and why you respect him or her.

Topic 3:

Interview someone about his or her job. This could be a classmate or a friend who has done a part-time job or internship, or it could be a person who has had a permanent job for some time. Then, write up a description of the person's job. What are his or her responsibilities? What does he or she like and dislike about the job? Comment on whether or not this job would be of interest to you.

ARTICLES

Among the different types of stores, which do you most like to shop in and why? How much of your shopping do you do online?

GOALS

- Learn why mastering articles is important in writing

- Understand five problems writers commonly encounter with articles

- Learn and apply rules for the correct use of articles in exercises and writing assignments

LEARN WHAT THE ERROR IS

Errors with Articles

The **articles**, which belong to the group of modifiers called *determiners*, are *a(n)*, *the*, and the zero article (when no article is needed). The article *a* and the zero article are *indefinite articles*, and *the* is a *definite article*. Before vowel sounds, *an* is used instead of *a* (*a* celebration, but *an* elephant, *an* honest day's work). The editing symbol for an article error is *art*.

Errors in article use are local (less serious) errors and usually do not greatly affect how well the reader can understand what you have written. However, frequent article errors are distracting and can cause the reader to focus on article errors rather than on content. In spoken English, leaving out some articles, while incorrect, may be tolerated, but in formal written English, article errors cannot be ignored.

Suggestions for Reducing Errors

- Learn the rules presented in this unit to improve your article usage and make your writing easier to read. The rules for article usage are complex, and only the most frequent usages are covered. You can look up additional rules in an advanced ESL grammar textbook.

- Be aware that if your native language does not use articles, you must learn the rules for articles in English. However, even if your native language does use articles, you will need to become aware of any differences in their use in English.

- Memorize the use of the article with words or phrases that you often use. A particularly good strategy is to memorize phrases and terminology in your field of study, classes you are taking, or in your profession.

- Remember that listening will not help you very much in learning how to use articles because they are not stressed (said loudly and clearly) in spoken English. To learn how to use articles correctly, practice using them in writing and observe their use in your reading.

- Be careful when you read newspaper headlines because articles are often left out to save space as in, for example, "Amateur Astronomer Finds New Comet." (The article *an* has been left out before *Amateur Astronomer* and the article *a* has been left out before *New Comet*.)

Check Your Understanding

Write answers to the following questions. Share your answers with another student.

1. List the articles and label each one as a definite or indefinite article. Which article has two forms and why?

2. Why is it important for a writer to minimize article errors?

GRAMMAR JOURNAL ENTRY 11 ARTICLES

Respond to the following in your grammar journal.

1. Have you experienced difficulty with using articles? If so, discuss two strategies that you could adopt to improve your ability to use articles correctly. If you have not had many problems with article use, explain why it is not a problem for you.

2. Write a list of five nouns you use often in your daily life, at school, or in your profession. Use each word in a sentence. Then, check your sentences with a classmate, a tutor, or your instructor to see if you have used the article correctly.

UNDERSTAND COMMON PROBLEMS

This section presents five problems that writers commonly encounter with articles. First, take the pre-test to see what you already know about articles. When you finish, check your answers on page 353. Then, carefully study each problem and the examples that illustrate it. Pay particular attention to those problems that correspond to the pre-test questions you had difficulty with. Remember that becoming aware of the types of article errors you most often make will increase your chances of avoiding these errors in your writing.

Pre-test   **What Do You Already Know?**

Test your ability to recognize errors with articles.

A   Correct the marked article errors. These are examples of the five common problems that are presented in this unit.

art
Problem 1 When a person buys a car, he or she usually has to get loan.

art
Problem 2 Students often go to their advisor for an advice.

art
Problem 3 Many doctors in the U.S. no longer wear the white coat during office hours.

Problem 4 My friend called the police because <u>one of neighbors</u> ^{*art*} was having a loud party.

Problem 5 My cousin always makes sure she has <u>the driver's license</u> ^{*art*} when she goes out.

B Underline and correct the one error in each of the following sentences. (The errors are not in any particular order.)

1. In her application, Isabelle stated that she had the green card, meaning that she had a work permit.

2. We always have a fun when we go to Disneyland.

3. I am about to finish the bachelor's degree in comparative literature.

4. Most students found that one of questions on the test was difficult to answer.

5. Gustavo forgot to bring pen to the exam, so he had to borrow one from his friend.

Five Common Problems

Problem 1

No article has been used when *a(n)* or *the* is needed.

Incorrect: Yesterday, I finally went to pay my overdue fine at ^*art* library.

Correct: Yesterday, I finally went to pay my overdue fine at <u>the</u> library.

Incorrect: She bought ^*art* book and ^*art* ballpoint pen as ^*art* birthday gift.

Correct: She bought <u>a</u> book and <u>a</u> ballpoint pen as <u>a</u> birthday gift.

Problem 2

An article has been used where no article is needed.

Incorrect: A good friend gives <u>an</u> ^{*art*} advice when asked.

Incorrect: A good friend gives <u>the</u> ^{*art*} advice when asked.

Correct: A good friend gives <u>advice</u> when asked.

Incorrect: My uncle has <u>an</u> ^{*art*} obvious reasons for his decision.

Correct: My uncle has <u>obvious reasons</u> for his decision.

Correct: My uncle has <u>an obvious reason</u> for his decision.

Problem 3
The wrong article has been used where an article is needed.

Incorrect: My cousin lived <u>the</u> *art* productive life as a pharmacist.

Correct: My cousin lived <u>a</u> productive life as a pharmacist.

Incorrect: My lab partner has <u>a</u> *art* books you wanted him to find.

Correct: My lab partner has <u>the</u> books you wanted him to find.

> SELF-HELP STRATEGY: Remember that you must first determine whether the noun is countable or uncountable. Then, if you are classifying (as opposed to identifying) a countable noun, use *a*. If you are classifying an uncountable or plural noun, do not use an article. To identify a noun, countable or uncountable, singular or plural, use *the*.

Problem 4
The article *the* has not been used after an *of*-phrase showing quantity.

Incorrect: All of textbooks for this class have been sold. *art*

Correct: All of <u>the</u> textbooks for this class have been sold.

Note: Some *of*-phrases are *one of the, most of the, some of the,* or *half of the.*

> SELF-HELP STRATEGY: Always use *the* after an *of*-phrase showing quantity whether the noun is countable or uncountable.

Problem 5
An article has been used where another determiner is needed.

Incorrect: Whenever I go to the library, I remember that I need <u>the</u> *art* library card.

Correct: Whenever I go to the library, I remember that I need <u>my</u> library card.
(*I need <u>a</u> library* card would also be correct but would not show possession.)

Incorrect: Restaurant employees need to wash <u>the</u> *art* hands frequently.

Correct: Restaurant employees need to wash <u>their</u> hands frequently.

Incorrect: She wants <u>a</u> *art* meat for dinner.

Correct: She wants <u>some</u> meat for dinner. (The emphasis is on the amount.)

Correct: She wants meat for dinner.
(The emphasis is not on the amount but on what she wants to eat for dinner.)

Note: Articles are part of the whole system of determiners, which includes possessive pronouns (for example: *my, your*), demonstrative adjectives (*this, these, that, those*), and quantifiers (for example: *some, any,* or *every*). Remember that articles classify or identify nouns; they do not show quantity or possession.

REVIEW GRAMMAR SOLUTIONS

Every time you use a common noun, a proper noun, or a noun phrase (the noun plus its modifiers) in English, you must decide between *a(n), the,* or no article. Articles are used to identify or not identify a noun as specified below.

Identifying or Classifying a Common Noun

The article *the* identifies common nouns (nouns that are not capitalized).

Example:

> I ate <u>the apple in my lunch</u>. (*The apple* identifies which apple it is: the one with my lunch.)

The article *a(n)* or no article (the zero article) does not identify a common noun but shows to what class or group the noun belongs. In the examples below, the nouns are not specifically identified.

Examples:

> I eat <u>an apple</u> every day. (*an apple* = something that can be classified as an apple)
>
> Your pen needs <u>ink</u>. (*ink* = something that can be classified as ink)
>
> I like <u>foreign films</u>. (*foreign films* = things that can be classified as foreign films)

1. **When you are not identifying a noun, use *a(n)* or no article.**

    Use *a(n)* or no article depending upon whether the noun is countable or uncountable. Countable nouns (like *book, test,* or *car*) can be counted and made plural, but uncountable nouns (like *writing, advice,* and *intelligence*) cannot be counted and do not have a plural form. Most learner's dictionaries indicate if a noun is countable or uncountable. Some nouns (like *paper* or *change*) can be either countable or uncountable depending on their meaning.

    a. **If the common noun is a singular countable noun, use *a(n)*.**

    Incorrect: Last week I bought chemistry textbook at Discount Books.

    Correct: Last week I bought <u>a</u> chemistry textbook at Discount Books.
    (The chemistry textbook is one of many chemistry texts the bookstore has; the writer has not identified a particular one.)

Incorrect: When students are taking <u>the</u> composition class, they often complain about the time they must spend working on their essays.

Correct: When students are taking <u>a</u> composition class, they often complain about the time they must spend working on their essays.
(The writer has not identified a specific class but is talking about any composition class.)

b. If the common noun is uncountable or if it is plural, use no article.

Note: The determiner *some* can be used with uncountable and plural nouns but only when an amount can be indicated.

Incorrect: Many people drink <u>the</u> bottled water as they prefer its taste.

Incorrect: Many people drink <u>a</u> bottled water as they prefer its taste.

Correct: Many people drink <u>bottled water</u> as they prefer its taste.
(Water is uncountable and no special type of water has been indicated.)

Incorrect: <u>The</u> playing badminton is my favorite activity.

Correct: <u>Playing badminton</u> is my favorite activity.
(Gerunds and gerund phrases [the gerund with its object and modifiers] are uncountable.)

Incorrect: Before I go to class, I had better buy <u>a</u> ruled notebook paper.

Correct: Before I go to class, I had better buy <u>ruled notebook paper</u>.
(Paper is uncountable and no amount is specified.)

Correct: Before I go to class, I had better buy <u>some</u> ruled notebook paper.
(Paper is uncountable and a nonspecific amount is indicated.)

Incorrect: <u>The</u> soft-soled shoes are to be worn at all times in the

gymnasium.

Correct: <u>Soft-soled shoes</u> are to be worn at all times in the

gymnasium.
(The writer means soft-soled shoes of any kind.)

Incorrect: <u>The</u> ballpoint pens must be used during the final exam.

Correct: <u>Ballpoint pens</u> must be used during the final exam.
(The writer has not identified any specific ballpoint pens.)

2. **When you are identifying a common noun, use *the*.**

a. **After you have classified a noun with *a(n)*, use *the* when you use the noun again.**

Incorrect: Yesterday, I found <u>a</u> used car that I liked and bought it.

I now have to buy insurance for <u>a</u> car.

Correct: Yesterday, I found <u>a</u> used car that I liked and bought it.

I now have to buy insurance for <u>the</u> car.
(*The car* means specifically the car that has already been mentioned.)

b. **In the following cases, use *the*.** The noun can be singular or plural, countable or uncountable.

i. The noun is identified by an adjective that identifies it as one of a kind.

Correct: <u>The best</u> ice cream is sold at that shop. (a superlative)

Correct: In <u>the next</u> chapter, we will examine verb tenses. (sequential)

Correct: She is <u>the only</u> student with whom I will study. (unique)

ii. The noun is identifiable to the reader and the writer through shared knowledge.

Correct: <u>The sun</u> is going to rise at 5:43 AM tomorrow.
(Both the reader and the writer know it is the sun we see from Earth.)

Correct: My roommate left her backpack in <u>the computer room</u>.
(Both the reader and the writer know which room it is.)

Correct: Some of <u>the students</u> will need to take a makeup test.
(Both the reader and the writer know who the students are.)

iii. The noun phrase is identified by the modification that follows it.

Correct: Last week, I finally read <u>the article about thunderstorms</u>

<u>that Professor Johns recommended to us.</u>
(The article has been identified as the one about thunderstorms and the one that was recommended.)

Correct: Most of <u>the textbooks for this class</u> have been sold.
(The textbooks have been identified as the ones for a certain class.)

Correct: <u>The laughter of the children</u> made my grandfather

happy.
(The noun has been identified by an *of*-phrase.)

Correct: <u>The laughing of his grandchildren</u> made my grandfather

happy.
(Note that when a gerund or gerund phrase is identified [e.g., *of his grandchildren*], *the* is used.)

iv. The noun is part of an *of*-phrase showing quantity.

Correct: Raymond noticed that <u>half of the cake</u> had already been

eaten.

Correct: My supervisor said that <u>all of the fruit</u> in that box was

spoiled.

Correct: <u>Some of the monkeys</u> will be transferred to a bigger cage.

Using Articles with Proper Nouns

In academic and professional writing, you will often need to use the names of people, places, and things. When you are naming a particular person, place, or thing, you will use a proper noun, which is always capitalized. The rules for using articles with proper nouns have many exceptions, so it is best to learn only a few general rules and to memorize article use for those proper nouns you frequently use. You can also check article use for individual cases in an advanced ESL grammar textbook or in a learner's dictionary, or you can simply ask a fluent speaker what is correct.

Guidelines for Names of People

1. With singular names of people, no article is usually used.

Examples:

Have you read *A Tale of Two Cities* by <u>Charles Dickens</u>?

<u>Miriam</u> has just finished a French quiz.

<u>Dr. Hendrickson</u> will be a guest lecturer in my history class today.

2. With plural family names, *the* is usually used.

Example:

Next week, <u>the Campbells</u> will leave for their vacation.

Guidelines for Names of Places

1. States, lakes, individual mountains, cities, streets, and universities usually use no article unless the name is introduced by a capitalized common noun (such as *City* or *University*) and *of*.

Examples:

<u>Mount McKinley</u> is in Alaska.

Last night, I telephoned my brother who attends <u>Stanford University</u> in Palo Alto, California.

The bank is located on <u>State Street</u>.

Ana's new job title is Public Defender for <u>the City of New York</u>.

<u>The University of Arizona</u> is on the semester system.

2. Oceans, rivers, mountain ranges, and public buildings usually use *the*.

Examples:

<u>The Pacific Ocean</u> keeps San Francisco cool.

<u>The Mississippi River</u> starts in Minnesota and ends in Louisiana.

<u>The Rocky Mountains</u> have good snow for skiing.

<u>The Metropolitan Museum of Art</u> is on Fifth Avenue in New York City.

3. Singular names of countries usually use no article.

Examples:

In <u>Switzerland</u>, four languages are spoken.

<u>Australia</u> has many unusual species of animals.

4. Plural names of countries or names of countries that contain the words *united, union, kingdom,* or *republic* use *the*.

Examples:

>The United States is a country with wide expanses of land.

>The Central African Republic borders Chad.

>The Seychelles are in the Indian Ocean.

Using Articles with Set Expressions

Certain set (or common) expressions use *the* or no article. To make sure that you are using the correct article, look up the expression in a learner's dictionary or ask a fluent speaker what is correct. It is also a good idea to memorize set expressions that you use frequently. The following lists will help you become aware of article use in set expressions.

COMMON SET EXPRESSIONS

WITH NO ARTICLE	WITH *THE*
after breakfast, after lunch, after dinner	in the afternoon
at home, at school	in the evening
at night	in the morning
at seven o'clock	on the other hand
by train, by plane, by car	to get the gist of
in class	to get the point
to school, to church	to play the part

IMPROVE YOUR WRITING STYLE
VARYING ARTICLES IN WRITING

In the following paragraph, pay attention to how the writer has varied the use of articles to talk about grizzly bears. Notice that the writer is talking about all *bears as members of that class of animals known as grizzly bears.*

>The grizzly bear is a large animal that lives in North America. Grizzly bears are wild animals, but it is not uncommon for them to be seen near garbage cans in national parks. Many people feel a grizzly bear is the most frightening of animals because of its size and ferocious look. The grizzly is a very dangerous animal and should never be offered food because it has been known to kill humans.

Continued on page 248.

Improve Your Writing Style (*cont.*)

In the following paragraph, notice how the writer has varied the use of articles to talk about computers in general.

> Since the 1970s, the computer has come into everyday use. At one time, computers were only used in business, but now they are used by everyone. In fact, the computer now is within the price range of most people. If we were to compare inventions, the invention of the personal computer in the late 1900s has been as significant as the invention of the car was in the early 1900s.

Note: *No article is used with an uncountable noun when talking about a class or when generalizing.*

Examples:

> Cadmium is a heavy metal.
>
> Some people like to drink mineral water at restaurants.

Being Specific with Uncountable Nouns

Examples:

> I want water. (no amount has been specified)
>
> I want some water. (an unidentified amount of water)
>
> I want a glass of water. (a specific amount)
>
> She likes to give advice. (general)
>
> She gave me a useful piece of advice. (more specific)
>
> She gave me the best piece of advice that I have ever received. (more specific)

PRACTICE WHAT YOU HAVE LEARNED

EXERCISE 1

Directions: Decide whether each of the following sentences is correct (C) or if it contains any article errors, making it incorrect (I). Then, correct each article error. Some sentences may have more than one article error, and some errors can be corrected in more than one way.

Examples: __*I*__ Cheryl forgot to turn in $\overset{an/the}{\wedge}$ assignment for her math class.

__*C*__ Will you stop at the grocery store on your way home?

_____ 1. At the end of each quarter, final exams are held.

_____ 2. Most of students in Chemistry 1 have to study very hard.

_____ 3. She went to the bookstore and bought pencils, a textbook, and glue.

_____ 4. At the night, good street lighting is essential for safety.

_____ 5. If I have problems with my car, I take bus to work.

_____ 6. Be sure that you study night before exam.

_____ 7. Instant noodles are quick and easy to prepare.

_____ 8. When there is full moon, I like to walk down the Beach Avenue.

_____ 9. In a dry state like California, the water is a precious commodity for agriculture.

_____10. Although I like to write down my thoughts, I do not have time to write in the journal.

EXERCISE 2

Directions: In the following student paragraph, the articles have been used correctly. Explain why *a(n)*, no article, or *the* was used in the underlined nouns and noun phrases. The first one has been done for you.

uncountable, not identified

When I was still very young, my parents taught me to love <u>learning</u>. Every evening after <u>dinner</u>, my father would teach me <u>simple math</u> and my mother would teach me how to write and read <u>Chinese characters</u>. At the age of five, I already knew a number of Chinese characters and was able to do addition, <u>subtraction</u>, and <u>simple multiplication problems</u>. It was not that I was <u>a genius</u> or even a precocious child; it was <u>the simple fact</u> that my parents encouraged me to learn by praising me whenever I gave them <u>the correct answer</u> to their questions. Their praise made me feel that I was smart and could learn. What also helped me learn was that I had <u>few distractions</u>. I did not grow up with <u>a television</u>, a radio, or <u>video games</u> as children do now, for it was not common in <u>China</u> at that time to have a television or a radio at home. Therefore, our usual source of entertainment after dinner was <u>playing games</u>, <u>reading</u>, and learning. When I began school, I never had to depend on <u>the teacher</u> to motivate me to learn because I had already developed a love of learning. I also entered <u>school</u> with the attitude that I could learn because my parents' early teaching and <u>the learning</u> that had taken place in my house had helped me develop not only <u>confidence</u> in my abilities but also <u>a sense</u> that learning was enjoyable.

EXERCISE 3

Directions: The following student paragraph has ten missing articles. Supply the correct articles where needed. The first one has been done for you.

My attitude toward English is negatively affecting my writing. I think *the* problem is that as mathematics major, I love to spend time doing as much math as possible. Often my homework for math and other classes occupies most of evening. As result, I do not have much time or energy to devote to writing essays required for my English class. In addition, I usually have trouble getting started. I waste time eating, listening to music, or even looking in mirror instead of trying to work on paper, which is due on next day. Furthermore, I always have negative feeling toward writing. Even before writing paper, I assume that it will not turn out well. Because of this negative attitude, my grade in English is suffering.

EXERCISE 4

Directions: Choose a short news article to read. Then, underline all the nouns or noun phrases in the first two or three paragraphs and explain why the author used *a(n)*, no article, or *the.*

Post-test   **What Do You Know Now?**

A   Add the missing article —*a(n)* or *the*—to each marked error.

1.   In most countries, students who want to enter a university must <u>pass</u> <u>difficult</u> entrance examination.

2.   One <u>of advantages</u> of learning a second language is the opportunity to learn more about another culture.

3.   I am always very nervous about speaking in class; <u>as result</u>, I am usually very quiet even when I know the correct answer.

4.   Although there are many ways to improve your ability to speak English, <u>best way</u> is to spend time with native speakers.

5.   If you practice giving your next oral presentation in front of friends and family, it will help you <u>give presentation</u> with confidence.

B   Fill in the blanks with *a(n)*, *the*, or *X* (no article) in the following sentences.

1.   It is _____ well-known fact that peeling onions can make people cry.

2.   By going on _____ Internet, the student was able to get a definition of the term.

3.   There are three editions of this book, but you need to buy _____ latest one for this class.

4.   A few of _____ students who lived in the dorms this year chose to remain next year.

5.   Do you want to put _____ sugar and cream in your coffee?

6.   In many states, it is against the law to send _____ text messages while driving.

7.   Before starting my paper, I need to write _____ outline.

8.   In _____ United States, many people commute to work by car.

C Find and correct the 12 errors with articles in this paragraph. The first one has been done for you. There may be more than one way to correct an error.

Many people discover the discomfort of ~~the~~ traveling by air after experiencing their first case of the jet lag. This condition occurs when traveler's brain releases neurochemicals according to the schedule of day and a night (light and dark) which was established at traveler's previous geographical location. During these times, people find that their bodies do not respond way that they did just day before; simply falling asleep at night or the staying awake in the afternoon can be struggle until their bodies learn to adjust to the new time zone. It would be possible to avoid jet lag if we could find a ways to adjust our biological rhythms to time zone at the destination before leaving home. However, the scientists have not yet found the answer to this problem.

APPLY WHAT YOU HAVE LEARNED TO WRITING

Select a writing topic and follow the steps in Appendix A on page 337.

Topic 1:

Do you generally prefer to do most of your shopping online, or do you prefer to shop in stores? What are some of the advantages and disadvantages of online shopping? With the increasing popularity and convenience of online shopping, what do stores need to do to keep customers coming in to shop in person?

Topic 2:

Think of a friend who has never seen where you live. Write a letter to this friend and describe your room or your apartment. If you live in a house, describe only your room. In your letter, tell your friend how comfortable you are living in this place or room. Alternatively, you may wish to describe your office or place of work to your friend, noting how comfortable it is for the kind of work you do.

Topic 3:

Some parents choose to have their children begin formal learning, such as learning to read or write or do simple math, before they are old enough to go to school. Do you think children should be given formal learning tasks at an early age, or do you think that children should be given maximum time to play before they are old enough to go to school? Explain your answer.

SINGULAR AND PLURAL OF NOUNS

GOALS

- Learn why mastering the singular and plural of nouns is important

- Identify seven common problems writers encounter with the singular and plural of nouns

- Form and use the singular and plural of nouns correctly in exercises and writing

Do you spend much time outdoors? Why or why not? What are your favorite outdoor places and activities near where you live?

plural = countable

LEARN WHAT THE ERROR IS

Errors with Singular and Plural of Nouns

Nouns (names of persons, places, or things) in English can be made plural if they are countable but not if they are uncountable. A singular/plural noun error is one in which the singular form of a noun has been used instead of the plural or vice versa. For example, in the sentence *I have two sister,* there is a singular/plural noun error because *sister* should be *sisters.* Likewise, in the sentence *He gave me some informations,* there is a singular/plural noun error because *informations* should be *information.* The editing symbol for an error with the singular/plural of nouns is *s/pl.*

A singular/plural noun error is a local error and usually does not affect the meaning of a sentence, but frequent errors of this type can distract the reader's attention from the content of a piece of writing. In formal written English, readers expect to see correct use of the singular and plural of nouns.

Suggestions for Reducing Errors

• Become aware of the rules for the singular and plural of nouns so that you can reduce your singular/plural errors in writing.

• Look up a noun in a learner's dictionary if you are unsure whether it is countable or not. While writing, you may want to simply mark nouns that you need to check later for singular/plural forms. In that way, you can focus on content while you write and later go back and check singular/plural forms in the dictionary.

• Memorize the singular and plural forms of nouns that you use often in your classes or in your field of study.

• Train yourself to use the singular and plural of nouns correctly in English if your native language does not have a plural form. If your native language indicates singular and plural of nouns much as English does, focus on learning those nouns in English whose singular or plural is formed or used differently than in your own language.

• Listen closely to hear plurals in speaking. Because the plural *-s* is often difficult to hear in spoken English, plural nouns may sometimes sound singular to you.

• Pay careful attention to the singular and plural of nouns while you are reading.

Check Your Understanding

Write answers to the following questions. Share your answers with another student.

    1. What is an error with the singular or plural of a noun?

    2. What is a suggested strategy for checking the singular or plural of a noun while writing? Why would such a strategy be helpful?

GRAMMAR JOURNAL ENTRY 12   SINGULAR AND PLURAL OF NOUNS

Respond to the following in your grammar journal.

1. Write a list of five nouns you often use in your daily life, at school, or in your profession. Then, use each word in a sentence. Check your sentences with a native speaker, a tutor, or your instructor to see if you have formed the singular or the plural correctly.

2. If you are multilingual, write three sentences in your native language, using at least one plural noun in each. Then, write those same sentences in English and check the use of the plural in both your native language and English. Explain briefly how the use of the plural is similar or different.

UNDERSTAND COMMON PROBLEMS

This section presents seven problems that writers commonly encounter with the singular and plural of nouns. First, take the pre-test to see what you already know about the singular and plural of nouns. When you finish, check your answers on page 353. Then, carefully study each problem and the examples that illustrate it. Pay particular attention to those problems that correspond to the pre-test questions you had difficulty with. Remember that becoming aware of the types of errors you most often make with the singular and plural of nouns will increase your chances of avoiding these errors in your writing.

Pre-test   **What Do You Already Know?**

Test your ability to recognize errors with the singular and plural of nouns.

    A   Correct the marked errors with the singular and plural of nouns. These are examples of the seven common problems that are presented in this unit.

                                                            s/pl

       Problem 1 When I travel, I always take two <u>suitcase</u>.

Problem 2   My older sister is always willing to give me advices. ✓

Problem 3   Perhaps you might like to read this two novels.   *these*

Problem 4   The little girl is selling red and yellows apples.

Problem 5   An old proverb says, "An eye for an eye and a tooths for a tooths."   *teeth*

Problem 6   On Valentine's Day, Andrea received one of the biggest box of   *es*
chocolates I have ever seen.

Problem 7   When the meeting started, only two woman were in the audience.   *women*

B   Underline and correct the one error in each of the following sentences.
(The errors are not in any particular order.)

1.   During the middle of the semester, we will start to review this chapter
and this handouts.   *handout*

2.   Tonight I have to stay home and work on the difficults problem sets
that I have not yet finished for my algebra class.

3.   My professor said that he was unable to work with me this summer
because he had to supervise five thesis.   *es*

4.   During a laboratory class, students need to make sure that they handle
the equipments carefully.

5.   One of the most difficult adjustment that students need to make their   *s*
first year in college is how to manage their study time.

6.   In order to finish the lab, we have to work out the calculations steps
by steps.

7.   Before going into an exam, students should make sure that they have
the materials they will need, such as a calculator and some writing
instrument.   *s*

Seven Common Problems

Problem 1

A countable
noun is singular
when it should
be plural.

Incorrect: The student in the class were asking question.

Correct: The students in the class were asking questions.

Incorrect: I solved all but two problem on my calculus test.

Correct: I solved all but two problems on my calculus test.

homework

Problem 2
An uncountable noun has been made plural.

Incorrect: You should seek *s/pl* <u>advices</u> when you are making an important decision.

Correct: You should seek <u>advice</u> when you are making an important decision.

Incorrect: Water consists of two parts <u>hydrogens</u> *s/pl* and one part <u>oxygens</u> *s/pl*.

Correct: Water consists of two parts <u>hydrogen</u> and one part <u>oxygen</u>.

> SELF-HELP STRATEGY: Look at the noun and ask yourself whether it is countable or uncountable. If it is uncountable, do not add -s or -es. If you are unsure, check the noun in a learner's dictionary. Regular dictionaries do not contain this information.

Problem 3
A noun and its demonstrative adjective do not agree.

Incorrect: <u>These book</u> *s/pl* are for the other class, not yours.

Correct: <u>These books</u> are for the other class, not yours.

Correct: <u>This book</u> is for the other class, not yours.

> SELF-HELP STRATEGY: Remember that, unlike adjectives, demonstrative adjectives agree in number with the noun they modify. If you are unsure, refer to the demonstrative adjectives in the Review Grammar Solutions section of this unit.

Problem 4
A noun or an adjective modifying a noun has been made plural.

Incorrect: The campus is made up of <u>reds bricks</u> *s/pl* buildings.

Correct: The campus is made up of <u>red brick</u> buildings.

Incorrect: Next week we have to write a <u>five-hundreds</u>-word essay. *s/pl*

Correct: Next week we have to write a <u>five-hundred</u>-word essay.

> SELF-HELP STRATEGY: If your native language makes adjectives plural to agree with the noun, be especially careful to avoid this error in English.

Problem 5

An idiomatic expression has incorrectly been made singular or plural.

Incorrect: To make a good decision, you need to weigh the *s/pl* <u>pro and con</u>.

Correct: To make a good decision, you need to weigh the <u>pros and cons</u>.

Incorrect: Robert promised to keep *s/pl* <u>eyes out</u> for the blue shirt I want.

Correct: Robert promised to keep <u>an eye out</u> for the blue shirt I want.

> SELF-HELP STRATEGY: Idiomatic expressions often have to be memorized. If you are unsure, look up the expression in a learner's dictionary.

Problem 6

After an *of*-phrase that shows quantity, a countable noun has not been made plural or an uncountable noun has been made plural.

Incorrect: One of the oldest *s/pl* <u>building</u> on campus is North Hall.

Correct: One of the oldest <u>buildings</u> on campus is North Hall.

Incorrect: Some of the *s/pl* <u>milks</u> has gone sour.

Correct: Some of the <u>milk</u> has gone sour. (milk is not countable)

Correct: Some of the <u>quarts of milk</u> have gone sour.

Note: Some of the quantity phrases are *one of the, most of the, any of the, half of the,* or *some of the.*

Problem 7

A countable noun that has an irregular plural has been incorrectly formed.

Incorrect: Five *s/pl* <u>womans</u> signed up for the class in auto mechanics.

Correct: Five <u>women</u> signed up for the class in auto mechanics.

> SELF-HELP STRATEGY: Be aware that some nouns in English have an irregular plural. Common examples are *tooth-teeth; fish-fish; thesis-theses.* If you are unsure, look up the noun in a dictionary. The dictionary entry will show irregular plural forms.

REVIEW GRAMMAR SOLUTIONS

Rules for Forming the Singular and Plural of Nouns

1. **Nouns are either countable or uncountable (also called *mass* or *noncountable* nouns).**

    Examples of countable nouns:

    table, building, road, carrot, horse

    Examples of uncountable nouns:

    luggage, research, advice, potassium, swimming

    Note: Gerunds (*-ing* forms as nouns) are uncountable and do not take an *-s* ending.

2. **Countable nouns have singular and plural forms (*book, books*).** Individual members of a group can be counted (*one book, two books, three books*). Countable nouns (*textbook, test,* or *assignment*) can be made plural by adding *-s* or *-es*.

3. **Uncountable nouns have only one form (*equipment, air, happiness, vocabulary, homework*) and cannot be counted.** We cannot say *one equipment, one air,* or *one happiness*. Note that uncountable nouns take a singular verb (*The air <u>is</u> fresh*).

4. **Some nouns can be either countable or uncountable depending on their meaning.**

    Examples:

    Learning English is hard <u>work</u>.

    The complete <u>works</u> of Dickens will be published in a new edition soon. (meaning all the different types of literature he wrote)

    Many painters like southern France because of its intense <u>light</u>.

    From that hill, the <u>lights</u> of the town are beautiful at night. (meaning all the different types of lights)

5. **Some nouns have irregular plural forms.** The plural form of some nouns is the same as the singular.

    Examples:

    child, children; life, lives; goose, geese

    deer, deer; sheep, sheep; fish, fish

6. **Adjectives can never be made plural in English.** Nouns used as adjectives are also singular.

    Examples:

    a <u>long</u> day, five <u>long</u> days

    one <u>chocolate</u> bar, two <u>chocolate</u> bars

7. **Demonstrative adjectives agree in number with the noun they modify.** The demonstrative adjectives are *this, that* = singular; *these, those* = plural.

Examples:

this room, these rooms

that castle, those castles

8. **A countable noun after an *of*-phrase that shows quantity is always plural.** An uncountable noun after these phrases is always singular.

Examples:

<u>Many of the workers</u> at that company would like higher pay.

<u>Two-thirds of the water</u> in that pond will be dried up by summer.

IMPROVE YOUR WRITING STYLE
USING WEEK(S), YEAR(S), AND MONTH(S)

When week, year, *or* month *is used as an adjective, it does not take an* -s *ending.*

Examples:

Our school is on a ten-<u>week</u> quarter system.

When I was a four-<u>year</u>-old child, I was still living in Taiwan.

That problem is so simple that a two-<u>year</u>-old could figure it out. (Here, *old* is a noun denoting a person or thing of a certain age.)

My aunt will be taking a three-<u>month</u> vacation in Europe.

When week, year, *or* month *is used as a noun, it takes an* -s *ending.*

Examples:

Ferdinand traveled in Africa for four <u>weeks</u>.

Ten <u>months</u> ago, my uncle immigrated to the United States.

You must be at least sixty <u>years</u> old to take advantage of the senior discount. (*Years* is a noun and *sixty* and *old* are adjectives.)

1. These frequently used nouns are uncountable. They do not take an -s ending.

advice	honesty	progress
air	ignorance	sadness
clothing	information	scenery
enjoyment	intelligence	snow
equipment	luggage	traffic
evidence	machinery	violence
fun	patience	vocabulary
furniture	peace	wealth
homework	poverty	

Examples:

Incorrect: Most students feel they need to improve their academic <u>vocabularies</u>.

Correct: Most students feel they need to improve their academic <u>vocabulary</u>.

Incorrect: When doing a chemistry lab assignment, students use many different kinds of <u>equipments</u>.

Correct: When doing a chemistry lab assignment, students use many different kinds of <u>equipment</u>.

2. These frequently used nouns are both countable and uncountable depending on meaning.

cereal	oil	tea
chicken	paper	temperature
density	rain	velocity
glass	rice	voltage
hair	salt	water
light	sand	work

Examples:

Most people like dishes made with <u>chicken</u>. (the type of meat)

My sister's fifth-grade class is raising <u>chickens</u> and will sell their eggs. (the animal)

My grandmother wears <u>glasses</u> for reading. (device that improves vision)

The fake diamond was made of <u>glass</u>. (the material)

Ken eats <u>cereal</u> for breakfast.

Different <u>cereals</u> are popular for breakfast. (meaning types or kinds of)

PRACTICE WHAT YOU HAVE LEARNED

EXERCISE 1

Directions: Underline and correct errors with the singular or plural. Some sentences may have more than one error.

Example: Please don't forget to buy some _banana_ on your way home.   *bananas*

1. When I read, I mark unfamiliar vocabularies, which I later look up in a dictionary.   *vocabulary*

2. This boys needs to sign up for the camping trip.   *boy*

3. One of the best way to practice your English is to join a conversation club.   *ways*

4. Many cultures teach respect for the elderlies.

5. I had three piece of candies and some cake at the party.   *pieces   candy*

6. My writing needs improvements, so I am going to work with a tutor.

7. My friends are renting a hundreds-year-old house.

8. The professor is hiring students to analyze the datas she collected.

9. You need to follow the instructions steps by steps to make your experiment come out as planned.

10. I had almost given up on finding my watch when it caught my eyes from under a pillow.

11. My aunt has five childs: two sons and three daughter.   *children*

12. My roommate has excellent computers skills.

EXERCISE 2

Directions: In the following student paragraph, selected nouns and adjectives are underlined. Decide whether you need to make the noun plural or leave the noun or adjective singular. Make any necessary corrections. The first one has been done for you.

assignments

During the fall quarter, I was overwhelmed with many <u>assignment</u>. The most

unexpected one was writing. Even though I knew that my two education <u>class</u>

required <u>writing</u>, the professors I had were especially fond of <u>essay</u> writing.

Both of my education <u>class</u> required a total of eight <u>paper</u>, each of which were

four to six <u>page</u> long; in addition, the final papers in both classes were 20-page

<u>research</u> papers. Furthermore, both of my biochemistry <u>class</u> required a total of

eight lab write-ups and three essays. In sum, I had to write more than 20 papers

last quarter, and <u>that</u> papers were a nightmare for me. Previously, I thought

that only English classes would require a lot of writing, which is not one of my

favorite <u>activity</u>. In fact, last semester was the only time during my four years in

college that I had to write so much. Thus, I lost much of my fear of writing. While

I have learned that revision is time-consuming work, it has helped me improve

my writing and my grades.

EXERCISE 3

Directions: Correct any singular or plural errors by underlining the
incorrect noun or adjective and writing the correct form
above it. Use a learner's dictionary if needed. There are
15 errors. The first one has been done for you.

States

Online shopping has become very popular in the United <u>State</u>, and sales

have been growing annually, sometimes at twice the <u>rates</u> of retail store sale.

With so many website these day, online shopping has indeed become fast

and convenients. For examples, you can avoid the tedious works of filling

out a mail order form by hands, a great frustrations with a paper catalog.

With online shopping, the website quickly does all the calculations, such as

taxes and shipping. Without even setting feet in a store, you can buy a simple

white blouse, a bouquet of flower, or a whole set of patio furnitures. However,

you do not always save time with online shopping. If your order meets your

satisfactions, you certainly have saved time. If not, it is time-consuming to

repack your purchase and send it back to the company. To avoid this problem,

you can find what you want in the store's online catalog. Then, you can go

to the company's nearest store to make sure it is what you want. With this

approach, you have the best of both world—online and in-store shopping.

EXERCISE 4

Directions: Read a short news article. Then, underline ten nouns in the article and decide why each noun is singular or plural. If you are unsure why a noun is singular, check a learner's dictionary to determine whether it is an uncountable noun and, therefore, it cannot be made plural. Remember that set phrases are an exception to this rule.

Post-test

What Do You Know Now?

A Write the plural for the following words. If there is no plural form of the noun, write an *X*.

information _____X_____   advice _____X_____

assignment __assignments__   violence __X__

vocabulary __vocabularies__   problem __problems__

this ____these____   university __universities__

child ____children____   woman ____women____

B Correct the underlined singular and plural errors in the following student paragraph.

It is a commonly known fact that dairy <u>product</u>, such as <u>milks</u>, yogurt,

                                        X
and cheese are rich sources of <u>calciums</u>, but how many people know that

        ✓   this
these <u>foods</u> products are also loaded with protein? It is for <u>these</u> reason

that <u>dietitian</u> recommend that people consume two to four <u>serving</u> of this

                                                        X
food group each day. A glass of milk or a cup of <u>yogurts</u> has high-quality

                                          X
protein that is equivalent to an ounce of <u>meats</u> or cheese or one egg. These

          s   X
food <u>item</u> are certainly good for our <u>healths</u>. Whenever possible, however,

we should opt for low-fat dairy products.

C Find and correct the one error in each of the following sentences. Then, explain what the error is.

1. Our school accepted 800 transfers students for next year.

   Our school accepted 800 transfers student for next year

   X

2. In the mountains, deers come to eat in people's yards.

   In the mountains, deer

3. Three of the student finished the exam early.

   ⌣ ⌣ ⌣ S

4. Jane washed all of her clothings after the camping trip.

   ⌣ ⌣ ⌣ ⌣ ⌣ NOX ⌣ ⌣ ⌣ ⌣ ⌣

5. The weakened hurricane brought six inch of rain to Florida.
   es

   ⌣ ⌣ ⌣ ⌣ ⌣ ⌣ ⌣ ⌣

6. Would you like to borrow this books to read on your vacation?

   ⌣ ⌣ ⌣ ⌣ these

7. I have visited that museum many time.

   ⌣ ⌣ ⌣ S

D Write sentences to show the difference in meaning between a noun that is both countable and uncountable.

1. Write a sentence with the noun "paper" as an uncountable noun.

   _____

2. Write a sentence with the noun "papers" as a countable noun.

   _____

3. Write a sentence with the noun "work" as an uncountable noun.

   _____

4. Write a sentence with the noun "works" as a countable noun.

   _____

APPLY WHAT YOU HAVE LEARNED TO WRITING

Select a writing topic and follow the steps in Appendix A on page 337.

Topic 1:

Look at the rose in the photo and consider how you might describe it to someone. Then, find an interesting item located outdoors to describe. It could be a leaf, a plant, a rock, a flower, a window, or any other item. In your description, include color, shape, size, and any unique markings. Conclude by saying why you are interested in this item or what you particularly like about it.

Topic 2:

To what extent is your current life or job stressful? Discuss your favorite ways to relieve stress and explain how they are beneficial to you.

Topic 3:

We often hear about changes that are destroying the earth, such as habitat destruction, invasive species, over-population, over-harvesting of resources, and global warming. Which situation do you think is the most important for people in your area or country to address now? Why? What is being done (or should be done) to lessen the negative impact on the environment?

Unit 13 WORD CHOICE

GOALS

- Learn why mastering word choice is important in writing

- Understand five problems writers commonly encounter with word choice

- Choose words accurately in exercises and writing assignments

What are some of your favorite holidays or celebrations and what are some of the customs, foods, and symbols associated with each?

LEARN WHAT THE ERROR IS

Errors in Word Choice

A **word-choice** error is one in which the wrong word has been used in a sentence. For example, in the sentence *Even though she spoke very little English when she first arrived in the United States, my mother did not <u>abundant</u> her dream of being a bookkeeper,* the word *abundant* should be *abandon*. The editing symbol for a word-choice error is *wc.*

Word-choice errors, although usually local (less serious) and affecting only part of a sentence, can become global (more serious) when they occur frequently or affect a reader's ability to understand a significant portion of a text.

To convey exact meaning, the writer must master word choice. When a writer uses a word incorrectly, the reader must then either guess at the meaning or skip the word altogether. Thus, the reader, instead of the writer, is supplying meaning that may or may not be correct. Such work tires the reader and can cause him or her to lose interest in a piece of writing.

It is equally important that writers expand their vocabulary so that they can choose effective words to convey exact meaning. See Section 3, "Expand Your Vocabulary," page 320 for strategies to help you expand your vocabulary.

Suggestions for Reducing Errors

- Remember that word choice is governed not by rules but by usage. For this reason, you will sometimes need to ask an instructor or a tutor if you have used a word correctly.

- Memorize how certain words are used, particularly words that you use frequently in your major fields of interest or on the job.

- Become familiar with collocations, words that are commonly used together, such as *mutual trust, breaking news,* or *crucial development.* Many learner's dictionaries now include such word partnerships.

- Use a learner's dictionary that shows how a word is used in a sample sentence. When using a thesaurus, choose words carefully from it, making sure that each word you have selected fits the sentence you have written.

- Avoid, as much as possible, translating from your language into English since direct translation often results in word-choice errors.

Check Your Understanding

Write answers to the following questions. Share your answers with another student.

1. Why can word-choice errors become global (more serious) errors?

2. What are two strategies you can employ to avoid errors in word choice?

GRAMMAR JOURNAL ENTRY 13   WORD CHOICE

Respond to the following in your grammar journal.

1. What, in your opinion, are two good strategies for you to use to expand your vocabulary in English? For some ideas, you might want to look at Section 3, Part A, "Expand Your Vocabulary on page 320."

2. Write a list of five words you have had difficulty with in the past but have now mastered. Then, write a list of five words that you are currently having difficulty with. Look up each word in a dictionary that has example sentences. Write your own sample sentences and check them with your teacher or a writing tutor.

UNDERSTAND COMMON PROBLEMS

Prepositions are covered in Unit 15, "Prepositions," and conjunctions are covered in Unit 9, "Connecting Words," as well as in Unit 6, "Relative, Adverbial and Noun Clauses."

This section presents five problems that writers commonly encounter with word choice. First, take the pre-test to see what you already know about word choice. When you finish, check your answers on page 354. Then, carefully study each problem and the examples that illustrate it. Pay particular attention to those problems that correspond to the pre-test questions you had difficulty with. Remember that becoming aware of the types of errors you most often make with word choice will increase your chances of avoiding these errors in your writing.

Pre-test   **What Do You Already Know?**

Test your ability to recognize and correct errors with word choice.

A Correct the marked word-choice errors. These are examples of the five common problems that are presented in this unit.

wc
Problem 1 <u>Intuition</u> fees will be increased 40 percent next year.

Problem 2 The driver was unconscious, so the police could only <u>spectaculate</u> *wc* about what had caused the accident.

Problem 3 The <u>rules expect</u> *wc* that library books will be returned on time.

Problem 4 Most teachers <u>discuss about</u> *wc* the importance of attending class.

Problem 5 His students all think Dr. Stern is an <u>awesome</u> *wc* teacher.

B Underline and correct the one error in each of the following sentences. (The errors are not in any particular order.)

1. Before going to the laboratory, we have to read an article online and do some other stuff.

2. Being around leaders in a field can exhilarate a young person's attitude.

3. Many first-year students find that eating in the student cafeteria is very convient.

4. Good coaches emphasize on the importance of good sportsmanship.

5. From my perceptive, a trip to Europe is very expensive.

Five Common Problems

Problem 1

A wrong word has been used in a sentence. Sometimes the incorrect word may sound like the target word, but it is not correct.

Incorrect: The essay we just read is an <u>exception</u> *wc* from a longer work.

Correct: The essay we just read is an <u>excerpt</u> from a longer work.

Incorrect: Adults have been complaining about the younger generation for <u>decays</u> *wc*.

Correct: Adults have been complaining about the younger generation for <u>decades</u>.

Incorrect: My limited vocabulary <u>bounds</u> *wc* my friendships at a superficial level.

Correct: My limited vocabulary <u>keeps</u> my friendships at a superficial level.

Incorrect: A serious student is not easily <u>allured</u> *wc* away from studying.

Correct: A serious student is not easily <u>lured</u> away from studying.

Incorrect: Most first-year students eat their dinner in the dining <u>columns</u>. ^{wc}

Correct: Most first-year students eat their dinner in the dining <u>commons</u>.

> **SELF-HELP STRATEGY:** Be aware that you might often confuse words that sound somewhat alike when you write them if you have learned English primarily through listening to it. The more you read, the less likely you will encounter this problem because you will see the word used in written form in the proper context.

Problem 2

A word has been used that does not exist in English.

Incorrect: The article was fairly easy to read and <u>comprehenced</u>. ^{wc}

Correct: The article was fairly easy to read and <u>comprehend</u>.

Incorrect: Being a student is <u>literarily</u> a full-time job. ^{wc}

Correct: Being a student is <u>literally</u> a full-time job.

> **SELF-HELP STRATEGY:** Keep in mind that the spell-check on your computer can sometimes help, as it will indicate if a word is unknown. Some spell-checks also give suggested words that may help you find the correct word.

Problem 3

A verb has been used that does not fit the subject and/or predicate.

Incorrect: <u>Reading collaborated</u> in opening Andrew's mind to a better ^{wc}

understanding of the lives of the people around him.
(Reading cannot collaborate.)

Correct: Reading <u>helped Andrew better understand</u> the lives of the people

around him.

Incorrect: Reiko's mother <u>suffered a struggle</u> to balance work and family. ^{wc}
(A struggle cannot be suffered.)

Correct: Reiko's mother <u>suffered while struggling</u> to balance work and family.

Note: This serious error in word choice affects the subject and/ or predicate of the sentence and affects meaning, making it a global error. This error is also covered in English writing textbooks and handbooks, where it may be referred to as a predication error.

SELF-HELP STRATEGY: Make sure that the subject or predicate and the verb fit together; that is, you need to verify that the verb you have chosen can do the action required by the subject or predicate. You may need to change the verb, rewrite the subject or predicate, or rewrite the whole sentence.

Problem 4

Two closely-related expressions have been confused.

Incorrect: She did not <u>just as exactly</u> know <u>how</u> to reach the airport.

Incorrect: She did not know <u>exactly as how</u> to reach the airport.

Correct: She did not know <u>just how</u> to reach the airport.

Correct: She did not know <u>exactly how</u> to reach the airport.

Incorrect: Jerome's lack of sleep will <u>directly effect on</u> his concentration.

Correct: Jerome's lack of sleep will <u>have a direct effect on</u> his concentration.

Correct: Jerome's lack of sleep will <u>directly affect</u> his concentration.

Incorrect: Jack is <u>seeking for</u> the answer on the Internet.

Correct: Jack is <u>looking for</u> the answer on the Internet.

Correct: Jack is <u>seeking</u> the answer on the Internet.

Problem 5

An informal word or expression has been used in formal writing.

Incorrect: My brother is a person with a lot of <u>smarts</u>.

Correct: My brother is an <u>intelligent person</u>.

Incorrect: Many people feel that the test for a driver's license is a <u>tough</u> exam.

Correct: Many people feel that the test for a driver's license is a <u>difficult</u> exam.

SELF-HELP STRATEGY: Be aware that in speaking, we frequently use informal words that are not acceptable in formal writing. Also, remember that shortcuts like "r" for "are" and "u" for "you" are not used in formal writing.

Note: There is no Review Grammar Solutions section in this unit.

IMPROVE YOUR WRITING STYLE

COLLOCATIONS

Be aware that certain words are commonly used together, like the adjective and noun, high expectations, *or the verb and noun,* set a goal. *If another word is used, as in the sentence* My parents have powerful expectations for me, *it will sound unnatural to fluent speakers even though they will understand the general meaning. Words that are commonly used together are called collocations. Many learner's dictionaries as well as ESL textbooks include notes about collocations.*

USING ONE-WORD VERBS

In written academic English, the writer needs to maintain a formal tone. One way to achieve such formality is to replace a two- or three-word verb (called a phrasal verb) with a one-word verb.

Examples:

This paper will <u>talk about</u> the effects of wildfires on birds.

This paper will <u>discuss</u> the effects of wildfires on birds.

Students will <u>look into</u> methods of recycling batteries.

Students will <u>investigate</u> methods of recycling batteries.

Good writers strive for the appropriate level of formality to suit their audience and purpose. For example, academic papers and professional reports are generally formal while e-mail and text messages tend to be relatively informal.

USING PRECISE VERBS

To make your writing as precise as possible, use a specific verb in place of a more general verb. In the examples below, the verb goes from general to very specific.

Examples:

The captain <u>threw away</u> nonessential items in order to lighten the ship's load.

The captain <u>discarded</u> nonessential items in order to lighten the ship's load.

The captain <u>jettisoned</u> nonessential items in order to lighten the ship's load.

The server is <u>talking</u> about the fish special.

The server is <u>promoting</u> the fish special.

The server <u>is touting</u> the fish special.

Continued on page 276.

IMPROVE YOUR WRITING STYLE (*CONT.*)

The little girl was holding her balloon when it <u>broke</u>.

The little girl was holding her balloon when it <u>popped</u>.

Although in English an exact verb can be found to describe most actions, it takes time and exposure to the language to be able to choose words accurately.

USING SPECIFIC NOUNS

To make your writing as precise as possible, use a specific noun in place of a more general noun.

Examples:

The doctor needed 25 <u>people</u> for her study. (general)

The doctor needed 25 <u>individuals</u> for her study. (more specific)

The doctor needed 25 <u>subjects</u> for her study. (more specific)

PRACTICE WHAT YOU HAVE LEARNED

EXERCISE 1

Directions: For each sentence, underline and correct the word-choice error.

1. Because she did not know anyone there, Leah felt very
   uncomfortable
   <u>discomfortable</u> at the party.

2. Arturo called to say he would be late; in the meanwhile, I read a book.

3. My parents, who immigrated from China two years ago, are inliterated in English.

4. I once was in a math class where everyone was motivated to conquer the best test score.

5. When Samir cannot answer in class, he does not feel cool.

6. Jennifer's bad grade on her final exam in French unabled her from passing the course.

7. I became so courteous that I decided to investigate the noise.

8. Students are also putting their part to keep the school clean by not littering.

9. At first, I was speakless in class because of my English.

10. After she had been studying English for six weeks, Madeleine expected to know everything, but in replacement she found she had just begun to learn.

EXERCISE 2

Directions: This student paragraph has six word-choice errors. With a classmate, read the paragraph and make the corrections, deciding on the correct word. If you are unsure, check the word in a learner's dictionary. The first one has been done for you.

When I was a senior in high school, I dreamed about being a college student
and often wondered what college would ~~appear~~ *be like*. I also wondered about how much difference there would be between college and high school, particularly in class size. I assisted to a big-city high school, which was crowded; each class had an enrollment of 40 students. Therefore, when I sent in my application for college, I hoped that classes in college would be small. However, here at college, especially in chemistry and economics classes, the lecture halls are crowding over. For instance, my chemistry class has more than 300 students in it and some of them cannot get a seat when they come late. Some students stand in the back, and others sit in the alleys. Unfortunately, when a class is very crowded, I cannot focus on what the teacher is emphasizing on. Therefore, I do not feel satisfied with what I am learning. Unfortunately, my wish that classes would be small in college has not been realized.

EXERCISE 3

Directions: Replace each underlined phrasal (two- or three-word) verb with a more formal, one-word verb from the list given. Be sure to use the appropriate tense of the verb.

investigate	summarize	find	mature
encounter	increase	determine	~~collapse~~

1. During the baseball game, the rain-damaged roof of the stadium
   collapsed
   <u>fell in</u>, injuring several spectators.

2. When certain weather conditions occur, smog <u>builds up</u> in the Los Angeles area.

3. The little Airedale puppy <u>has grown up</u> into a prize-winning champion.

4. When the rain stops, the police are going to <u>look into</u> the crime and take fingerprints.

5. At the next class meeting, the cancer specialist will <u>briefly tell about</u> his research on preventing skin cancer.

6. I am in the process of talking to a number of professors to <u>figure out</u> what research topic I might be interested in.

7. Mathematicians have <u>come up with</u> a new way to solve the equation.

8. We never expected to <u>run into</u> these types of problems.

EXERCISE 4

Directions: Read a short news article and underline any words that are new to you. Then, check the meaning of each new word in a dictionary, preferably a learner's dictionary. Finally, write a sentence using the new word.

Post-test   ## What Do You Know Now?

A   Complete each sentence by underlining the correct word.

1.   When we are at the beach, it is a lot of fun to swim around and (recover/uncover) the mystery of the ocean.

2.   My friends like to go hiking on a weekly (base/basis).

3.   When Tracy moved to Chicago last fall, at first she felt homesick and (unsettled/unpeaceful).

4.   We are usually in a good mood outdoors because all the fresh air and beautiful scenery are refreshing to our (spirits/heads).

5.   It is (obvious/easy) to find evidence in our daily life of why we gain weight.

6.   We have plenty of (stuff/assignments) to complete before the winter break starts.

7.   People usually prefer to (watch/see) television when sitting on a comfortable sofa.

8.   When I visited the (desert/dessert), I was surprised to see all the flowers that had come out after the spring rains.

9.   For most people, giving a speech is not difficult if they have a variety of points to (talk/say) about.

10.   The presence of friends and acquaintances at a party (decorates/enriches) one's experience.

B   Replace each underlined two-word verb with a more formal, one-word verb from the list given.

collect   submit   establish   determine   dedicate

1.   The students can <u>pick up</u> their graded papers today from the teaching assistant's office.

2.   We are still trying to <u>figure out</u> where to have the party.

3.   Can we <u>turn in</u> our papers next Thursday instead of Monday?

4. Many students do not want to <u>put in</u> time to doing meaningless homework.

5. My brother-in-law <u>set</u> himself <u>up</u> as a lawyer 20 years ago and has been very successful as a defense attorney.

C Correct the seven underlined errors with word choice.

Our happiness as children is related to the environment that is created for us <u>buy</u> our parents. There are parents who do not let kids <u>feel</u> anything in the kitchen, for example; they have decided the surroundings are too dangerous for the children to explore. However, during my childhood, my <u>mom</u> let me play with anything I wanted to handle. I collected stones, caught frogs, chased rabbits, and fed turtles. A couple of times I was <u>pained</u>, but I learned how to avoid getting hurt. I also helped my mother cook and do housework. Although I was a <u>pest</u> when I was helping, I gained knowledge and learned how to survive independently. I had a wonderful childhood, and today I can laugh with my mother for hours when we talk about some <u>brainless</u> mistakes I made. Young people who are not allowed or encouraged to explore their worlds freely are at a disadvantage; there is no freedom and no fun for these <u>kids</u>.

APPLY WHAT YOU HAVE LEARNED TO WRITING

Select a writing topic and follow the steps in Appendix A on page 337.

Topic 1:

Choose a holiday or celebration that is important in your culture or that you particularly enjoy. Describe this holiday or celebration, giving details on the customs associated with it and showing why you enjoy it or why it is important. Comment on whether there are any parts of the holiday or celebration that you do not like.

Topic 2:

Think of several strategies that you could use to improve your English skills. Then, write about the two or three strategies you think would help you the most, indicating how and why they would work for you.

Topic 3:

Interview at least two people and find out about some interesting places they like to visit or businesses they like to frequent. Write a report on what you found out, including what the places are, what people can do or see at each, and why the people you interviewed like these places. Conclude by saying whether or not you, personally, would like to go to these places.

Unit 14   WORD FORMS

Aside from your academic work or your job, what are some of your hobbies, special interests, or talents?

GOALS

- Learn why mastering word forms is important in writing

- Understand four problems writers commonly encounter with word forms

- Use different parts of speech (nouns, verbs, adjectives, and adverbs) and their most common forms correctly in exercises and writing assignments

LEARN WHAT THE ERROR IS

Errors with Word Forms

A **word-form** error is one in which the choice of the word is correct but the wrong form of it has been used. For example, in the sentence *I had a happiness day,* the adjective *happy* should be used instead of the noun *happiness.* Note that the parts of speech we will address in this unit are nouns, verbs, adjectives, adverbs, and present and past participles used as adjectives. The editing symbol for a word-form error is *wf.*

A word in English can have several different forms, depending on whether the word functions as a noun, verb, adjective, or adverb. Examine the following forms of the word *success.* Notice how each form has a different grammatical function.

- His <u>success</u> surprised everyone. (noun)

- She has been <u>successful</u> in persuading others. (adjective)

- I certainly hope she <u>succeeds</u>! (verb)

- Ana could hardly believe that she had <u>successfully</u> finished the race. (adverb)

Errors with present and past participles that are used as adjectives are also covered in this unit. For example, the sentence *I am <u>interesting</u> in molecular genetics* is incorrect because the past participle *interested* should be used rather than the present participle *interesting.* Errors with infinitives, gerunds, participles, and base forms are treated in Unit 2, "Verb Forms."

Note that word-<u>choice</u> errors (Unit 13) are errors in which an incorrect word has been chosen. Word-<u>form</u> errors (this unit), on the other hand, are those in which the correct word has been chosen but the grammatical form of the word (noun, verb, adjective, or adverb) is incorrect.

Academic and professional writers are expected to use word forms correctly. Although word-form errors are classified as local (less serious) errors because they affect individual clauses rather than larger parts of a text, they are highly noticeable to the reader because they affect content words (nouns, verbs, adjectives, and adverbs)—words that carry the most meaning in a sentence. Thus, writers need to be aware that numerous word-form errors will make a piece of writing appear flawed to the reader.

Suggestions for Reducing Errors

- When you are unsure whether you are using the correct form of a word, look up the word in a dictionary to check its different forms. Almost all dictionaries indicate the part of speech (noun, verb, adjective, adverb) next to the word. Some dictionaries also include example sentences, which can be very helpful.

- Become aware of common word endings, called **suffixes**, that identify words as nouns, verbs, adjectives, or adverbs. For example, *-ness* and *-tion* are common noun endings; *-ous* and *-ful* are common adjective endings; *-en* and *-ify* are common verb endings; and *-ly* is a common adverb ending. A list of the most common word endings is included in this unit.

- Be aware of word formation when you read in English. Take time to analyze sentences, making sure you can identify nouns, verbs, adjectives, and adverbs in each sentence.

Check Your Understanding

Write answers to the following questions. Share your answers with another student.

1. Choose two suffixes that you already know. Give two examples of words that take each suffix.

2. How can a dictionary help you with accurate word formation?

GRAMMAR JOURNAL ENTRY 14   WORD FORMS

Respond to the following in your grammar journal.

1. What is your definition of success and/or a successful person?

2. Choose two words that you use frequently, such as *friend, education, environment,* or any other words you wish. Then, list all of the different forms of these two words that you can think of. Label the different forms as nouns, adjectives, verbs, or adverbs. Then, in a dictionary, verify whether the parts of speech are correct.

UNDERSTAND COMMON PROBLEMS

This section presents four problems that writers commonly encounter with word forms. First, take the pre-test to see what you already know about word forms. When you finish, check your answers on page 354. Then, carefully study each problem and the examples that illustrate it.

Pay particular attention to those problems that correspond to the pre-test questions you had difficulty with. Remember that becoming aware of the types of errors you most often make with word forms will increase your chances of avoiding these errors in your writing.

Pre-test

What Do You Already Know?

Test your ability to recognize and correct errors with word forms.

A   Correct the marked word-form errors. These are examples of the four common problems that are presented in this unit.

Problem 1   Electronic <u>communicate</u> *wc* via e-mail, Facebook, and texting has become commonplace around the world.

Problem 2   Employees must submit weekly progress reports in a <u>timeful</u> *wc* manner.

Problem 3   Heating up a frozen dinner is sometimes <u>convenient</u> *wc* than cooking a meal.

Problem 4   As a possible career goal, I am <u>interesting</u> *wc* in computer science.

B   Underline and correct the one error in each of the following sentences. (The errors are not in any particular order.)

1.   Most of the students thought that the second quiz was more easy than the first one.

2.   When my friends are late, I always start to get impatience.

3.   The pharmacy is locating right behind the bank.

4.   My roommate needs to straightize her room.

Four Common Problems

Problem 1

The choice of a word is correct, but the wrong part of speech has been used.

Incorrect: She was <u>easy</u> *wf* persuaded to change her vote.

Correct: She was <u>easily</u> persuaded to change her vote.
   (An adverb instead of an adjective is needed to modify the verb *persuaded*.)

Incorrect: The students will clearly feel the *wf* <u>lost</u> of Mr. Jensen, who will retire soon.

Correct: The students will clearly feel the <u>loss</u> of Mr. Jensen, who will retire soon.

(A noun instead of an adjective is needed as the direct object of the verb *feel*.)

Incorrect: Her attitude is a *wf* <u>reflect</u> of the views of society.

Correct: Her attitude is a <u>reflection</u> of the views of society.

(A noun instead of a verb is needed in this position.)

Problem 2

A suffix has been used incorrectly.

Incorrect: I am a graduate student in the Department of Management and *wf* <u>Financement</u>.

Correct: I am a graduate student in the Department of Management and <u>Finance</u>.

Incorrect: I studied *wf* <u>hardly</u> before I took the TOEFL exam.

Correct: I studied <u>hard</u> before I took the TOEFL exam.

> SELF-HELP STRATEGY: Study the list of common word suffixes in this unit to become familiar with noun, verb, adjective, and adverb suffixes. However, keep in mind that there are no rules that will tell you whether a word requires a specific suffix to mark it as a certain part of speech. For example, the noun form of the verb *manage* requires the *-ment* ending, while the verb *finance* does not require an ending to form the noun *finance*. To verify word forms that you are unsure of, check your dictionary.

Problem 3

The incorrect adjective or adverb form has been used in a comparison.

Incorrect: That was the *wf* <u>worse</u> movie I have seen in a long time.

Correct: That was the <u>worst</u> movie I have seen in a long time.

Incorrect: This semester, Faizah has been <u>more busier</u> *wf* than usual.

Correct: This semester, Faizah has been <u>busier</u> than usual.

Incorrect: Mario is working <u>hard</u> *wf* this year than last year.

Correct: Mario is working <u>harder</u> this year than last year.

Problem 4

The incorrect present or past participle form has been used as an adjective.

Incorrect: The essay was <u>interested</u> *wf*.

Correct: The essay was <u>interesting</u>.

Incorrect: The <u>interesting</u> *wf* members of the audience stayed after the lecture to ask further questions.

Correct: The <u>interested</u> members of the audience stayed after the lecture to ask further questions.

REVIEW GRAMMAR SOLUTIONS

Common Word Suffixes

The following lists will help you recognize common noun, verb, adjective, and adverb suffixes. After you study each list, add your own examples of suffixes.

1. Noun Suffixes

SUFFIX	EXAMPLES
-ance	importance, distance, *reliance* _____
-ancy	expectancy, redundancy, _____
-ant	hydrant, participant, _____
-arium	planetarium, aquarium, _____
-ary	diary, commentary, _____
-ation	education, dedication, _____
-cide	genocide, herbicide, _____
-dom	kingdom, martyrdom, _____
-eer	volunteer, engineer, _____
-ence	presence, emergence, _____
-ency	potency, transparency, _____
-er	teacher, speaker, _____
-ess	princess, actress, _____

SUFFIX	EXAMPLES
-hood	likelihood, childhood, _____
-ian	guardian, librarian, _____
-ion	fusion, religion, _____
-ism	socialism, sexism, _____
-ist	specialist, artist, _____
-istics	statistics, logistics, _____
-ity	legibility, impossibility, _____
-logy	geology, analogy, _____
-ment	argument, establishment, _____
-ness	sadness, likeness, _____
-ology	terminology, ecology, _____
-or	instructor, doctor, _____
-orium	auditorium, moratorium, _____
-ory	observatory, laboratory, _____
-ship	scholarship, friendship, _____
-sion	expression, admission, _____
-tion	application, indication, _____
-ure	closure, departure, _____
-work	network, homework, _____

2. Verb Suffixes

SUFFIX	EXAMPLES
-ate	mediate, delegate, _regulate_ _____
-en	lengthen, brighten, _____
-ify	solidify, intensify, _____
-ize	finalize, customize, _____

3. Adjective Suffixes

SUFFIX	EXAMPLES
-able	agreeable, understandable, _believable_ _____
-al	emotional, lethal, _____
-an	American, Italian, _____
-ant	important, hesitant, _____
-ate	considerate, subordinate, _____
-ative	superlative, demonstrative, _____
-ed	interested, challenged, _____
-ent	different, excellent, _____
-ese	Japanese, Maltese, _____

Continued on page 290.

SUFFIX	EXAMPLES
-ful	colorful, useful, _____
-ible	responsible, infallible, _____
-ic	characteristic, electric, _____
-ing	interesting, challenging, _____
-ious	delicious, cautious, _____
-ish	childish, foolish, _____
-ive	expressive, competitive, _____
-less	colorless, useless, _____
-like	childlike, lifelike, _____
-ly	friendly, lonely, _____
-ous	famous, dangerous, _____
-some	wholesome, bothersome, _____
-y	dressy, noisy, _____

4. Adverb Suffixes

SUFFIX	EXAMPLES
-ly	usually, legibly, *quietly* _____
-ward	afterward, upward, _____
-wise	clockwise, likewise, _____

Comparative and Superlative Forms of Adjectives

1. **One-syllable adjectives and adverbs:** Add *-er* + *than* for the comparative form and *the* + *-est* for the superlative form.

Examples:

The midterm test was <u>harder than</u> the final test. (comparative)

Some students think that essay tests are <u>the hardest</u>. (superlative)

My roommate usually stays up <u>later</u> than I do. (comparative)

Monica stays up <u>the latest</u> of all my friends. (superlative)

2. **Most adjectives and adverbs of two or more syllables:** Use *more … than* for the comparative form and *the most* for the superlative form.

Examples:

The Mexican restaurant downtown is <u>more popular than</u> the Chinese restaurant. (comparative)

The Vietnamese restaurant is <u>the most popular</u>. (superlative)

3. **Two-syllable words that end in -*y*: Change the -*y* to -*i*.** Then, add -*er* + *than* for the comparative form and *the* + -*est* for the superlative form.

Examples:

The red car is <u>sportier than</u> the blue car. (comparative)

The black convertible is <u>the sportiest</u> of all. (superlative)

4. **The following words have irregular comparative and superlative forms.**

	COMPARATIVE	SUPERLATIVE
good	*better than*	*the best*
bad	*worse than*	*the worst*
little	*less than*	*the least*
much/many	*more than*	*the most*

Examples:

I like my chemistry class <u>better than</u> my math class. (comparative)

I like my history class <u>the best</u> of all. (superlative)

I am earning <u>less</u> money this year <u>than</u> last year. (comparative)

Of all my friends, Juan earns <u>the least</u> money. (superlative)

Jogging is <u>better</u> exercise <u>than</u> walking. (comparative)

The <u>best</u> exercise program is a daily workout. (superlative)

Choosing the Appropriate Participle as an Adjective

1. **Use the past participle form of the verb when you are describing something or someone affected by someone or something else.**

Examples:

The reader was <u>interested</u> in the essay.

An <u>interested</u> reader can read an essay for hours.

(In both cases, the focus is on the reader's being interested in the essay.)

2. **Use the present participle form of the verb when you are describing something that affects someone or something else.**

Examples:

The essay was <u>interesting</u>.

An <u>interesting</u> essay holds the reader's attention.

(In both cases, the focus is on the essay's being interesting.)

IMPROVE YOUR WRITING STYLE
WORDS WITH MULTIPLE FORMS

Be aware that many English words have more than one form for the same part of speech. However, the different forms have different meanings. As you encounter these different forms and uses, you will need to memorize them, since their usage is not rule-based but instead is vocabulary-based. The more you read and listen to English, the sooner you will become acquainted with these different forms. Below you will find selected examples.

1. **friend** (noun)   **friendship** (noun)

   My <u>friend</u> helped me move to a new apartment.

   My <u>friendship</u> with Mr. Jones led me to go into the engineering field.

2. **comparable** (adjective)   **comparative** (adjective)

   This hotel is <u>comparable</u> to the one we stayed at last year.

   Kevin's research is a <u>comparative</u> study of health services in India.

3. **various** (adjective)   **variable** (adjective)   **varied** (adjective)

   Her job requires her to travel to <u>various</u> countries each year.

   The weather is <u>variable</u> in the spring.

   The climate of the United States is <u>varied</u>, with some parts having a cold climate and others having a hot and humid climate.

4. **characteristic** (noun)   **character** (noun)

   Conscientiousness is one of John's <u>characteristics</u>.

   Tran's current behavior seems to contradict his <u>character</u>.

PRACTICE WHAT YOU HAVE LEARNED

EXERCISE 1

Directions: For the following nouns commonly used by academic and professional writers, fill in the other word forms.

Noun	Verb	Adjective	Adverb
1. characteristic	characterize	characteristic	characteristically
2. approximation	_____	_____	_____
3. production	_____	_____	_____
4. origin	_____	_____	_____
5. category	_____	_____	_____
6. significance	_____	_____	_____
7. theory	_____	_____	_____

EXERCISE 2

Directions: Decide if a sentence is correct (C) or if it contains any word-form errors (I). If it is incorrect, underline the error and make the correction.

Example: _I__ The young child did not receive much <u>encourage</u> *encouragement* to speak her native language.

_____ 1. Taking timed writing tests often gives students the beneficial of becoming more accustomed to writing quickly under pressure.

_____ 2. The article very precisively and effectively explains the advantages and disadvantages of taking a class online.

_____ 3. Many young immigrants become maturity by dealing with adult problems at an early age.

_____ 4. My supervisor quickly approval of my request for a two-week leave from work.

_____ 5. Gregorio came to Canada to pursuit his Ph.D.

_____ 6. In order to succeed, one must be able to make sacrifices.

_____ 7. My suggest is aimed at easing the problem.

_____ 8. If I keep writing in this fashion, my writing skills might even become worst, for I might get used to making those mistakes.

_____ 9. When my roommate cooks, I have to clean up the messiness he makes.

_____10. Being able to interact with a variety of people makes my job thorough enjoyable.

EXERCISE 3

Directions: Fill in each blank with the correct form of the verb in parentheses.

Examples: Writing in English is quite <u>challenging</u> (challenge) for me.

I am <u>confused</u> (confuse) about what the lecturer meant by some of his statements.

1. My professor's absence was _____ (surprise) to all of us in the class.

2. The room, with its chipping paint, leaking roof, and lack of light, was _____ (depress).

3. Mario is _____ (interest) in the topic of the lecture because it is related to his research.

4. Natalie was _____ (puzzle) by the grade she received on her test.

5. Your ability to type quickly and accurately is _____ (amaze).

6. The amount of money raised by the walkathon was _____ (astonish).

7. Jack was completely ＿＿＿＿＿＿ (surprise) by the party his

friends gave for him.

8. This book is one of the most ＿＿＿＿＿＿ (entertain) books

that I have ever read.

EXERCISE 4

Directions: Practice making comparisons by writing sentences following
the example given below.

Example: Compare two academic courses you have taken or are
familiar with.

*The new course on cultural anthropology is more popular than
the old one.*

1. Compare two different makes of cars.

2. Compare this month's weather to last month's.

3. Compare two cities you have lived in or visited.

4. Compare the price of food in your country of origin with that of

another country.

5. Compare an aspect of your school or job with your expectation of

it before you started.

EXERCISE 5

Directions: In the following student paragraph, correct the underlined
word-form errors. Write the correct form of the word above
each incorrect word form. The first one has been done for you.

My bilingualism may benefit me in terms of job opportunities. First of all,

immigrants
more and more ~~immigrates~~ arrive in the United States every year. To help these

newcomers or to do business with them, bilingual and multilingual employees

are needed. For example, banks, law firms, and insurance agencies often

need employees who can <u>communicative</u> with both non-English speakers

and English-speaking clients. Therefore, because I speak Spanish <u>good</u>,

I might find many job opportunities in places where there are a lot of Spanish speakers, such as Los Angeles, New York, Chicago, and Miami. Second, if I can <u>achievement</u> my goal of having my own <u>dentist</u> clinic, Spanish-speaking clients may be a good source for my <u>earns</u>. Many Spanish speakers <u>tendency</u> to feel more <u>comfort</u> with Spanish-speaking doctors and dentists. Even Hispanics who speak English very well would <u>preference</u> a Spanish-speaking dentist to an English-speaking one. So, overall, I may benefit <u>economical</u> from my <u>knowledgement</u> of two languages.

EXERCISE 6

Directions: The following student paragraph contains nine errors in word form. Correct each word-form error. The first one has been done for you.

directly
Being multilingual enables me to communicate ~~direct~~ with many people. Even though I mostly use English in my everyday life, especially at the university, I still use Cantonese to communicate with my relatives. My grandmother, for example, who just recently came to the United States from Vietnam and is now living with my family, cannot understand English. The only language she speaks fluent is Cantonese. Therefore, knowing how to speak Cantonese allows me to communicate easy with her. By talking with her, I have learned some of my family's historical. She told me that she and my grandfather were originally from China, and she explanation what her life was like there. She has also told me interest stories about China that I never would have heard if I did not speak Cantonese. Besides Cantonese, I also speak Vietnamese. Being able to speak these languages in Asian restaurants has also been benefit to me. The restaurant employees recognize that they and I are from similar backgrounds because we speak the same language. They, therefore, give more attentive to me than to customers who do not speak the language. Thus, being able to speak these languages opens the door for me to communication closely with many different people.

EXERCISE 7

Directions: Read a short news article. Then, underline all of the words with noun, verb, adjective, or adverb suffixes in two paragraphs of the article. Identify the part of speech (noun, verb, adjective, or adverb) of each word you have underlined.

Post-test **What Do You Know Now?**

A Fill in the blanks with the correct word forms for these words, which are commonly used in academic and professional writing.

Noun	Verb	Adjective	Adverb
1. _____	analyze	_____	_____
2. recovery	_____	_____	
3. _____	_____	contributed	
4. _____	facilitate	_____	
5. norm	_____	_____	_____
6. _____	promote	_____	
7. _____	_____	involved	
8. modification	_____	_____	
9. _____	_____	_____	finally
10. _____	predict	_____	_____

B Check (✓) the part of speech for each of the words listed. Then, underline the suffix that indicates the part of speech.

	Noun	Verb	Adjective	Adverb
1. equate	____	____	____	____
2. individually	____	____	____	____
3. generosity	____	____	____	____
4. calmly	____	____	____	____
5. attentiveness	____	____	____	____
6. ability	____	____	____	____
7. dependable	____	____	____	____
8. regulation	____	____	____	____
9. strengthen	____	____	____	____
10. doubtful	____	____	____	____

C Circle the correct word form to complete each sentence.

1. Deborah decided that she would like to major in biochemistry in preparation for (graduation/graduate) school in pharmacy.

2. The school cafeteria is (periodical/periodically) inspected by the health department.

3. We need to (considerate/consider) what to add to our grocery list for the party.

4. Gerald needs to find his anatomy textbook to (refer/reference) to some diagrams.

5. My advisor has given me much care and (supporting/support).

D Fill in each blank with the present or past participle of the word in parentheses.

1. The student found several _____ (confuse) sentences on the test.

2. A run-on sentence is also known as a _____ (fuse) sentence.

3. The newest theory about the 1918 flu virus is _____ (interest).

4. The new student union building is _____ (locate) behind the administration building.

5. Some of the Halloween costumes were very _____ (amuse).

E Write the comparative and the superlative forms for the following adjectives.

Adjective	Comparative Form	Superlative Form
1. good	_____	_____
2. difficult	_____	_____
3. fast	_____	_____
4. bad	_____	_____
5. light	_____	_____
6. foggy	_____	_____

F In the following e-mail a student wrote to her tutor, find and correct the five errors with word forms.

Dear Barbara,

How are you? I have not had a chance to visit you late since school keeps

me very busy. However, I really appreciated your input on my application

for pharmacy school, particularly the part where I talked about learning

American Sign Language and the causes of deaf.

Thank you, too, for sending me such a detailed e-mail on how to success in

taking the entrance exam.

I made a quick visiting to my father yesterday. He was happiness to see me

and to find out that I am doing well in school.

Best,

Tuyet

APPLY WHAT YOU HAVE LEARNED TO WRITING

Select a writing topic and follow the steps in Appendix A on page 337.

Topic 1:

Describe in detail one of your hobbies, special interests, or talents. How long have you been pursuing this activity and why is it important to you? How does it enrich your life?

Topic 2:

Think about your birth order among your brothers and sisters. Are you the youngest, the oldest, or somewhere in the middle? First, explain where you are in the order of birth of the siblings in your family. Then, explain how you think this birth order has affected you as a person. If you are an only child, explain how this situation has affected you.

Topic 3:

Choose a book that you enjoyed reading or a movie that you enjoyed seeing. Briefly explain what the book or movie was about. Then, explain what you particularly liked about it or in what way it influenced you.

PREPOSITIONS

GOALS

- Learn why mastering prepositions is important in writing

- Understand three problems writers commonly encounter when using prepositions

- Use prepositions correctly in exercises and writing assignments

Think about some of your favorite foods. What is one food item that you particularly like? What are the ingredients and how is it prepared? How and when is it usually eaten?

LEARN WHAT THE ERROR IS

Errors with Prepositions

An error with a preposition occurs when a preposition has been incorrectly used or not used when needed. **Prepositions** (for example, *in, at, towards,* or *in spite of*) link nouns, pronouns, and adjectives to other words in a sentence. Prepositions can be used in a phrase (*during the daytime*), as a particle with a two- or three-word verb (*turn in, check up on*), or after an adjective or noun (*be happy about, take credit for*). The editing symbol for a preposition error is *prep*.

Knowing how to use prepositions correctly is very important in formal writing. Although an error with a preposition is a local (less serious) error and thus affects only part of a sentence, many errors with prepositions in a piece of writing make it difficult for the reader to concentrate on the content while he or she is trying to mentally correct the prepositions.

In academic and professional writing, the reader expects to see correct use of prepositions. Preposition use is generally idiomatic (unpredictable) rather than rule-based, so which preposition to use must often be memorized. While mastering prepositions is challenging, each small improvement in preposition use makes a text easier to read.

Suggestions for Reducing Errors

- Remember that there are few rules for prepositions, so preposition use is learned mainly through listening and reading.

- Memorize **phrasal verbs** (two- and three-word verbs) so that you can use them correctly and automatically. Use a learner's dictionary to look up phrasal verbs that you are unsure of.

- Improve your control of prepositions by paying attention to them when you read and listening for them when people speak.

- Ask an instructor or a fluent speaker for help when you are unsure about a preposition.

Check Your Understanding

Write answers to the following questions. Share your answers with another student.

1. What happens when a reader encounters too many errors with prepositions in a piece of writing?

2. Why is it necessary to learn preposition use through usage and memorization?

GRAMMAR JOURNAL ENTRY 15   PREPOSITIONS

Respond to the following in your grammar journal.

1. What are three things that you usually do in the morning, at noon, and at night? List what these activities are and at what time you do them. Then, write a paragraph about whether or not you would like to change any of these activities to another time. Underline five prepositions in your paragraph.

2. Look in a magazine or a newspaper for an article that interests you. Then, underline five two- or three-word verbs that you find. Write sentences with each of those verbs.

UNDERSTAND COMMON PROBLEMS

This section presents three problems that writers commonly encounter with prepositions. First, take the pre-test to see what you already know about prepositions. When you finish, check your answers on page 354. Then, carefully study each problem and the examples that illustrate it. Pay particular attention to those problems that correspond to the pre-test questions you had difficulty with. Remember that becoming aware of the types of errors you most often make with prepositions will increase your chances of avoiding these errors in your writing.

Pre-test   **What Do You Already Know?**

Test your ability to recognize and correct errors with prepositions.

A   Correct the marked preposition errors. These are examples of the three common problems that are presented in this unit.

> *prep*
> **Problem 1** Erik is taking summer school classes <u>in</u> Harvard University.

> *prep*
> **Problem 2** The dentist said that there are three reasons <u>of</u> my new cavities: too much candy, too little flossing, and too soft a toothbrush.

> *prep*
> **Problem 3** Jack is seeking <u>for</u> information about snakes on the Internet.

B   Underline and correct the one error in each of the following sentences. (The errors are not in any particular order.)

1.   Registration of next semester's classes starts next week.

2.   Linh wanted to study the grammar rules with herself to get ready for the test.

3.   When I arrived, the class was already discussing about the Civil War.

Three Common Problems

Problem 1

The wrong preposition has been used in a prepositional phrase or in an idiomatic expression using a preposition.

Incorrect: My brother lives <u>*prep*</u>in Anderson Street.

Correct: My brother lives <u>on</u> Anderson Street.

Incorrect: Tran always gives the correct answers <u>*prep*</u>of the math homework questions.

Correct: Tran always gives the correct answers <u>to</u> the math homework questions.

Incorrect: Jaime gets frustrated if he makes the same error time <u>*prep*</u>by time.

Correct: Jaime gets frustrated if he makes the same error time <u>after</u> time.

Incorrect: Marjan will often meet us for coffee <u>*prep*</u>in the night.

Correct: Marjan will often meet us for coffee <u>at</u> night (or <u>in</u> the evening).

> SELF-HELP STRATEGY: Be aware that because the rules for preposition use are very limited, you may want to ask an instructor or a fluent speaker for help, as he or she knows intuitively whether the preposition "sounds right" in that particular case. However, since some rules do exist, it is a good idea not only to learn the rules below but also to read about preposition use in a comprehensive ESL grammar textbook.

Problem 2

The incorrect preposition has been used following an adjective or a noun.

Incorrect: My mother worked, so the <u>responsibility of</u> *prep* the housework was mine.

Correct: My mother worked, so the <u>responsibility for</u> the housework was mine.

Incorrect: I sometimes feel <u>uncomfortable in</u> *prep* speaking up in class.

Correct: I sometimes feel <u>uncomfortable about</u> speaking up in class.

Correct: I sometimes feel <u>uncomfortable</u> speaking up in class.
(no preposition needed)

> SELF-HELP STRATEGY: Remember that you can look up the adjective or noun in a learner's dictionary to see which preposition(s) it can be used with. Remember that some nouns or adjectives can take more than one preposition depending on meaning.
>
> EXAMPLES:
>
> I am <u>happy about</u> getting a part-time job. (A learner's dictionary will show various prepositions that can be used with *happy*.)
>
> I am <u>happy to</u> help you.

Problem 3

A verb + preposition problem has occurred.

1. The preposition that should be used with a given verb is missing.

prep

Incorrect: I will have to study more tonight <u>to compensate</u>∧the time I lost yesterday.

Correct: I will have to study more tonight <u>to compensate for</u> the time I lost yesterday.

prep

Incorrect: The two teams will <u>compete</u>∧each other next week.

Correct: The two teams will <u>compete with</u> each other next week.
(or <u>compete against</u>)

2. A preposition is used when it is not needed after a given verb.

prep

Incorrect: In my paper, I <u>emphasized about</u> the need for smaller classes.

Correct: In my paper, I <u>emphasized</u> the need for smaller classes.

prep

Incorrect: The reporter got her information by <u>interviewing with</u> three people.

Correct: The reporter got her information by <u>interviewing</u> three people.

3. The wrong preposition has been used after a given verb.

prep

Incorrect: The professor often <u>refers on</u> the textbook.

Correct: The professor often <u>refers to</u> the textbook.

prep

Incorrect: In the spring, Mike often <u>suffers of</u> allergies.

Correct: In the spring, Mike often <u>suffers from</u> allergies.

4. A preposition that is part of a phrasal verb (two- or three-word verb) is incorrect or missing.

Incorrect: He just <u>hung off</u> the phone.
prep

Correct: He just <u>hung up</u> the phone.

Incorrect: We will have to <u>call over</u> the birthday party.
prep

Correct: We will have to <u>call off</u> the birthday party.

Incorrect: After being sick, I had to <u>catch up</u> my assignments.
prep

Correct: After being sick, I had to <u>catch up on</u> my assignments.

> SELF-HELP STRATEGY: Many errors with verbs and prepositions can be avoided by checking the verbs in a learner's dictionary.

REVIEW GRAMMAR SOLUTIONS

In this section, you will learn selected rules and be given guidelines that will help you use prepositions correctly.

Prepositions of Direction, Place, Position, and Time

1. Prepositions of Direction

PREPOSITION	MOVEMENT	EXAMPLE
around	in a circular fashion	around the block
into	to an interior location	into the room; into the box
onto	to a surface	onto the desk
to	in the direction of	to work
toward(s)	in the direction of	toward the school

2. Prepositions of Place

PREPOSITION	PLACE	EXAMPLE
at	an address	at 1123 Harvard Drive
at	a specific place	at school; at home; at the airport; at the store; at the movies
in	a city, country	in Dallas; in Canada
in	inside of a place	in the language lab; in the library
on	a street	on First Street

3. Prepositions of Position

PREPOSITION	POSITION	EXAMPLE
above; over	higher than	(an airplane) above us; (hit the ball) over the net; above the line
behind	in back of	behind the building
below; under	lower than	under the magazine; below the window
between	somewhere in the middle of	between San Diego and Los Angeles
in	inside of	in my room; in the car
in front of	ahead of something or someone	in front of the building
near	close to	near Chicago
next to; beside	adjacent to	the house next to Jim's; beside the sofa
on	on top of; on a surface	on the desk; on the wall

4. Prepositions of Time

PREPOSITION	TIME	EXAMPLE
at	specific time of day	at 8:00 AM; at 3:30 PM sharp
in	month, year	in February; in 2012
in	time of day	in the morning; in the afternoon; in the evening (but at night)
on	day of the week, date	on Monday; on June 1

Using Prepositions with Phrasal Verbs

A phrasal verb is a verb + a preposition. In a phrasal verb, the preposition is sometimes called a **particle**. Together, the verb and its preposition or prepositions create the meaning of the verb. Although phrasal verbs are used more frequently in speaking than in formal writing, they are also used in written English.

Phrasal verbs and their synonyms are also treated in Unit 13, "Word Choice."

1. **Phrasal verbs frequently have a more formal one-word synonym that can be used in written English.**

Examples:

We had to <u>call off</u> the party. (*call off* has the same meaning as *cancel*)

Could you <u>turn down</u> the volume? (*turn down* has the same meaning as *decrease* or *lower*)

I am trying <u>to get hold</u> of my friend. (*get hold of* has the same meaning as *contact* or *reach*)

2. **Phrasal verbs are highly complex in that a preposition can completely change the meaning of the verb.** Read the following examples and note how the meaning changes.

Examples:

Please <u>turn on</u> the light. (meaning = start the operation of)

Please <u>turn in</u> the assignment on Friday. (meaning = submit)

I usually <u>turn over</u> a lot when I sleep. (meaning = roll from one side to the other)

3. **Another complexity is that some phrasal verbs have more than one meaning depending on the context.**

Examples:

Please <u>turn down</u> the volume. (meaning = decrease or lower)

I hope you will not <u>turn down</u> the job because of the pay. (meaning = refuse)

Five thousand people <u>turned out</u> to hear the concert. (meaning = came)

Please <u>turn out</u> the light. (meaning = extinguish)

The best way to learn these two- and three-word verbs is to listen for them in conversations and to look for them in written material. They are also listed in dictionaries.

IMPROVE YOUR WRITING STYLE

THE NINE MOST COMMON PREPOSITIONS

Improve your ability to use prepositions by becoming aware of the most commonly used prepositions. The nine most common prepositions are at, in, on, by, from, to, for, of, *and* with.

Examples:

I met my professor <u>at</u> a conference in Illinois.

<u>At</u> present, I am a fourth-year Ph.D. student in economics.

I plan to take a biochemistry course <u>in</u> the spring.

<u>In</u> this laboratory course, I developed skills <u>in</u> recording data.

<u>On</u> Friday, the president visited an elementary school in Washington, D.C.

The children loved his visit. <u>On</u> the other hand, critics questioned it as political.

We obtained our information <u>by</u> performing studies in five states.

One study was conducted <u>by</u> a marketing company in Texas.

We obtained our blood samples <u>from</u> patients who volunteered.

Phase II of our research will take place <u>from</u> May to July of this year.

After class, I need to go <u>to</u> the bookstore and <u>to</u> the library.

According <u>to</u> some studies, second-hand smoke is dangerous <u>to</u> children.

The manager was absent, so her assistant chaired the meeting <u>for</u> her.

The committee identified numerous reasons <u>for</u> the problem.

The price <u>of</u> gasoline seems to go up every year.

Fifty percent <u>of</u> the survey respondents said they were trying to drive less.

Jacob is writing a report <u>with</u> two other graduate students.

They have not finished <u>with</u> their research yet.

AVOIDING WORDINESS

Overuse of prepositional phrases can make a piece of writing very wordy as well as difficult to read. Below are some suggestions to edit out wordiness with prepositional phrases.

Continued on page 310.

IMPROVE YOUR WRITING STYLE (CONT.)

You can replace the prepositional phrase with a verb.

Example:

> What are the effects <u>of large chains and superstores on smaller, family-owned businesses</u>?

> How <u>do large chains and superstores affect smaller, family-owned businesses</u>?

You can replace the prepositional phrase with a possessive.

Example:

> The illness <u>of her mother</u> left the family in turmoil.

> <u>Her mother's illness</u> left the family in turmoil.

You can replace the prepositional phrase with an adjective.

Examples:

> A country needs a president <u>with intelligence</u> and with good people skills.

> A country needs an <u>intelligent</u> president with good people skills.

> That school district requires students to wear shirts or blouses <u>with navy and white stripes</u>.

> That school district requires students to wear <u>navy and white striped</u> shirts or blouses.

PRACTICE WHAT YOU HAVE LEARNED

EXERCISE 1

Directions: Underline and correct the preposition errors. Each sentence has one error. The first one has been done for you.

1. They had to be nice <u>with</u> their neighbors. *to*

2. I am a student in the music department in the University of Michigan.

3. The revised schedule gives students a choice with dates.

4. All the graduate classes in this department are held at the early afternoon and evening.

5. It is easy to clean the kitchen when all you have to do is load the dishes to the dishwasher.

6. My lab partner lives in 1003 Rosemont Avenue.

7. Living in an apartment is difficult if you are not happy of your roommates.

8. If you are looking for your car keys, I saw them lying in the table.

9. If my trip goes as planned, I will see you at Monday.

10. My uncle, who owns a successful business, has had a big influence in me.

EXERCISE 2

Directions: Fill in each blank with the correct preposition to accompany a verb, noun, or adjective. You may want to refer to a dictionary.

Example: My sister is very proud __*of*__ her swimming award.

1. My neighbors make so much noise that I have trouble concentrating _____ my work.

2. I dreamed _____ you last night.

3. I do not know if I can ever forgive you _____ misleading me.

4. Are you interested _____ going camping with us next weekend?

5. My advisor insisted _____ my submitting a research proposal by January.

6. I will have to think _____ what you have said before I give you an answer.

7. I am hopeful that I will succeed _____ finishing my
bachelor's degree by next year.

8. My parents do not object _____ my borrowing their car
on weekends.

9. We want to take advantage _____ the nice weather and
go on a picnic.

10. My brother's carelessness about food safety resulted _____
his getting food poisoning.

EXERCISE 3

Directions: Check your knowledge of prepositions in two- and three-word
verbs by filling in each blank with the correct preposition.

Example: When her fever got worse, she was sorry she had put _off_
going to the doctor.

1. The school has not yet found _____ who gave that
generous gift of $500.

2. If you have not finished your homework before class, you had
better come up _____ a good excuse for the teacher.

3. He was so angry about being overcharged that he tore
_____ the bill.

4. If you are not going to use that equipment, please get rid
_____ it.

5. My cousin is very sociable; he likes to interact _____
people.

EXERCISE 4

Directions: Fill in each blank in the following e-mail message with the correct preposition.

Dear World Bank Internship Coordinator:

I am very pleased to apply _____ an internship with the World Bank
(1)
for next summer. I am a second-year graduate student _____ the
(2)
Economics Department _____ the University of California, Davis. My
(3)
research focuses _____ International Economics.
(4)

I am certain that your internship program will provide me with valuable hands-
on experience that I will be able to use _____ my future career.
(5)
Before becoming a graduate student, I worked _____ the Bank of
(6)
Korea from 2009 _____ 2011, mainly _____ the Foreign
(7)   (8)
Exchange department.

I would be honored to work _____ your organization _____
(9)   (10)
my summer vacation. I have attached my résumé and would also be happy to
participate _____ a phone or face-to-face interview. Please feel free
(11)
to contact me _____ the following phone number or e-mail address:
(12)
550-327-6655; jsmithstone@somewhere.net

Thank you for your consideration, and I look forward _____ hearing
(13)
from you.

Sincerely,

Jason Smithstone

Graduate Student in Economics

University of California, Davis

Post-test   **What Do You Know Now?**

A Fill in the blanks with the correct commonly used prepositions.

1. I live _____ Chicago.

2. I am a student _____ Northwestern University.

3. A botanical garden can be found _____ the college campus.

4. Chelsea is a student _____ the Environmental Science Department. Cindy is _____ the field of computer science.

5. Lin is doing research _____ the effects of vitamins on the immune system. Sandra is doing research _____ wireless networks.

6. The lecture for the entrance exam was _____ the topic of homelessness in small towns.

7. Frank's work focuses _____ human memory processes.

8. My calculus class meets _____ the afternoon _____ Tuesdays and Thursdays _____ 2:10 PM.

9. Rashid was admitted _____ Ohio State University to study maternal and child nutrition.

10. Moe is interested _____ a career in advertising.

11. I have enrolled _____ three classes this quarter.

12. This semester, classes began _____ Thursday, September 15.

B Fill in the blank in each sentence with the correct preposition to follow a noun or adjective.

1. Sharif was very nervous _____ taking the driving test for the first time.

2. Some stores are happy to give refunds while others are hesitant _____ giving refunds and would rather give credit instead.

3. The reason _____ the delay in the flight's arrival was not explained.

4. During the summer months, there is an abundance _____ produce in the farmers' markets.

5. Many students say that the preparation _____ taking an entrance exam is often harder than the exam itself.

C Fill in the blank in each sentence with the correct preposition or prepositions to complete the verb.

1. In mid-April, we need to register _____ summer school to get the classes we want.

2. When Jacques looked up _____ the clock, he saw he had only ten minutes left to complete the exam.

3. Before I give you a definite answer, I feel I need to think _____ the situation further.

4. Mark was asked to write an article _____ the conference that he attended.

5. The professor has referred _____ Shakespeare's works numerous times.

D Correct the marked errors in each paragraph in the short biographical statements by writing the correct preposition, adding a preposition, or deleting a preposition. The first one has been done for you.

1.   *in*
    Gail Wong is a senior <u>of</u> chemistry and expects to graduate <u>at</u> June of this year. After she graduates, she hopes to do graduate work <u>on</u> the area of organic chemistry. She just completed one year as a study-abroad student <u>for</u> Beijing University, where she learned to speak Chinese. Besides her academic studies, Gail <u>serves student</u> body vice president, and she is <u>interested swimming</u>. Her hobbies include listening to classical music and reading.

2.   Michael Miyagi is a first-year graduate student working <u>in</u> a master's degree <u>for</u> civil engineering. He has a bachelor's <u>degree civil</u> engineering from Hokkaido University <u>at</u> Japan. Before coming to the United States, he <u>worked a</u> Japanese company that plans, designs, and constructs urban freeway systems <u>on</u> the Tokyo metropolitan area. While in Japan, he was <u>involved designing</u> new freeways. Currently, his research focuses <u>in</u> ways to reduce traffic congestion and air pollution. In his free time, he likes to play baseball and spend time <u>for</u> his family.

APPLY WHAT YOU HAVE LEARNED TO WRITING

Select a writing topic and follow the steps in Appendix A on page 337.

Topic 1:

Think about your favorite restaurants. Choose one of them and describe what it is like in terms of food, atmosphere, service, and any other aspects you would like to focus on. Then, say why you would recommend this restaurant to your friends.

Topic 2:

Advise someone on how to be a successful student. What should a student do to be successful? If you are working, you may want to give advice on how to be successful in your line of work.

Topic 3:

Compare and contrast the person you are today with the person you were two or more years ago. What are the major changes in yourself? What has stayed the same?

SECTION 3

BEYOND GRAMMAR: OTHER WAYS TO MAKE YOUR WRITING CLEAR

This section has five parts:
A. Expand Your Vocabulary;
B. Achieve an Academic Writing Style;
C. Avoid Nonidiomatic and Unclear Sentences;
D. Improve Flow of Ideas;
E. Revise Your Writing.

Each part focuses on an aspect of writing that goes beyond grammatical errors and addresses clarity and style. This section will help you develop an effective writing style.

PART A: EXPAND YOUR VOCABULARY

Language learners, in general, are always working to expand their vocabulary. As a writer, you want to be more precise and accurate in your choice of words. Similar to the way you acquired words in your first language, learning vocabulary in another language is a gradual process. It happens over a period of time by exposure to the language through reading, listening, and interacting with others who speak it. Following these suggestions will help you take a more active role in expanding your academic English vocabulary.

1. Read in English as much as possible.

One of the best ways to acquire new vocabulary is through reading. Make it your goal to understand what you are reading. Guess the meanings of words from their context whenever possible but look up key words (those central to the meaning of the text) in a dictionary.

2. Make vocabulary expansion a daily habit.

Find the learning strategy that works best for you and use it daily. You may wish to make vocabulary cards and review them regularly. It can also be helpful to keep a vocabulary notebook, paper or electronic, which you can carry with you.

3. Become an active learner of vocabulary.

When you learn a new word, you will have a better chance of making it a part of your active vocabulary if you focus on learning more than just its meaning. For example, you should also learn how to pronounce the word, a task that has become much easier now that online dictionaries provide pronunciation. It is also important to learn collocations, that is, words that are commonly used together, such as *the right price* or *a successful outcome*. Many learner's dictionaries now include collocations. In addition, the example sentences given in many dictionary definitions are also very useful. Focus on how to use the word in context by writing it in a phrase or a sentence of your own.

4. Decide which words you need to know and focus on learning those.

Generally, words you should learn are those that are used frequently in your field of study or work. Make a note of words that appear frequently in your textbooks, during class, in articles you read, and in discussions with your classmates and professors. It is also very useful to study words in the Academic Word List, a list of words commonly used in academic texts, which was developed at Victoria University in New Zealand. Many vocabulary textbooks are now based on the Academic Word List and can be used for independent study.

5. **Become familiar with the meanings of common prefixes, suffixes, and roots of words.**

By knowing the meanings of common prefixes, suffixes, and roots of words, you can guess the meaning of words that contain them. For example, if you know that the meaning of the prefix *anti-* is *against* and that the meaning of the prefix *post-* is *after*, you can more easily guess the meaning of words such as *antisocial, antibiotic, postwar,* or *postgraduate.* If you know that the root *dict* means *say*, you can guess that the words *predict, diction, dictionary, dictation,* and *valedictorian* have something to do with *saying* or *words.* Similarly, if you know the root *hydro* means *water*, you will know that the words *hydrology* and *hydraulic* have something to do with *water.*

Knowing suffixes will also help you identify the part of speech (noun, verb, adjective, adverb) of a word. For example, the suffix *-ment* as in *requirement* or *agreement* identifies a word as a noun. The suffix *-en,* on the other hand, as in *widen* or *straighten*, identifies a word as a verb and also has the meaning of *to make,* as in *to make wide* or *to make straight.* The suffix *-ee,* as in *employee* or *payee*, identifies a word as a noun and also has the meaning of a person who is doing or has received a certain action. For more information on common suffixes, see Unit 14, "Word Forms." For information on common prefixes and word roots, consult vocabulary textbooks or dictionaries.

6. **Put yourself in an English-speaking environment as much as possible and become an active listener.**

Listen actively for new words and phrases. Do not be afraid to ask the speaker, when possible, to explain words you do not understand. For example, you can ask, *"What did you mean by . . . ?"* or *"I'm not sure I understand what . . . means."*

Electronic media are good sources for active listening. Many radio stations and TV networks, such as National Public Radio (NPR) and Cable News Network (CNN), offer informational programs that can serve as a source of new vocabulary. Websites, ranging from educational sites to news sites, are also excellent resources for vocabulary building. With electronic media, you can watch or listen to something over and over.

7. **Relax and take your time.**

Realize that expanding your vocabulary *will* take time. However, commit yourself to working actively to expand it by using some of the above strategies. Most importantly, whenever possible, try to use the new words that you have learned in your own speaking and writing in order to move them from your passive vocabulary—words that you have heard and are familiar with—to your active vocabulary—words that you can confidently use in speaking and writing.

Exercises for Practice

EXERCISE 1

Interview at least two fluent speakers of English. Ask them how they learn new words and expand their vocabulary. Then, interview at least two nonnative speakers of English and ask them how they learn new words and what strategies they find useful for expanding their vocabulary. Finally, write up a list of all the ways that people you have interviewed expand their vocabulary. Explain which strategies you feel would be most useful and appropriate for you to use for expanding your own vocabulary.

EXERCISE 2

Choose an article that interests you in a newspaper, magazine, or online, or choose a section in a chapter from one of your textbooks. As you read, underline or highlight all the words that are new or unfamiliar to you. Decide which of the underlined words are important for you to know in order to understand the text and look those up in a dictionary. After you have read the article or section, make a list of the words you want to learn and incorporate into your active vocabulary. On your list, include each new word and its definition, along with a sentence that illustrates its use.

PART B: ACHIEVE AN ACADEMIC WRITING STYLE

Academic writing in English is clear and concise. It is also formal in its use of vocabulary and sentence structure, whereas spoken English is often more informal. When writing in the academic or professional world, you need to adopt an academic or formal writing style. Although style is covered throughout this textbook, Part B highlights certain features of academic writing style you can readily incorporate into your own writing.

One of the best ways to become familiar with academic style is to read authentic samples of writing, such as articles and reports, and to use them as models for your own writing. These samples not only will help familiarize you with formal word choice and sentence structure but also will help you become familiar with standard formats and common language used in many types of academic and professional writing, such as term papers, lab reports, journal articles, business letters, memos, grant proposals, and progress reports. The following specific suggestions will get you started on your way to achieving an academic writing style.

Suggestions for Achieving an Academic Writing Style

1. **Avoid informal or colloquial language.**

   Original: I need to spend some time sorting the <u>junk</u> in my office.

   Revision: I need to spend some time sorting the <u>material</u> in my office.

   Original: Analyzing the data has been <u>rough</u>.

   Revision: Analyzing the data has been <u>challenging</u> (or <u>difficult</u>).

2. **Use single-word verbs as much as possible rather than phrasal verbs (two- and three-word verbs), as single-word verbs are generally more formal and concise.**

   Original: First, heat the solution to the boiling point. Then, <u>keep on</u> boiling it for at least two minutes.

   Revision: First, heat the solution to the boiling point. Then, <u>continue</u> boiling it for at least two minutes.

   Original: The medicine will not <u>get rid of</u> the problem, but it will lessen the symptoms.

   Revision: The medicine will not <u>cure</u> (or <u>alleviate</u>) the problem, but it will lessen the symptoms.

   > **Note:** For more information on using single-word verbs, see Unit 13, "Word Choice," beginning on page 269.

3. **Avoid contractions.**

   Original: Applicants who <u>don't</u> have strong computer skills <u>won't</u> be as competitive as those who do.

   Revision: Applicants who <u>do not</u> have strong computer skills <u>will not</u> be as competitive as those who do.

4. Avoid addressing the reader directly as "you."

Original: If you receive less than 80 on the TOEFL iBT™, <u>you</u> may not be able to enter some U.S. universities.

Revision: <u>Applicants who receive less than 80 on the TOEFL iBT™</u> may not be able to enter some U.S. universities.

Original: First, <u>you heat</u> the solution. Then, <u>you let</u> it boil for five minutes.

Revision: First, <u>heat</u> the solution. Then, <u>let</u> it boil for five minutes.

5. Avoid asking the reader direct questions.

Original: What are the reasons for global warming?

Revision: The reasons for global warming include . . .

Original: How were the data collected?

Revision: The data were collected by . . .

> **Note:** Direct questions are common in textbooks and are also often used as essay titles.

6. As much as possible, place adverbs before the main verb or in a verb phrase after the first auxiliary verb rather than at the beginning or the ending of a sentence.

Original: I will be able to expand my vocabulary <u>eventually</u>.

Revision: I will <u>eventually</u> be able to expand my vocabulary.

Original: Mark uses the writing center <u>regularly</u>.

Revision: Mark <u>regularly</u> uses the writing center.

> **Note:** Transitional words and phrases, many of which are adverbs, often come at the beginning of a sentence. For example: <u>Currently,</u> I am taking four classes.

7. **Use formal negative forms.**

Original: Many programs <u>do not admit any</u> new students in spring semester.

Revision: Many programs <u>admit no new students</u> in spring semester.

Original: <u>Not very much</u> research has been done in this area.

Revision: <u>Little research has been</u> done in this area.

8. **Avoid the use of *etc.*, *and so on*, and *and so forth* because these terms are vague.**

Original: In my free time, I enjoy sports, <u>etc.</u>

Revision: In my free time, I enjoy sports <u>and other activities, such as reading</u>

<u>and cooking</u>.

> **Note:** The term *such as* in the revised sentence above tells the reader that not all examples have been given.

Original: At the meeting, the new project, the old project, the new pay scale,

<u>etc.</u> were discussed.

Revision: At the meeting, the new project, the old project, the new pay scale,

<u>and several other agenda items</u> were discussed.

9. **Try to vary the sentences in your writing by using simple, compound, and complex sentences.**

Examples:

Flooding has been a serious problem in the past few weeks. (a simple sentence)

Although flooding has been a serious problem recently, our area has not been affected so far. (a complex sentence made up of an adverbial clause + an independent clause)

Flooding has been a serious problem recently, causing mandatory evacuation of houses in some areas. (a complex sentence made up of an independent clause + a reduced relative clause)

Ski resorts are affected in that they have suffered lack of business because of road closures. (a complex sentence made up of an independent clause + a noun clause)

A huge amount of rain and unusually warm weather melting the snow led to the flooding we have recently experienced. (a compound subject)

Most of the reservoirs are almost full to capacity, yet farmers are still worried about a possible shortage of irrigation water. (a compound sentence)

Note: For more information on complex sentences (sentences with dependent clauses), see Unit 6, "Relative, Adverbial, and Noun Clauses." For more information on compound sentences and ways to connect sentences, see Unit 9, "Connecting Words."

10. Use passive voice when appropriate.

Examples:

The fruit was <u>harvested,</u> <u>cleaned,</u> and <u>dried</u>.

In the past five years, a number of studies <u>have been done</u> on this topic.

Note: The passive voice is common in some types of academic writing, especially when the writer is describing methods and procedures. For more information on passive voice, see Unit 5, "Passive Voice."

11. Use words that indicate the strength of your claims.

Examples:

The data <u>clearly show</u> that . . . (strong claim)

The data <u>indicate</u> that . . . (weaker claim)

The data <u>suggest</u> that . . . (weaker claim)

Examples:

A <u>dramatic</u> difference was observed. (a very big difference)

A <u>significant</u> difference was observed. (a clearly noticeable difference)

A <u>slight</u> difference was observed. (a minor difference)

Note: See *Improve Your Writing Style*, page 69, in Unit 3, "Modals," for other ways to show the strength of a claim.

Exercises for Practice

EXERCISE 1

Directions: Revise each of the following sentences to make its style more academic. The parts that you should revise are underlined.

1. When <u>you</u> are applying for a job, <u>you</u> may want to use the services of the Career Placement Center on <u>your</u> campus.

2. There <u>has not been any</u> snow this year.

3. Although <u>they've</u> lived here for ten years, my parents <u>haven't</u> learned to write English well.

4. <u>Usually</u>, I communicate with my parents in our native language, Chinese.

5. I have a number of tasks I need to accomplish today: errands, <u>etc.</u>

6. <u>Why is this procedure helpful?</u> First, it is simple and inexpensive to perform.

EXERCISE 2

Directions: Revise each sentence by choosing a more formal or precise word for each of the underlined words or phrases.

Example:

Original: I could not <u>figure out</u> which method to use.

Revision: I could not <u>determine</u> which method to use.

1. The job description <u>talks about</u> the requirements for potential candidates.

2. In my research, I will <u>look at</u> the effects of pesticides on soil.

3. <u>Now</u>, I am finishing my senior year as a chemistry major.

4. I am <u>thinking about</u> applying for the position available at your company.

5. I am writing to inquire about <u>some more</u> details on the research I will be expected to do.

6. I am <u>really</u> interested in a technology support job with your company.

7. Today has been a <u>tough</u> day.

8. Due to advances in medical research, thousands of people can now survive <u>bad</u> diseases.

9. The website contains <u>good</u> information on our research topic.

10. The job applicant has <u>a lot of</u> teaching experience.

PART C: AVOID NONIDIOMATIC AND UNCLEAR SENTENCES

The two causes of unclear sentences are nonidiomatic (awkward or unnatural) language and unclear language. Idiomatic language is the language most commonly used by native and fluent speakers. Do not confuse idiomatic language with an *idiomatic expression* or *idiom*, which is a set expression that means something other than the literal meaning of the words that make it up. For example, "I am all ears" does not mean that a person has many ears; it means "I am eagerly listening."

Unclear and nonidiomatic sentences (or phrases) are not grammar errors; instead, the writer is simply having a problem expressing a particular idea or concept clearly or idiomatically in English. Making such errors is part of learning a new language. You can minimize such errors through exposure to the new language over a period of time.

Nonidiomatic Language

Idiomatic language reflects the way a native or fluent speaker would express an idea or thought. The meaning of a nonidiomatic phrase or sentence is clear, but a native or fluent speaker would not say it that way.

Example

Nonidiomatic: When I write under pressure, I feel that <u>I lack of knowledge of expressing myself with sophisticated English words</u>.

Idiomatic: When I write under pressure, I feel <u>that I cannot use sophisticated English words to express myself</u>.

Idiomatic: <u>I lack the knowledge to express myself in sophisticated English</u>.

Nonidiomatic errors are local (less serious) because they do not prevent understanding; however, if too much of a piece of writing is nonidiomatic, the error can become global (more serious). The editing symbol for a nonidiomatic error is *nonidiom*.

Errors with idiomatic expressions (idioms) are different. Various grammar errors can occur with these expressions. In the sentence *I would rather use a computer than write <u>by a hand</u>*, the idiomatic expression *by a hand* should be *by hand*, an article error. In *I make the same mistakes in English times after times*, <u>*times after times*</u> should be *time after time*, a singular-plural error.

Why Writing Idiomatically Is Important

When reading nonidiomatic phrases or sentences, a fluent speaker will think: "I can understand what the writer is saying, but it sounds awkward to me." Writers need to understand that the closer their writing is to idiomatic English, the easier it will be for the reader to understand.

Suggestions for Improving Your Use of Idiomatic English

Writing idiomatic English is a challenge because idiomatic English is based on usage, not rules. Therefore, how well you master idiomatic English depends to a great extent on your commitment to writing in English and your desire to write as precisely and accurately as possible. Start by focusing on using more idiomatic English in your major or the field in which you will most likely be doing the majority of your writing.

These four suggestions will help you improve your idiomatic use of English.

1. Read in English as much as possible. Doing so is an excellent way to learn new collocations in context.

2. Listen attentively to the way English is used. Realize that learning a language involves more than studying rules. For example, the more you interact with native or fluent English speakers, the more you will tune your ear to idiomatic usage in English; that is, you will use the language the way fluent speakers do.

3. Make it a habit to learn the collocations of words you commonly use or encounter in your studies. Collocations are combinations of words that commonly go together. Some examples include *writing effectively* or *minimum wage*. Using correct collocations is an important aspect of using idiomatic language; collocations offer you a richer way of expressing yourself. Learner's dictionaries will often give common collocations.

4. Ask fluent speakers how they would say a phrase or sentence if one has been marked nonidiomatic on a paper you have written. Then, rewrite that sentence or phrase and memorize it for later use. Writing or saying it three times in a row can help you learn it.

EXERCISE 1

In the following sets of sentences, the writer is attempting to say the same thing in sentence a and sentence b, but one of the sentences is nonidiomatic. Read each set of sentences and then decide whether the underlined part is idiomatic or not. Mark the sentence with an *I* for idiomatic or an *NI* for nonidiomatic.

_____ 1a. Because the next history test is worth 100 points, I will have to study <u>to my fullest</u>.

_____ b. Because the history test is worth 100 points, I will have to study <u>very hard</u>.

_____ 2a. <u>The students in the residence halls</u> waved and smiled at me as I jogged by.

_____ b. <u>The residential students</u> waved and smiled at me as I jogged by.

_____ 3a. I like to study on the first floor of the library because of the <u>vast bloodline</u> of people I can see entering the library.

_____ b. I like to study on the first floor of the library because of the <u>variety</u> of people I can see entering the library.

_____ 4a. Writing compositions for my French class is <u>causing me struggles</u>.

_____ b. Writing compositions for my French class is <u>a struggle for me</u>.

EXERCISE 2

Directions: Underline the nonidiomatic parts of these sentences and then rewrite them in idiomatic English.

Example:

Based on my experience
<u>As my feeling</u> during the last year, the biggest challenge for a new university student is gaining enough confidence to participate fully in class discussions.

1. My mother did not let us go to the mall alone when we were small ages.

2. By talking to people who live in the U.S., I can have a little bit of knowledge about American customs.

3. According to an essay in *Time* for May 20th issue, job openings for college graduates dropped ten percent during the last year.

4. That red blouse does not suit of those purple jeans.

5. My aunt, who lives in Los Angeles, takes the bus everywhere because she is afraid to drive freeway.

6. Now that my English has improved, I can make communication with my friends.

7. After talking with my teacher, I am more understanding of the lecture.

8. It was blowing very hard and then the wind died down in a sudden.

Unclear Language

In an unclear sentence, the reader cannot understand the writer's message. In contrast, a nonidiomatic sentence is usually understandable to the reader. In an unclear sentence, the whole sentence or just part of the sentence may be unclear. The error is global (more serious). The editing symbol for an unclear error is *unclear*.

An unclear message may or may not be ungrammatical. For example, the following unclear sentences are grammatically incorrect and have an unclear message: *Pressure is one of equipment to bring up our skill by ourself* or *I can experienced the truth of studying by a coffee*. In contrast, unclear sentences like *Waiting for these negatives to grow is not a particular way* or *I felt sick that I missed some tasteful water* are correct grammatically but their message is unclear.

Why Writing Clearly Is Important

In academic and professional writing, the reader should not have to guess at meaning. In an unclear sentence, however, the reader must try to guess what the writer is saying—without the writer there. In other words, the meaning of that part of the text is lost. Remember, as a writer, you have the responsibility for conveying your ideas clearly to the reader.

Notice how the unclear sentences in the following passage affect its clarity.

> An example of how decorations can identify us is a stuffed toy stuck on the car's windshield. These toys bring our car to people's attention, and therefore people in other cars [can outline our *unclear* message] even at a very fast speed. [These toys mostly show that *unclear* person really the car and animals.]

Suggestions for Reducing Unclear Sentences

Writers who can write clearly about their personal experiences are often less able to write clearly when they begin to write on more abstract topics in academic or professional writing. The following six suggestions will help pave the way toward clear formal writing.

1. Read examples of academic or professional writing in textbooks, journals, newspapers, or magazines to become familiar with the language and structures you will need to use.

2. Avoid translating from your native language. Try to think and write in English as much as possible.

3. Explain to a classmate or your teacher the idea you are trying to express in writing. Then, write it the way you said it. Do not worry that your English is "too simple." Being clear is more important than sounding sophisticated.

4. Use words that you know rather than "big words" whose meanings you are unsure of. You can refine your language when you revise your writing.

5. Take a sentence that has been marked unclear on your paper and try to rewrite it yourself. Rethink the idea you want to express, determine what you really want to say, and then restate the sentence.

6. Do not be afraid to write some short, simple sentences to clarify your meaning to yourself when you are writing a draft and are in the process of formulating your ideas. Then, in later drafts, you can combine some of these ideas into more complex sentences.

EXERCISE 3

Directions: This student paragraph has been edited so that the only errors in grammar are unclear sentences. With a partner, read the paragraph out loud and listen for unclear sentences. As you listen, put brackets around any unclear sentences or unclear parts of sentences. Then, read the paragraph silently to check it again for unclear sentences. Rewrite the unclear sentences to make them clear. Be prepared to discuss how easy or difficult it is to revise the unclear sentences of another writer.

There are many differences between developing and industrialized nations. One important difference is in the types of worries individuals have in their daily lives. All humans have worries, but one hard tension for some people may differ hardness other people. In many parts of the world, people never think about buying new clothes or the latest model TV or car. All that they think about is how they can get a food from hunger. People have a great terror and this thing has a lot of tension. In contrast, people who live in wealthy nations usually never think about food except where or when they are going to eat, but they have different problems in their lives, such as too much work, family problems, and stress. In both types of countries, rich or poor, people are never free from worry.

PART D: IMPROVE FLOW OF IDEAS

Suggestions for Improving Flow of Ideas in Writing

1. **Combine ideas using subordination and coordination. While you may use some simple sentences consisting of one independent clause, avoid strings of simple sentences.**

Original: The houses are made of mud bricks. They vary in size. They contain no modern conveniences. A few have electricity.

Revision: The houses, which vary in size, are made of mud bricks. Although they contain no modern conveniences, a few have electricity.

Original: Albert Einstein was a theoretical physicist and professor. He taught physics at the Institute for Advanced Study at Princeton University. He was a native of Germany. He began teaching at Princeton in 1939.

Revision: Albert Einstein was a theoretical physicist and professor who taught physics at the Institute for Advanced Study at Princeton University. A native of Germany, he began teaching at Princeton in 1939.

> **Note:** For more information on combining ideas using dependent clauses and connectors, see Unit 6, "Relative, Adverbial, and Noun Clauses," and Unit 9, "Connecting Words."

2. **Refer back to old information using *this* or *these* plus a noun that refers to the old information (for example, *this feature, this process, these difficulties*).**

Examples:

On the first day of class, students write a short essay. This essay is used to help determine the strengths and weaknesses of each student's writing.

Some of the students in the course have asked for more time on their group project. This request is being considered by the course coordinator.

3. **Point back to old information using pronouns (for example *he, she, it, they*) as reference words.**

Examples:

The new factory produces a variety of electronic equipment. According to production statistics, its output has increased significantly despite some initial problems.

The new residential subdivision features three different sizes and models of houses. They are all energy-efficient and reasonably priced.

4. Use introductory prepositional phrases.

Example:

> As a graduate student in computer science, I am concerned about the small number of women compared to men in my field. <u>In my department</u>, there are only a few female graduate students.

> I like to study in a variety of places, depending on the time of day. <u>During the daytime</u>, I like to study at one of several local cafés. <u>At night</u>, on the other hand, I prefer to study at home.

5. Repeat key words and ideas.

Example:

> <u>Caffeine</u> withdrawal can indeed cause headaches. Many <u>coffee</u> drinkers find that if they stop drinking <u>coffee</u> for one day, they get a headache. The result is the same whether or not the <u>coffee</u> drinker has a large or small amount of <u>coffee</u> every day.

6. Use connecting words.

Note: Although you should not rely on connectors alone to achieve flow of ideas in your writing, connecting words are certainly one important aspect of maintaining flow of ideas in writing.

Example:

> The effect of color on an individual's emotions has been studied by a number of researchers in various fields. Some researchers think that red is a tense and stimulating color. Blue, <u>on the other hand</u>, is considered to be calm, cool, and soothing.

Exercises for Practice

EXERCISE 1

Directions: Read this student paragraph. Find and underline the techniques used to make the ideas flow smoothly.

This quarter, I am taking four courses. Because I am doing my Ph.D. degree in the Epidemiology Graduate Group, it is necessary for me to take one required course, Principles of Epidemiology, and two prerequisite courses, Statistics and Short Calculus. The other important course is Academic Writing. Since I am an international student in my first year, I will be spending a lot of time adjusting to the different teaching style here as well as working on improving my English. Also, I have gotten a job as a research assistant doing some laboratory work, which is scheduled on Wednesday and Friday afternoons. In short, I think this quarter will be very challenging for me, especially in terms of adapting to a new academic culture and handling a busy time schedule.

EXERCISE 2

Directions: Read the following student writing. Revise it in order to make the ideas flow more smoothly.

I am taking an engineering course (Advanced Dynamics), an English course, a seminar, and doing research. Totally, it is 12 units. It is a light load for me. I only pay attention to dynamics and English. Because this is my first semester, what is the most important is to improve my English.

PART E: REVISE YOUR WRITING

Once you have written your first draft, you are ready to begin the process of revision. Revision involves rereading and reworking your writing in order to improve it, both in terms of content and language use. Although revising is hard work, the reward is clear, polished writing. Language learners, even though they may initially be afraid of adding more grammatical errors to a piece of writing, can and should revise. As you become accustomed to revising your drafts, you will begin to see your writing as words and ideas in progress, not as words and ideas set in stone as soon as they have been written.

Guidelines for Revision

1. Make a commitment to revision. Realize that good writing is worked and reworked and that it is done to provide clarity, accuracy, and precision for the reader. Good writers know that it may take much rewriting to "get it right."

2. Do not try to revise a large piece of writing all at one time. It takes mental energy to rewrite; trying to do too much at one time will result in uneven revision, with the writing getting noticeably less polished as you become tired.

3. Think of revising in terms of an abstract-to-concrete approach. Divide the revision into three parts: organization, development, and sentences. During revision for organization, make sure that what you have written has a beginning, a middle, and an end. Also make sure that the whole piece of writing fits together—that meaning flows from one sentence to another and

from one paragraph to another. For development, make sure that you have provided enough detail for the reader to "see" what you are writing about. In revising for clear and correct sentences, prioritize your errors, working first on those that you, as an efficient self-editor, know need the most work. For example, you might first choose to edit for verb tenses and subject-verb agreement. Then, you can go back and look carefully at another possible problem area, such as use of dependent clauses or word choice.

4. Work with the whole manuscript. If you are using a computer, too much work with only the screen is not efficient. To see your text, you need, from time to time, to work with the entire text during revision, not only with what you see on one screen.

5. Once you have revised heavily, read your writing out loud to hear its rhythm. As practice, read formal prose out loud, on a regular basis, and you will begin to hear how the words fit together in a steady beat. Good writers recognize that spoken English uses different structures and, thus, has a different rhythm than that of formal written English.

6. Know that you can become a skilled self-editor. That is, you will be able to consciously recognize and correct grammatical errors based on the rules that you have learned. Decide whether it is more efficient for you to monitor for your errors as you are composing your text or to compose your text and then go back and edit for your most serious and frequent errors.

7. Be patient. The rewards of a well-written, revised text are well worth the effort. Moreover, all good writers revise, even the most widely published authors.

EXERCISE 1

Directions: Think about and answer the following questions. Then, discuss your answers with a classmate.

1. How do you approach revising what you have written? Explain the steps you currently use?

2. Would you like to incorporate some of the strategies from the previous guidelines? If so, which ones?

EXERCISE 2

Directions: Think about and answer the following questions. Then, discuss your answers with a classmate.

1. To what extent do you feel you have developed a self-monitor for finding and correcting grammatical errors?

2. At this time, what errors do you look for and how successful are you at finding and correcting them?

3. During the writing process, when do you monitor for errors?

STEPS TO WRITING AND REVISING

After you have chosen a writing topic, follow these steps.

Step 1: Brainstorming Ideas and Gathering Information

Brainstorm ideas about your topic by listing ideas in a format that is comfortable for you. Then, discuss your ideas with a classmate or in a small group.

Step 2: Prewriting

Working by yourself, list some of the ideas you discussed and write down any other ideas that come to mind related to your topic.

Step 3: Writing Your First Draft

Use your list from prewriting to help you write your first draft. Focus on content.

Step 4: Sharing Your Draft

Working with a classmate, read each other's draft. Give feedback to each other using the format given below.

A. Reading for Content

1. What do you like most about this paper?
2. What would you still like to know more about?
3. What suggestions for revision do you have for the writer?

B. Checking for Language Errors

1. What language errors do you notice in the response?
2. Do you notice any errors of the type you have been studying in this unit (e.g., verb-tense errors or preposition errors)?
3. Discuss with your classmate how to correct the above errors.

Step 5: Revising Your Writing

Using your classmate's suggestions as well as your own ideas for revising, write your second draft. Focus on content and accuracy of language and check for the types of errors that you most commonly make. You may wish to rewrite your final draft.

Step 6: Proofreading Your Final Draft

Read your final draft, paying particular attention to the grammatical structure(s) you have studied in this text. Make any necessary changes.

EDITING SYMBOLS

Editing Symbols with Examples

Global Errors More serious errors which usually interfere with understanding

cl clause
A dependent clause is incorrectly formed.

Incorrect: I have a grandmother <u>which her wisdom</u> I value greatly. *(cl)*

Correct: I have a grandmother <u>whose wisdom</u> I value greatly.

Incorrect: Diane Ackerman is an author <u>has written many books I admire</u>. *(cl)*

Correct: Diane Ackerman is an author <u>who has written many books I admire</u>.

Incorrect: The students do not like to ride their bikes <u>because of</u> it is raining. *(cl)*

Correct: The students do not like to ride their bikes <u>because</u> it is raining.

cond conditional
A conditional sentence has been incorrectly used or formed.

Incorrect: If the bus <u>did come</u> on time, I would not have been ten minutes late. *(cond)*

Correct: If the bus <u>had come</u> on time, I would not have been ten minutes late.

Incorrect: If the book does not arrive, I <u>would not be able</u> to read the chapters. *(cond)*

Correct: If the book does not arrive, I <u>will not be able</u> to read the chapters.

conn connector
The connector is incorrect or missing.

Incorrect: The instructor has already written the test. <u>Therefore</u>, he is not completely satisfied with his work and wants to do more revising. *(conn)*

Correct: The instructor has already written the test. <u>However</u>, he is not completely satisfied with his work and wants to do more revising.

modal modal
The modal has been incorrectly used or formed.

Incorrect: The student said that he must not <u>had</u> clicked on the right icon to send his essay. *(modal)*

Correct: The student said that he must not <u>have</u> clicked on the right icon to send his essay.

modal modal	Incorrect: When my calculator broke down, I <u>*modal* must have done</u> the problems on paper.
	Correct: When my calculator broke down, I <u>had to do</u> the problems on paper.
pass passive The passive voice has not been formed or used correctly.	Incorrect: She <u>*pass* has be called</u> to jury duty at the courthouse.
	Correct: She <u>has been called</u> to jury duty at the courthouse.
	Incorrect: If I used a dictionary, my writing <u>*pass* would be improved</u> even more.
	Correct: If I used a dictionary, my writing <u>would improve</u> even more.
ss sentence structure There are missing words, extra words, incorrect syntax, mixed structures, or non-parallel structures.	Incorrect: <u>She ^{*ss*}happy</u> that she passed the exam.
	Correct: She <u>is</u> happy that she passed the exam.
	Incorrect: <u>As for studying ^{*ss*}is not an option</u> this weekend as I am going to Los Angeles.
	Correct: <u>Studying is not an option</u> this weekend as I am going to Los Angeles.
	<u>It is not an option to study</u> this weekend as I am going to Los Angeles.
	Incorrect: My grandmother and I talk about things like <u>dating, falling in love, ^{*ss*} and get married</u>.
	Correct: My grandmother and I talk about things like <u>dating, falling in love, and getting married</u>.
vf incorrect verb form The main verb, verb phrase, or verbal has been incorrectly formed.	Incorrect: The teacher will help<u>s</u> us <u>*vf* learning</u> to control verb tense.
	Correct: The teacher will hel<u>p</u> us <u>to learn</u> to control verb tense.
	Incorrect: These problems <u>*vf* making</u> my writing so horrible.
	Correct: These problems <u>are making</u> my writing so horrible.

vf   incorrect verb form

Incorrect: I will use their writing and reading strategies to improve on *[vf]* my grammar.

Correct: I will use their writing and reading strategies to improve my grammar.

Incorrect: I have decided to take a course on public speaking and keeping *[vf]* working on my oral presentation skills.

Correct: I have decided to take a course on public speaking and keep working on my oral presentation skills.

Incorrect: I did not passed *[vf]* Friday's math quiz.

Correct: I did not pass Friday's math quiz.

vt   incorrect verb tense

The time expressed by the verb is incorrect.

Incorrect: In fact, writing skills are *[vt]* valuable next year when I get a job.

Correct: In fact, writing skills will be valuable next year when I get a job.

Incorrect: On our first day of the linguistics class, our instructor has summed *[vt]* up the importance of developing good academic skills.

Correct: On our first day of the linguistics class, our instructor summed up the importance of developing good academic skills.

Incorrect: I always learn something when I read; for example, I learned *[vt]* new vocabulary.

Correct: I always learn something when I read; for example, I learn new vocabulary.

wo   word order

The word order is incorrect or awkward.

Incorrect: I do not remember when is the job application due *[wo]*.

Correct: I do not remember when the job application is due.

Incorrect: The meeting has been postponed because the chairperson is getting the flu over *[wo]*.

Correct: The meeting has been postponed because the chairperson is getting over the flu.

Local Errors Less serious errors, which, while distracting, usually do not interfere with understanding

art article
The article (*a, an, the*) or determiner (*this, that, these, those*) is incorrect or missing.

Incorrect: I want to give my opinion in *art* <u>right</u> way.

Correct: I want to give my opinion in <u>the right</u> way.

rep preposition
The wrong preposition has been used.

Incorrect: The students *prep* <u>in</u> this university are usually very studious.

Correct: The students <u>at</u> this university are usually very studious.

s/pl incorrect singular or plural noun
The noun is singular when it should be plural or vice versa.

Incorrect: The purpose of rereading is to look for *s/pl* <u>error</u>.

Correct: The purpose of rereading is to look for <u>errors</u>.

sv incorrect subject-verb agreement
The subject and verb do not agree.

Incorrect: When I read history, my reading *sv* <u>slow</u> down because I am unfamiliar with many words.

Correct: When I read history, my reading <u>slows</u> down because I am unfamiliar with many words.

wc word choice
The word does not say what the writer means.

Incorrect: In the medical *wc* <u>industry</u>, a doctor must be a good communicator.

Correct: In the medical <u>field</u>, a doctor must be a good communicator.

wf incorrect word form
The word is correct but its formation is incorrect.

Incorrect: It is *wf* <u>importance</u> to develop good writing skills.

Correct: It is <u>important</u> to develop good writing skills.

Other Errors These errors, commonly made by native speakers, are also common to English learners.

coh coherence

One idea does not flow into the next, either sentence to sentence or paragraph to paragraph. See "Improve Flow of Ideas," page 333.

dm dangling modifier
A phrase or clause has no word to modify.

Incorrect: Hurrying to catch the bus, my essay *dm* was left on my desk.

Correct: Hurrying to catch the bus, I left my essay on my desk.

p punctuation
The punctuation is incorrect or missing.

Incorrect: Also *p* I should try to make friends with them.

Correct: Also, I should try to make friends with them.

pro agree pronoun agreement
The pronoun and its antecedent do not agree.

Incorrect: Shoppers like to go to malls because it *pro agree* has a lot of stores in one place.

Correct: Shoppers like to go to malls because they have a lot of stores in one place.

pro ref pronoun reference
The pronoun reference is not clear.

Incorrect: My supervisor has revised my work schedule several times. This *pro ref* has made organizing my study time difficult.

Correct: My supervisor has revised my work schedule several times. All these changes have made organizing my study time difficult.

sb sentence boundary

There is a fragment, run on, or comma splice.

frag fragment
The sentence is incomplete.

Incorrect: Although he could be a good student *frag*.

Correct: Although he could be a good student, he does not work very hard.

cs comma splice
Two sentences have been joined with a comma.

Incorrect: The administration plans to raise fees, many *cs* students will not be able to afford this university as a consequence.

Correct: The administration plans to raise fees, and many students will not be able to afford this university as a consequence.

ro run on
Two sentences have been joined together without punctuation or a connector between them.

Incorrect: I can see how the writer organized the ideas, also *ro* I may learn some new words in this article.

Correct: I can see how the writer organized the ideas; also, I may learn some new words in this article.

unclear unclear
The meaning is not clear.

Incorrect: Final exams are coming up first *unclear* we will have spring break.

Correct: Final exams are coming up, but first we will have spring break.

ERROR AWARENESS SHEET

This Error Awareness Sheet will help you discover what your sentence-level errors are and prioritize them. When you receive a corrected writing assignment, review your errors and put a check in the second column for each error marked. Then, look at your most frequent errors in the second column and select two or three to begin working on. Put a check next to them in the third column. Work on your most frequent global errors first.

TYPE OF ERROR	TOTAL NUMBER OF ERRORS	TOP-PRIORITY ERRORS TO WORK ON
GLOBAL ERRORS (more serious)		
cl		
cond		
conn		
modal		
pass		
ss		
vf		
vt		
wo		
LOCAL ERRORS (less serious)		
art		
prep		
s/pl		
sv		
wc		
wf		
OTHER ERRORS		
cap		
coh		
cs		
dm		
frag		
lc		
nonidiom		
p		
pro ref/agree		
ro		
sp		
unclear		

SAMPLE PAPER

Directions: Read the sample paper and the instructor's comments. Then, fill in an Error Awareness Sheet for this student. What are the most frequent global errors? What are the most frequent local errors? What should this student have as a priority to work on?

Writing Topic: Discuss the progress you have made so far on your English 25 term paper assignment. In addition to explaining what you have already done and what you are currently working on, comment on the aspect of writing a term paper that has been the most challenging for you.

                       vt   *art*

After five weeks of studies at this university, I learned many skills from English

                                   art

25 course. One of the most important is writing^ term paper. I would like to write

something about my term paper right now.

       vt   *wc*   *s/pl*

I scheduled my term-paper writing progress into ten parts: (1) deciding topics,

(2) collecting reference papers/books, (3) briefly reading those papers/books,

      wc

(4) <u>writing down</u> the outline, (5) reading the papers/books carefully and taking

      vf art

notes, (6) write^ first draft, (7) revising the draft, (8) asking my tutor to comment

                                                      vt

on my paper, (9) typing it, and (10) finally checking the paper. So far I finished

                     sv

the first four steps and is proceeding to the fifth step. I hope I can speed up;

   pro ref   *prep*   *ss*

otherwise <u>it</u> will be very busy <u>on</u> the end of November because [it dues] on

December 4.

     In order to type my term paper, I must learn how to operate Macintosh or

                                              vt

IBM compatible computers because I never use them before, especially two

kinds of word processing packages (Word for Macintosh and WordPerfect

                         vt?   *art*

for Windows). As a result, I attended several lab classes offered by^ computer

  pro ref   *pro ref*

center. <u>It</u> is really interesting and I enjoyed it very much. <u>It</u> is useful for my future

                    pro ref

career too, and I think <u>it</u> is most challenging to me in writing my term paper.

In this response, you have done a careful job of addressing both parts of the question and have illustrated your points with good specifics, including the names of word-processing programs. Good organization, too!

Because your organization is strong, I have marked most of your sentence-level errors as you requested. I would suggest, however, that you first work on verb tense and articles. Also, you will want to work on avoiding unclear references when you use the pronoun <u>it</u>.

ADDITIONAL EXERCISES FOR PRACTICE: EDITING FOR A VARIETY OF ERRORS

EXERCISE 1 Editing for errors with verb tense and verb form

Directions: The following paragraph, written by an exchange student from Korea who is studying in the United States, has ten errors in verb tense and seven errors in verb form. Find and correct these errors.

Aside from study for a degree, I have learned and experience many things from being a student here. First, I had many opportunities to broaden my views. By encounter people from many different backgrounds, I learned about many different points of view. I also came to understand more about the issues facing people from different countries and how people from many different cultures thought. Second, I have learned much about the American culture and people. In the United States, I have encounter many unfamiliar aspects of culture that I have never seen before. Also, the way American people interact is different from what I was used to in my home country. I have try to understand these differences and in the future hope to be a sort of "bridge" that can connect Americans and Koreans. In terms of customs, one of the best ones that I learn is to smile at people. Finally, I greatly improve my English. Now I do not have any fear of speak English, and think in English feels very natural to me. Sometimes, I even dream in English. In my dreams, I spoke in English even to my family! In conclusion, the experience of being here was a great asset for me. When I will return home after a year here, I will be a person who is more open-minded and a person who is a better "citizen of the world."

EXERCISE 2   Editing for errors with articles and singular/plural of nouns

Directions: The following passage was written by a student in an intensive English program. Find and correct the 20 errors with articles and with the singular/plural of nouns.

Note: *Onigiri* and *sushi* are uncountable nouns.

Rice balls (called onigiri) are a type of Japanese food that is much older than the sushi. It is the most popular food to take along while traveling in the Japan. Rice balls are taken on picnics and trips, found at school and work, and put in box lunch. They are made from a cooked rice and shaped into triangle or a ball. The three ingredient that are needed to make Japanese rice balls are cooked rice, salt, some type of filling that has strong flavor, and seaweeds. The filling is put in the center of ball of rice and then it is shaped by hand. Ball of rice is then wrapped in a seaweed.

In my opinion, onigiri could become as popular around the world as sushi. It is a delicious yet an easy-to-make food. A problem that has to be solved, however, is choice of a filling. In Japan, the most popular filling are dried plums, barbecued salmons, and flaked, dried bonito. Recently, tuna and chicken with the mayonnaise have been used and the barbecued beef is becoming more and more popular. In Japan, every family has its own favorites. However, it is difficult to know what kinds of fillings would be appropriate for foreigner. The people I interviewed in California said that they like various kinds of fish, cucumber, chicken, crab meats, or barbecued pork. To my surprise, all of them were very interested in onigiri. I am sure that if we experiment with recipes to get right taste, onigiri will become popular food around the world.

EXERCISE 3   Editing for errors with sentence structure and clauses

Directions: The following paragraph, written by an undergraduate student, contains nine errors with sentence structure and clauses. Find and correct these errors.

For immigrants to a different country, learning a new language is a challenge that they will inevitably face. Some Chinese-speaking immigrants to the United States have a hard time learning English because of their background. In their home country, because English is rarely used, so most people have had little contact with English before coming to the United States. Moreover,

English totally different from Mandarin or Cantonese in both grammar and pronunciation, so requires a lot of practice for an immigrant to be able to use English well and having the confidence to speak it. When immigrants arrive here, many of them have to learn English starting with the alphabet. Even though they may have had professional skills in their home country.

While it is difficult for immigrants to learn English, it also hard for them to find time to study the language. Immigrants usually start to work within a community uses the same language as they do because they need to go to work before they acquire good English skills. At work, they usually communicate with people only in their home language, and, unfortunately, even they want to take English classes, they often cannot find one that they are able to attend because of their busy schedules. By communicating in their home language at work and by not attending language classes, immigrants can spend the whole day without saying even one English sentence. This weekend I went home to San Francisco, I spoke no more than twenty complete sentences in English because I always communicate with my family and friends there in Mandarin. In some communities, a person can spend his or her entire life in this country without learning how to speak English. This situation is much more common the older the immigrants are and sometimes results in a feeling of isolation. Many immigrants feel have lost their social identities and become people without a voice in this "land of opportunity."

EXERCISE 4   Editing for errors with subject-verb agreement and prepositions

Directions: The following biographical statement has 10 errors in subject-verb agreement and with prepositions. Find and correct these errors.

Marie Williams is a first-year graduate student working in a master's degree in Animal Science. She received her undergraduate degree on the same field from the University of California, Los Angeles, last June. While she was an undergraduate student, she held summer jobs in Sea World and the Wild Animal Preserve in San Diego, California. Her research currently focus on reproduction physiology. Based on her Sea World experience, she is also very interested about animal breeding behavior at captivity and the factors that affects it. Aside from her studies, she like outdoor activities, including fishing, hiking and biking. She also play the guitar and sings on a local band.

EXERCISE 5   Editing for errors with modals and conditional sentences

Directions: In this passage, taken from a longer paper, a student in a composition class is analyzing one of the advantages of going to school via computer instead of attending class in person. Find and correct 10 errors with modals and conditional sentences.

If on-line courses became a reality in the adult school in my area, one positive effect would be that working adults who wanted to study English as a second language will be able to go to school at their convenience. Nowadays, many older people are eager to enrich their education by attending adult school. However, attending school on a daily basis would be very difficult for some because they have to work at night, the school is far away from their home, or because the classes are full. When I was a sophomore at Richmond High School, I earned some extra high school credits by attending Richmond Adult School. On the first day of class, the air was filled with excitement and the class was full. However, the very next week when I went to my English writing class, some students should have been missing because I overheard someone say, "Fong-Wai won't be here today because he's working at night. Mei-Ling's sick, so she is staying home."

If these students were there, my English instructor would not have been so frustrated. She would not have felt as if she were losing her audience. Moreover, the eager students from the first class had turned into exhausted human beings. Although I did not know their backgrounds at that time, some mothers can have three children to raise, or some people could had just gotten off work. Today, if these same students were enroll in an on-line course, they can just attend class by sitting in front of a computer at any time of day. They will not have to make a tremendous effort to get to class after a long and tiring day. While looking at a computer screen, they could relax and feel the joy of education instead of the exhaustion of adding hours to their day. For older students, studying at their own pace and having control over their time should be one of the major benefits of an on-line class. Their struggle between work, childrearing, and school will be alleviated, and they could get the education that they desire—but only if they have the willingness to sit down and pursue it via the computer screen.

EXERCISE 6   Editing for errors with word form and the passive voice and choosing appropriate connectors

Directions: The following paragraph, written by a teacher whose first language is not English, is about two of the factors that make his job satisfying. It has ten errors with word form and the passive. Find and correct these errors. Then, test your ability to use connectors by choosing the appropriate connector to fill in each blank from the list of connectors given below.

Choose an appropriate connector to fill in the blanks from this list: *first of all, nonetheless, of course, thus, for example.*

The two factors which make my job as a high school teacher satisfying are developing a sense of trust with the students and seeing their progress. _____, it is necessary to develop a sense of trust between my students and myself. I have always felt that it is indispensable for the teacher to build a good relation with students, including developing one with their parents, too. A good relationship with the students makes the atmosphere in class one of learning and the students find themselves eagerly to learn. _____, last year a student of mine, Juan, told me that he was very unsure of his ability to do mathematics because he had transferred from a school that had a poor math department. To help him gain confidence, I worked with him during lunch period and helped him catch up with the class. At the end of the semester, he was getting a B, and he said to me, "You trusted me and helped me learn to trust myself. Thank you."

The second factor that makes my job as a teacher satisfying is seeing the progress of my students. _____, it is part of my job to encouragement students to get good results on their examinations; yet, it gives me a sense of personal satisfaction when they are been accepted by the university of their choice or get a summer job based on some of the skills they have been teached. Their succeed encourages me to work harder so that their dreams, and those of their parents, will come true. While it is true that I am often evaluate by whether or not my students success, it is the personal investment in their future that makes me feel satisfy with my job. If I had to choice a career all over again, I would definitely choose teaching.

Answers to Pre-tests

UNIT 1: VERB TENSES

A **Problem 1** Since I moved to my new house 15 days ago, I <u>have been</u> very busy.
Problem 2 Human beings make mistakes. Sometimes, we do things we <u>regret</u> later.

B 1. Many students like to go abroad to study. Now I am in my second year of college, and I just <u>found out</u> yesterday that I have been accepted to go to Brazil. (Problem 2)
2. Last week, my parents sent me money for my tuition bill, and I <u>will pay</u> (OR <u>am paying</u>; OR <u>paid</u>) it today. (Problem 1)

UNIT 2: VERB FORMS

A **Problem 1** Mario <u>chose</u> to live in the dormitory rather than in an apartment.
Problem 2 The hikers <u>had walked</u> two miles before they realized their mistake.
Problem 3 Sometimes <u>I am</u> totally <u>confused</u> about English grammar.
Problem 4 The company clearly <u>deserved</u> to win the award for their research.
Problem 5 An effective speaker tries <u>to look</u> directly at his or her audience.
Problem 6 I hope <u>to present</u> a convincing argument during my presentation.
Problem 7 After <u>finishing</u> work, Margarita likes to work out in the gym for at least an hour.

B 1. Gwen <u>spends</u> (OR <u>does spend</u>) too much time texting her friends. (Problem 4)
2. My former roommate wants me <u>to call</u> her when I am in Washington, D.C. (Problem 7)
3. I <u>am interested</u> in seeing this new play. (Problem 3)
4. My sister <u>taught</u> me how to write my name when I was four years old. (Problem 1)
5. After the game was over, we wanted <u>to go</u> to a restaurant. (Problem 5)
6. We planned to <u>take</u> the TV back to the store because it was not working properly. (Problem 6)
7. Most of the students had <u>finished</u> their homework before class began. (Problem 2)

UNIT 3: MODALS

A **Problem 1** I have not seen my next-door neighbor for a week. She <u>might be</u> (OR <u>could be</u> OR <u>may be</u>) out of town.
Problem 2 In order to be successful, a person <u>must have</u> the determination to achieve goals.
Problem 3 I cannot find my favorite pen. I <u>must have left</u> it at home.

B 1. When we arrived, Lili was not at the station. She <u>must have forgotten</u> that we were coming at 3:00 PM (Problem 2)
2. My e-mail did not go through. I <u>must have forgotten</u> to press "send." (Problem 1)
3. Juan told me he <u>could</u> play the flute at age five. (Problem 3)

UNIT 4: CONDITIONAL SENTENCES

A **Problem 1** If the weather improves, I <u>will play</u> tennis after finishing my homework.
Problem 2 The flight attendant <u>would never have fixed</u> the problem if we had not brought it to her attention.
Problem 3 I am sorry I cannot join you because I moved to New York last month. If I <u>were</u> still in Chicago, I <u>would have gone</u> to the meeting with you.
Problem 4 If she had not brought her ATM card with her, Sheila would have been without any money soon after she arrived in San Diego. After a few days of not eating much, she <u>would have felt</u> very hungry.

B 1. If her apartment <u>were</u> closer to the university, she could walk to class instead of taking the bus or riding her bike. (Problem 1)

      2. The teaching assistant for my math class has very strict rules. If we do not turn in our homework on time, he deducts points. He also <u>refuses</u> to accept papers that are not stapled together. (Problem 4)

      3. The house <u>would have burned</u> down had the firefighters not arrived so quickly. (Problem 2)

      4. Last week, my teacher brought some candy bars containing peanuts to class to reward us for our hard work and good attendance. If she <u>had known</u> that two students are allergic to peanuts, she <u>would not have brought</u> the candy. (Problem 3)

UNIT 5: PASSIVE VOICE

A **Problem 1** Some math problems <u>can be solved</u> very easily.
     Problem 2 The speaker's question <u>was directed</u> at the younger members of the audience.
     Problem 3 While in New York City last month, we <u>stayed</u> in a hotel near Wall Street.

B 1. My friends <u>had already arrived</u> when I got to the airport. (Problem 3)
      2. The textbook <u>was sent</u> to him yesterday by priority mail. (Problem 2)
      3. Many of the books I want <u>have already been checked</u> out from the library. (Problem 1)

UNIT 6: RELATIVE, ADVERBIAL, AND NOUN CLAUSES

Part A: Relative Clauses

A **Problem 1** People <u>who</u> (OR <u>that</u>) <u>live</u> in Florida are used to warm, sunny weather for much of the year.
     Problem 2 The students <u>whose cars</u> were illegally parked will get a ticket.
     Problem 3 After college, David wants to find a job <u>in which</u> he will need to use math (OR <u>which</u> he will need to use math <u>in</u>).
     Problem 4 A chemistry experiment <u>that I did</u> in high school gave me the idea that I might want to major in chemistry in college.

B 1. The calculus student <u>whose test scores</u> were the highest won a prize. (Problem 2)
      2. When the semester started, most students did not know the buildings <u>in which</u> their classes were located (OR <u>which</u> their classes were located <u>in</u>). (Problem 3)
      3. Students <u>who</u> (OR <u>that</u>) transfer from a two-year college to a university say that it takes time to adjust. (Problem 1)
      4. One problem that the instructor solved ~~it~~ ended up having several possible answers. (Problem 4)

Part B: Adverbial Clauses

A **Problem 1** Although Henry hates grammar, ~~but~~ he studies it anyway. (OR: Henry hates grammar, <u>but</u> he studies it anyway.)
     Problem 2 We have purchased one of those pens <u>because</u> we like them.
     Problem 3 <u>Because</u> ~~of~~ the rain has stopped, we can go on our picnic.
     Problem 4 <u>Especially when</u> I see shoes, I want to buy them.
     Problem 5 While you were at the <u>movies, Alexander</u> called to ask about the weekend.
     Problem 6 Some travelers fly business <u>class because</u> they like the wider seats.
     Problem 7 While he <u>is working</u> in Australia, we will visit him.

B 1. <u>Because</u> children do not exercise enough, obesity in children has increased. (Problem 2)
      2. We will text you as soon as we ~~will~~ arrive in town. (Problem 7)
      3. The man was not allowed to board the plane because ~~of~~ his passport had expired. (Problem 3)
      4. Matthew promised to complete his part of the group project <u>as soon as he could</u>. (Problem 5)
      5. Even though Ron is not a vegetarian, ~~but~~ he prefers not to eat meat. (Problem 1)
      6. Although the weather has been cool in the past few <u>days,</u> hotter weather is expected. (Problem 6)
      7. <u>Since</u> Alison enjoys the outdoors, she goes hiking frequently. (Problem 4)

Part C: Noun Clauses

A **Problem 1** <u>That</u> she got a job so quickly is amazing.
     Problem 2 Barry needs to find out <u>if</u> his supervisor wants him to proceed on the project.
     Problem 3 Christy needs to face up to <u>the fact</u> that she is not prepared for the exam.
     Problem 4 Matthew promised that he <u>would</u> go to the potluck.
     Problem 5 Marcel is not sure what the assignment for tomorrow <u>is</u>.
     Problem 6 Her professor prefers that Marta <u>write</u> a thesis.
     Problem 7 The students were surprised <u>that the exam</u> was going to be on Monday.

B **1.** I cannot agree with <u>what</u> you just said. (Problem 2)

    2. Jill wonders what the next chapter <u>will</u> cover. (Problem 5)

    3. The students cannot understand <u>what the question says</u>. (Problem 7)

    4. The researcher said the experiment <u>was</u> a success. (Problem 4)

    5. <u>That</u> he received a scholarship is good news. (Problem 1)

    6. The professor insists that Paul <u>get</u> his essay finished by Monday. (Problem 6)

    7. We are very concerned about <u>the fact</u> that the test yesterday was so difficult. (OR: We are very concerned ~~about~~ that the test yesterday was so difficult.) (Problem 3)

UNIT 7: SENTENCE STRUCTURE

A **Problem 1** In my opinion, speaking in English <u>is</u> easier than writing in English.

    Problem 2 <u>It</u> is a very interesting point you have raised. (OR: You have raised a very interesting point.)

    Problem 3 My summer internship, for example, <u>is</u> one way for me to obtain valuable work experience.

    Problem 4 My parents are first-generation immigrants to the United States, and they communicate mostly <u>in their</u> native language.

    Problem 5 <u>It makes it difficult to start studying again after celebrating a holiday and having time off.</u> (OR: <u>Celebrating a holiday and having time off makes it difficult to start studying again.</u> OR: <u>It is difficult to start studying again after celebrating a holiday and having time off.</u>)

    Problem 6 At present, I am finishing a project and also <u>starting</u> a new one.

    Problem 7 If you are working as an attorney, the problem is not the quantity of work <u>itself; it</u> is the responsibility you feel for your clients. (OR . . . itself. It is . . .)

B **1.** Malnutrition in children is a problem in many poor countries<u>, but</u> childhood obesity is a growing problem in the United States. (Problem 7)

    2. <u>It is</u> a very hard adjustment to have a roommate if a student has always had a single room at home. (Problem 2)

    3. Unlike lots <u>of</u> friends who like dining out in restaurants, I prefer to eat at home. (Problem 4)

    4. Most of the athletes at my university ~~they~~ have full scholarships. (Problem 3)

    5. Students in a recent survey reported that they liked the new library but <u>wanted</u> a new gym as well. (Problem 6)

    6. If they have not studied enough, most students think the test they are taking <u>is</u> very hard. (Problem 1)

    7. ~~In~~ The beginning of a new school year is difficult for teachers and students. (Problem 5)

UNIT 8: WORD ORDER

A **Problem 1** I do not remember <u>when the job application is due</u>.

    Problem 2 Our alarm system went off unexpectedly, and I had trouble figuring out how <u>to turn it off</u>.

    Problem 3 O'Hare airport in Chicago is <u>extremely busy</u>.

    Problem 4 The <u>long-stemmed red roses</u> are the loveliest.

    Problem 5 My department <u>gave me an award</u> for ten years of service. (OR: My department gave an <u>award to me</u> for ten years of service.)

    Problem 6 The movies at the six-screen cinema <u>always change</u> on Fridays.

    Problem 7 We left the laboratory <u>at 7:00 PM</u> because we did not have time to finish the experiment.

B **1.** She is <u>always</u> tired after playing tennis. (Problem 3)

    2. The hikers walked <u>over ten miles</u> this afternoon. (Problem 7)

    3. The student felt he answered the question <u>adequately</u>, but he still lost five points. (Problem 3)

    4. On some products, the government determines what the price <u>is</u>. (Problem 1)

    5. That is a very difficult question, and I'll need to think <u>it</u> over. (Problem 2)

    6. The <u>light gray</u> laptop is the newest model. (Problem 4)

    7. The instructor gave ~~to~~ me an A- on my essay. (OR: The instructor gave <u>an A- to me</u> on my essay.) (Problem 5)

UNIT 9: CONNECTING WORDS

A Problem 1 Natasha hoped to find an acting job in Hollywood, but she had little talent. (OR: Natasha hoped to find an acting job in Hollywood; however, she had little talent.)

Problem 2 Global warming poses a continuing threat to our environment; therefore, we are trying to solve the problem.

Problem 3 Even though we should be saving money, ~~but~~ we are always going shopping. (OR: We should be saving money but we are always going shopping.)

Problem 4 There are three obstacles to losing weight; however, they can be overcome with a strong commitment to having a healthier, better-looking body.

B 1. Although most students would like to have brand-new textbooks, ~~but~~ those on a budget often buy used ones. (OR: ~~Although~~ Most students would like to have brand-new textbooks, but those on a budget often buy used ones.) (Problem 3)

2. Before we bought a car, we did research on car safety; in addition, we test drove different models. (Problem 4)

3. Our teacher wanted to schedule an extra class, but we did not like that idea. (OR: Our teacher wanted to schedule an extra class; however, we did not like that idea.) (Problem 1)

4. A new bookstore has just opened downtown; however, I do not have any money to spend on new books right now. (Problem 2)

UNIT 10: SUBJECT-VERB AGREEMENT

A Problem 1 A good scientist observes closely and records data accurately.

Problem 2 An attorney from one of the most distinguished law firms has agreed to represent the suspect.

Problem 3 A supervisor who listens to others and whose style is collaborative is often the most effective leader.

Problem 4 Taking regular breaks often helps a person work more efficiently.

Problem 5 There are six articles that I need to review this week in preparation for my presentation.

Problem 6 One of the two cars consumes significantly more gas than the other.

B 1. There are indications that global warming is more complex than scientists originally thought. (Problem 5)

2. One of the questions on the exam has a typing error in it and is hard to understand. (Problem 6)

3. Most people feel comfortable around a person who listens to them. (Problem 3)

4. Before buying a car, the smart consumer compares prices and checks the car's safety rating. (Problem 1)

5. Mica, like most of my friends, likes to go out to a restaurant at least once a week. (Problem 2)

6. Going shopping for clothes is something that always interests my sister. (Problem 4)

UNIT 11: ARTICLES

A Problem 1 When a person buys a car, he or she usually has to get a loan.

Problem 2 Students often go to their advisor for advice.

Problem 3 Many doctors in the U.S. no longer wear a white coat during office hours.

Problem 4 My friend called the police because one of the neighbors was having a loud party.

Problem 5 My cousin always makes sure she has her driver's license when she goes out.

B 1. In her application, Isabelle stated that she had a green card, meaning that she had a work permit. (Problem 3)

2. We always have fun when we go to Disneyland. (Problem 2)

3. I am about to finish my bachelor's degree in comparative literature. (Problem 5)

4. Most students found that one of the questions on the test was difficult to answer. (Problem 4)

5. Gustavo forgot to bring a pen to the exam, so he had to borrow one from his friend. (Problem 1)

UNIT 12: SINGULAR AND PLURAL OF NOUNS

A Problem 1 When I travel, I always take two suitcases.

Problem 2 My older sister is always willing to give me advice.

Problem 3 Perhaps you might like to read these two novels.

Problem 4 The little girl is selling red and yellow apples.

Problem 5 An old proverb says, "An eye for an eye and a tooth for a tooth."

Problem 6 On Valentine's Day, Andrea received one of the biggest boxes of chocolates I have ever seen.

Problem 7 When the meeting started, only two women were in the audience.

B 1. During the middle of the semester, we will start to review this chapter and <u>these</u> handouts. (Problem 3)
2. Tonight I have to stay home and work on the <u>difficult</u> problem sets that I have not yet finished for my algebra class. (Problem 4)
3. My professor said that he was unable to work with me this summer because he had to supervise five <u>theses</u>. (Problem 7)
4. During a laboratory class, students need to make sure that they handle the <u>equipment</u> carefully. (Problem 2)
5. One of the most difficult <u>adjustments</u> that students need to make their first year in college is how to manage their study time. (Problem 6)
6. In order to finish the lab, we have to work out the calculations <u>step</u> by <u>step</u>. (Problem 5)
7. Before going into an exam, students should make sure that they have the materials they will need, such as a calculator and some writing <u>instruments</u>. (Problem 1)

UNIT 13: WORD CHOICE

A Problem 1   <u>Tuition</u> fees will be increased 40 percent next year.
Problem 2   The driver was unconscious, so the police could only <u>speculate</u> about what had caused the accident.
Problem 3   The <u>rules clearly state</u> that library books will be returned on time.
Problem 4   Most teachers <u>discuss</u> (OR <u>talk about</u>) the importance of attending class.
Problem 5   His students all think Dr. Stern is an <u>excellent</u> teacher.

B 1. Before going to the laboratory, we have to read an article online and do some other <u>preparation</u>. (Problem 5)
2. Being around leaders in a field can <u>positively affect</u> a young person's attitude. (Problem 3)
3. Many first-year students find that eating in the student cafeteria is very <u>convenient</u>. (Problem 2)
4. Good coaches <u>emphasize</u> (OR <u>focus on</u>) the importance of good sportsmanship. (Problem 4)
5. From my <u>perspective</u>, a trip to Europe is very expensive. (Problem 1)

UNIT 14: WORD FORMS

A Problem 1   Electronic <u>communication</u> via e-mail, Facebook, and texting has become commonplace around the world.
Problem 2   Employees must submit weekly progress reports in a <u>timely</u> manner.
Problem 3   Heating up a frozen dinner is sometimes <u>more convenient</u> than cooking a meal.
Problem 4   As a possible career goal, I am <u>interested</u> in computer science.

B 1. Most of the students thought that the second quiz was <u>easier</u> than the first one. (Problem 3)
2. When my friends are late, I always start to get <u>impatient</u>. (Problem 1)
3. The pharmacy is <u>located</u> right behind the bank. (Problem 4)
4. My roommate needs to <u>straighten</u> her room. (Problem 2)

UNIT 15: PREPOSITIONS

A Problem 1   Erik is taking summer school classes <u>at</u> Harvard University.
Problem 2   The dentist said there are three reasons <u>for</u> my new cavities: too much candy, too little flossing, and too soft a toothbrush.
Problem 3   Jack is <u>seeking</u> information about snakes on the Internet.

B 1. Registration <u>for</u> next semester's classes starts next week. (Problem 2)
2. Linh wanted to study the grammar rules <u>by</u> herself to get ready for the test. (Problem 1)
3. When I arrived, the class was already <u>discussing</u> the Civil War (OR: When I arrived, the class was already <u>talking about</u> the Civil War.) (Problem 3)